MINNESOTA HISTORICAL SOCIETY
PUBLIC AFFAIRS CENTER PUBLICATIONS

RUSSELL W. FRIDLEY

Editor and Director

JUNE DRENNING HOLMQUIST

Managing Editor

The
Progressive Era
in Minnesota
1899–1918

By CARL H. CHRISLOCK

MINNESOTA HISTORICAL SOCIETY • ST. PAUL • 1971

Library of Congress Catalog Number: 79–178677
Standard Book Number : 87341– 067– 4

To the memory of my father

CARL H. CHRISLOCK, SR.

Preface

TWO BROAD GOALS have guided the writing of this book: (1) interpreting an important epoch in Minnesota's political development, and (2) illuminating the history of progressivism as a national phenomenon. Whether the second goal is attainable within the limits of the study may be debatable. The uniqueness of Minnesota politics is often proclaimed. Minnesota voters, we are frequently informed, are extraordinarily "independent" and "issue-oriented." We are further reminded that no other state has a record of third-party success comparable to that of the Minnesota Farmer-Labor party in the 1920s and 1930s. Minnesota also appears to have produced more than its quota of political mavericks, a classification broadly applied to such personalities as Ignatius Donnelly, Charles A. Lindbergh, Sr., Arthur C. Townley, Magnus Johnson, Elmer A. Benson, and Eugene J. McCarthy.

If the thesis of uniqueness is not open to qualification, Minnesota's political history can contribute little to an understanding of national politics. One can persuasively argue, however, that such a thesis is subject to qualification. While admittedly atypical in several respects, the political culture of Minnesota since the 1890s also has conformed to broad national trends. In the eighteen presidential contests held from 1896 through 1968, for example, the state's electorate voted for the winner fifteen times, usually by a margin roughly parallel to the national outcome. It failed to do so in 1912, a campaign year marked by unusual complications, in 1916 when Woodrow Wilson lost Minnesota to Charles E. Hughes by a plurality narrower than Wilson's slim margin of victory nationally, and in 1968 when Hubert H. Humphrey carried his home state.

A glance at the geographic, economic, and social forces shaping Minnesota politics in the early twentieth century reinforces confidence in the validity of the second goal. While by no means a microcosm of the country, Minnesota was sufficiently diverse to register broad national trends. Geographically its varied terrain traversed the boundary between the eastern and trans-Mississippi Middle West; by 1890 the dairy and corn-hog farmers of southern

Minnesota had more in common with agriculturists in Wisconsin and Illinois than with the wheat growers of the Red River Valley, whose interests paralleled those of North Dakota producers. Urbanization and diversification of economic activity also were well advanced. In 1900 nearly one-fourth of the state's inhabitants resided in the three cities of Minneapolis, St. Paul, and Duluth, and fifty-three incorporated municipalities had populations exceeding 2,000. Proportionately Minnesota's ethnic mix was heavily North European, but a variety of cultural traditions were represented.

On the controversial question of whether progressivism was a futile effort to recover an irretrievably lost past, a creative foray into the future, an attempt by established power structures to retain control of American society, or a genuine democratic renaissance, my position is flexible. To a greater or lesser extent it may have been all of these things. Progressive spokesmen employed a common rhetoric and apparently shared a number of broad assumptions concerning man, society, and American destiny, but they failed to achieve either ideological or programmatic unity.

The thesis of the book is that Minnesota progressivism was no more successful than its national counterpart in overcoming inner tensions or developing a sure sense of direction. Until about 1916 the primacy of issues on which state-wide consensus existed minimized the tensions and helped sustain an effective progressive coalition in Minnesota politics. Thereafter the rise of new concerns, dramatized and brought into focus by Arthur C. Townley's Nonpartisan League, together with the debilitating impact of World War I disrupted the coalition, brought the progressive era to a close, and produced the unique political alignment of the postwar years.

Some readers may feel that the book slights progressivism's first decade; only two chapters out of fifteen are devoted to the Lind-Van Sant-Johnson period. My defense would be that there was no need to duplicate two excellent studies of that period: George M. Stephenson, *John Lind of Minnesota*, and Winifred G. Helmes, *John A. Johnson: The People's Governor*. The Nonpartisan League era also has attracted scholarly attention, but the intervening years have not. Moreover, it was my conviction that focusing emphasis on progressivism's decline might contribute to an understanding of its nature.

A number of individuals and organizations deserve acknowledgment for their roles in producing this book. June D. Holmquist, the Minnesota Historical Society's managing editor, provided helpful counsel and encouragement at all stages of the writing. Rhoda R. Gilman edited the manuscript and in the process substantially improved it. Hermina Poatgieter expertly translated all the German-language materials cited, and Dorothy

D. Kidder assisted with the research. Lucile M. Kane and her staff made available the rich resources of the Society's manuscripts collection, and Dorothy J. Gimmestad of the audio-visual library was most helpful in locating the illustrations used in these pages. All of the photographs not otherwise credited were drawn from the Minnesota Historical Society's picture collection. Alan Ominsky is responsible for the book's design.

Two grants in 1964 and 1965 from the Minnesota Historical Society's McKnight Family Endowment research funds helped defray research expenses, and one from the Society's Public Affairs Center, supported by the Louis W. and Maud Hill Family Foundation, partially covered the cost of publication. I am pleased that this volume was selected as the first in what promises to be a fruitful series of studies supported by the Public Affairs Center, which was created in 1967 to call attention to the influence of Minnesotans and midwestern organizations on the course of politics and government in the nineteenth and twentieth centuries.

I am also grateful to Millard L. Gieske and James M. Youngdale for the many insights relating to recent Minnesota political history gained from conversations with them. At the same time, I, of course, assume full responsibility for any factual errors or faulty interpretations that may mar the book.

CARL H. CHRISLOCK

Minneapolis, Minnesota
September 27, 1971

Contents

Illustrations

THE PROGRESSIVE ERA

IN MINNESOTA

1899–1918

CHAPTER ONE

The Rise and Decline of American Progressivism

A PHENOMENON known as progressivism significantly influenced American politics from the beginning of the twentieth century down to the country's entry into World War I. During these years an agitated examination of American society by writers, journalists, clergymen, and other opinion makers produced a critique of that society which deplored its main drift. Specific complaints were directed against the concentration of wealth and economic power, the displacement of idealistic values by a selfish materialism, the debasement of the political process by corrupt machines, and the prodigal waste of natural resources. The mood of the times emphatically demanded a purification of politics and new departures in economic and social policy.[1]

Corrective measures were soon formulated. In the first decade of the twentieth century a variety of reform programs, all claiming the progressive label, emerged. Most of them called upon government to assume increased responsibility for the general welfare, but they did not agree as to which level of government — national, state, or local — should be primarily responsible. The degree of responsibility which government should assume was also a subject of debate. In the realm of economic policy some progressives wanted to combat monopoly by restoring competition through rigorous enforcement of the antitrust statutes. Others, claiming to see advantages in large-scale enterprise, recommended junking the antitrust laws in favor of regulated monopoly, an approach that called for day-to-day supervision of giant corporations by a federal administrative agency.

In part such diverse viewpoints grew out of a fundamental difference of outlook within the progressive camp. The so-called "old progressives" wanted, as far as possible, to restore the individualistic, small-town and rural society of the pre-urban period. Another wing of the progressive movement accepted the permanence of large-scale industrial and financial en-

1

terprises, proclaimed that the nation's future lay in the cities, affirmed
that old-fashioned individualism was dead, and accused those who refused
to accept these realities of being "rural tories." In short, progressivism
oscillated between a nostalgic hankering for an idyllic past and a confident
acceptance of the future.[2]

The competing interests of the many dissimilar groups affiliated with
progressivism multiplied the contradictions within the movement. While
middle-class hopes, values, and anxieties dominated it to a great degree,
other classes also identified with it. On the Eastern Seaboard established
elites utilized progressivism as a weapon to combat the aggressions of new
wealth. In the Midwest a fear that the financial power of the East threatened
regional economic independence led many top business leaders to support
such progressive causes as tariff reduction, banking and currency reform,
railroad regulation, and antitrust legislation. At the same time virtually
all business leaders remained sensitive to a danger that progressivism's
constant agitation might disturb the business climate.[3]

Wage earners, recent immigrants, and nonwhite minorities also found
their positions within the progressive camp ambiguous. On the one hand
the rhetoric of progressivism, which proclaimed hostility to all forms of
special privilege and professed concern for the rights of "small" people,
strengthened the determination of peripheral groups to improve their status
within American society. Up to a point the leaders of middle-class progressivism acknowledged the propriety of these aspirations. Demands for workmen's compensation programs, strengthened factory inspection, and prohibition of child labor were included in the typical progressive platform,
and in many states these measures found their way onto the statute books.
In a few instances, representatives of the urban foreign-born working class
became full participants in the progressive politics of their states—the
early careers of Alfred E. Smith and Robert F. Wagner in the New York
legislature are notable examples.[4]

On balance, however, middle-class progressivism remained basically
suspicious of the so-called lower strata of American society. Paternalistic
humanitarianism, a pronounced progressive trait, dictated the enactment
of minimal social legislation, but the disposition of slum residents to follow
corrupt political bosses seemed to some middle-class progressives to confirm
the thesis that the urban poor—particularly those who were recent immigrants—were not ready to assume full political responsibility. The social
settlement movement—one of progressivism's significant components
—sought not only to ameliorate urban poverty, but also to "Amer-
icanize" its foreign-born clients. Essentially this meant encouraging im-

migrants and their progeny to abandon inherited modes of thought and action in favor of values consonant with the white Anglo-Saxon Protestant tradition.[5]

Trade unionism also was distasteful in principle to many middle-class progressives. The closed shop, which limited employment in a given firm to union members, had monopolistic connotations that the opponents of organized labor cleverly exploited. The campaign to maintain the open shop in American industry reached a high point of effectiveness in the ten-year period from 1904 to 1914, which also saw the flowering of progressivism.[6]

Still another tension-creating factor within the progressive movement was the general acceptance of racist doctrines in the early twentieth century—a factor that had implications for progressivism's relationship to the Negro question. Southern progressives emphatically embraced segregation; indeed, the complete elimination of Black citizens from the political life of the South was one of their legacies to the future. Elsewhere a few reformers emerged as champions of Black America's claim to equality, but acceptance of the theory of white superiority in a biological sense inhibited solid identification with the Negro rights movement.[7]

No such barriers existed with respect to the drive for women's rights. By the turn of the century this movement had largely abandoned its earlier broad radicalism, including its identification with the cause of Black Americans. During the progressive era proponents of women's rights concentrated on the single issue of woman suffrage, basing their arguments heavily upon the regenerative moral influence which female voters would presumably bring to bear on American politics — a line of reasoning particularly congenial to the ethos of progressivism.[8] Closely allied to the woman suffrage cause was that of prohibition, and both became associated in varying degrees of intimacy with the progressive movement.

Despite inner tensions and a confused sense of direction, progressivism significantly shaped American development. Its most productive years extended from the beginning of Theodore Roosevelt's second administration (1905) through the four years of William Howard Taft's presidency and into Woodrow Wilson's first term (1913–17). Reform statutes of this time span provide a rough measure of the change that was achieved. The Hepburn act of 1906 and the Mann-Elkins act of 1911 brought railroad transportation under the effective supervision of the Interstate Commerce Commission.

The Federal Reserve act of 1913 strengthened national control — previously almost nonexistent — over money and banking. The Clayton law and the Federal Trade Commission act, both passed in 1914, expanded federal authority over business generally. Enactment in 1906 of the pure food and drug act and the federal meat inspection law invested the national government with what virtually amounted to a new responsibility: guardianship of the nation's health. At the same time, presidential action and exhortation, particularly while Roosevelt occupied the White House, helped to create a strong national consensus demanding a more provident utilization of the country's natural resources.

Progressivism also influenced public policy on the state and local levels. During the Roosevelt-Taft-Wilson period, most of the states wholly or partially scrapped the nominating convention in favor of the direct primary, and several experimented with some combination of the initiative (the proposal of legislation by popular petition), the referendum (submission of a proposed law to popular vote), and the recall (a procedure under which an elected official can be removed by the people before the expiration of his term). In addition, many states placed new restrictions on traditional forms of political campaigning, reorganized public administration along "business" lines, and expanded the regulation of public utilities. Other provisions in the typical state reform program included refinement of public supervision of insurance and banking, liberation of legislative power to tax from the limitations written into nineteenth-century state constitutions, passage of more stringent factory inspection laws, and creation of additional state welfare services.[9]

By 1915 signs of a widening rift within the progressive camp began to multiply. The moderates, by and large, believed that measures like the Federal Reserve act had carried reform far enough. The progressive left, an informal coalition including social justice advocates, spokesmen for organized labor, and a coterie of militant agrarians, felt otherwise. Organized labor wanted, above all, to improve its invidious position before the law. The social justice group championed, among other things, an effective ban on child labor. And several farm organizations demanded the creation of a rural credit system under federal sponsorship. Other unachieved goals, particularly woman suffrage and prohibition, gave additional impetus to the drive for more reform.

For a time Wilson identified with the moderates. In 1914–15 he held that tariff reduction, the Federal Reserve act, the Clayton act, and the Federal Trade Commission law had fulfilled his 1912 "covenant" with the American people. However, unrelenting pressure from the left changed the presidential mind. Shortly before the campaign of 1916 got under way, Wilson yielded to the reformers. In the spring and summer of 1916, he pushed through congress a substantial portion of the program advocated by advanced progressives. The more important measures included the Federal Farm Loan Bank act, which conformed essentially to the demands of the agrarians; the Owen-Keating child labor bill (later invalidated by the United States Supreme Court); and the Adamson eight-hour railway labor act, which averted a serious transportation strike by writing the Railroad Brotherhoods' basic demand into law.[10]

These successes, coupled with Wilson's narrow victory in the presidential election on a "peace and progressivism" platform, gratified left-wing progressives. But a new era of reform did not materialize. The country responded to Wilson's swing to the left with a divided mind. Conservatives were more determined than ever to resist innovation, and some moderates thought that measures like the Adamson law would encourage trade-union arrogance. More important, the entry of the United States into World War I on April 6, 1917, created a situation that, to say the least, discouraged initiative on behalf of domestic reform.

To a greater extent than was realized at the time, the European war, even during the period of American neutrality, confronted progressivism with a number of perils. For one thing, issues growing out of America's relationship to the conflict — neutral rights, preparedness, proposed arms embargoes, and the like — tended to divide the movement. Many progressives, particularly the midwestern variety, were staunch noninterventionists who regarded the war as an unwelcome diversion from the task of reforming American society. A number of influential reformers, however, accepted far-reaching American responsibility for global betterment, and a larger number wondered if the United States did not, indeed, have an obligation to uphold the rights of humanity in the submarine controversy with Germany. The *New Republic*, then as later a major spokesman for left-wing progressivism, vacillated in 1915 and 1916 between pro-Ally interventionism and uncompromising neutralism.[11]

The war also threatened the reform climate. By late spring of 1915 a developing conviction that German militarism might be a danger to the United States was generating a crusade for pure, undiluted Americanism — and, as usual, patriotism came to be identified with defense of the status quo rather than its alteration. Declarations by some of the more strident critics of American society that they would refuse to bear arms if the United States went to war made it all the easier to associate reform with sedition. The thesis that radicalism and patriotism were incompatible did not win general public acceptance during the period of American neutrality, but interventionists occasionally suggested that "unsound" reformist views might well coincide with a basic lack of loyalty to the United States.[12]

Following the break with Germany in early 1917, the dangers to progressivism became clear and present. Most progressives, to be sure, supported the war with apparent enthusiasm. Wilsonian rhetoric persuaded many of them that the American entry had transformed the conflict from a squalid militaristic encounter into an armed crusade for democracy and righteousness. Less idealistic motives also came into play. A spokesman for one militant reform organization asserted that it would be inexpedient for his movement to separate itself from the mainstream of American opinion by opposing the war.[13] Some progressives saw the war as a boon to their cause. Mobilization and revenue needs argued powerfully for comprehensive government control of the economy and a steeply graduated income tax — measures that advanced progressivism had advocated for several years. It was reasonable to hope that these policies — which congress to a considerable degree adopted in 1917 and 1918 — would remain in force after the war. The war also gave powerful impetus to two other reforms supported by many progressives — prohibition and woman suffrage, both of which were written into the United States Constitution by 1920.

For a number of reasons, progressivism's rally around the flag failed to avert the perils of wartime. Image was part of the problem. The patriotic militance of the war progressives could not obscure the reality that opposition — or apparent opposition — to the war came primarily from the left of the political spectrum. Senator Robert M. La Follette of Wisconsin, whose name was almost synonymous with radical progressivism, became the chief symbol of what the spirit of the times defined as antiwar sedition — a reputation resting primarily on the senator's continuing refusal to acknowledge that his vote against the war resolution had been a mistake. The pacifist stand taken by the majority wing of the American Socialist party further tarnished progressivism. Most progressives indignantly denied kinship with socialism, but many Americans vaguely thought of all reform movements as being basically in the same camp.

The superpatriotism of 1917 and 1918 exalted the nation's virtues and to a corresponding degree discouraged preoccupation with its shortcomings. Moreover, the prevailing mood demanded that winning the war receive first priority; competing concerns simply had to be set aside for the duration of the conflict. The conservative contention that debate on controversial domestic issues might compromise national unity and endanger military victory apparently gained wide acceptance. In other words, the advocacy of political and social change invited accusations of knowingly or unknowingly aiding the enemy.

The Bolshevik assumption of power in Russia on November 7, 1917, added to progressivism's burdens. Neither the socialist nor the progressive sectors of the American left knew how to interpret the Soviet regime, which in the name of egalitarian democracy and national self-determination established a tight dictatorship that harshly repressed basic civil liberties. A number of American reformers — the famous writer and journalist Lincoln Steffens, for example — wanted to believe that Bolshevism was leading Russia into a bright democratic future. Other progressives were not so sure. American conservatives did not share these uncertainties. They saw the excesses reported out of Russia as a warning that it was dangerous to let the reform spirit get out of hand. Moreover, the aid that imperial Germany had given the Bolshevik rise to power by permitting Nikolai Lenin to return to Russia in April, 1917, coupled with the treaty of Brest-Litovsk that contracted Russia out of the war in March, 1918, seemed to support the charge that the Soviet leaders were German agents. Bolshevism, in short, was linked to pro-Germanism, and the American left was suspected of being in league with both.[14]

The armistice of November 11, 1918, presumably lifted the moratorium on discussion of controversial questions, but progressivism remained on the defensive. Instead of ushering in the democratic millennium, the postwar period brought chaos, instability, and disillusionment. Overseas, Bolshevism threatened to extend its sway as hope for a new democratic world order faded at the peace conference. At home the outbreak of serious labor disturbances combined with a wave of terror bombings convinced many Americans that revolutionary radicalism of the Bolshevik variety seriously threatened the nation's stability. A steep rise in the cost of living reinforced other discontents.[15]

The progressive response to the situation in 1919 proved beyond doubt that the powerful reform movement of prewar days had lost its dynamism. A few progressives remained faithful to the old commitment, but a greater number joined the antiradical crusade, giving it some of the fervor that a few years earlier had animated the drive against political machines and unrestrained capitalism. Ole Hanson, mayor of Seattle, and A. Mitchell Palmer, United States attorney general, who had begun their careers as progressives, emerged in 1919 as the nation's leading "Red" hunters. In his battle for the League of Nations, Wilson retained the support of some reformers, while others took the position that the proposed world organization was an instrument for the maintenance of a reactionary Anglo-French imperialism rather than a potential parliament of man.[16]

Deprived of a stable base, the Wilson administration abandoned its commitment to the militant liberalism of 1916 even before illness partially incapacitated the president in September, 1919. The first postwar Wilson message to congress, delivered in December, 1918, commented that conversion from war to peace could be accomplished with only minimal help from government, a suggestion that scarcely reassured those progressives who had hoped for a continuation of comprehensive state regulation of the economy. Congress, which the election of 1918 had placed under conservative Republican domination, carried this recommendation further than Wilson intended. Not only did it speedily liquidate wartime controls, but it also threatened the regulatory policies established before the war. A retreat from progressivism also characterized the president's relationship to the anti-Red crusade. Although a few of his officials, notably Secretary of Labor Louis F. Post, tried to moderate the excesses of this crusade, Wilson failed to restrain the zeal of his attorney general, and he resolutely refused to pardon Eugene V. Debs, the Socialist party leader who was serving a sentence in Atlanta federal prison on a charge of seditious utterance.[17]

The victory of Warren G. Harding in the presidential election of 1920 confirmed the decline of progressivism that had begun during the war. Harding's rambling incoherence made a precise interpretation of his mandate difficult, but no one equated his "normalcy" with a revival of the reform spirit. Nevertheless, residual fragments of progressivism continued to influence American politics in the 1920s — to what extent is a moot point among historians. The challenge of the Great Depression of the 1930s encouraged a return to reform. The New Deal was much more than a simple revival of progressivism, but the legacy of the earlier movement became part of its substance.[18]

CHAPTER TWO

The Rise of the Progressive Movement In Minnesota — 1899–1909

THE INAUGURATION of Governor John Lind on January 2, 1899, heralded the progressive era in Minnesota. Lind's opening message to the legislature and people has been called "an inventory of Minnesota life and problems at the turn of the century."[1] It also served as a blueprint for reform that influenced the policies of both Lind's immediate successors in the governorship, Republican Samuel R. Van Sant and Democrat John A. Johnson.

The most urgent recommendations in Lind's message dealt with taxation. The new governor called for an immediate increase in the railroad gross earnings tax, a proposal that several previous legislative sessions had debated without adopting. He also requested that the legislature create a special commission to formulate a comprehensive reform of the existing tax structure. His other proposals included a reappraisal of Minnesota's antitrust statutes; the future retention by the state of title to mineral rights in state lands transferred to private ownership; the establishment of a board of control to supervise state institutions; and an investigation of the merits of the direct primary, the initiative, the referendum, and the recall.[2]

Minnesotans were familiar with both Lind and his program. The latter had been publicized by nearly a generation of reform agitation. In the 1870s the Patrons of Husbandry, popularly called the Grange, helped establish the right of state governments to control railroad transportation and related activities. Along with Illinois, Iowa, and Wisconsin, Minnesota was in the forefront of the granger movement. Oliver H. Kelley, founder and national leader of the organization, was a Minnesotan. His influence, coupled with that of such effective leaders as the colorful Ignatius Donnelly and with the frontier conviction that the railroads were bilking the public, helped build the Minnesota Grange into a powerful political force. In

9

response to its pressure, the legislative sessions of the early 1870s laid the foundations of Minnesota's railroad regulatory code.[3]

The Grange declined in power after its spectacular flowering in the 1870s, although it continued to operate as a nonpolitical farm organization. Within a few years the Farmers Alliance, a movement that reached a high point of influence in the late 1880s, filled the gap. Basically the Alliance resembled the Grange, but it aspired to become a broader movement than its predecessor. In addition to more stringent regulation of transportation, the Minnesota Alliance platform of 1886 demanded legislation that would define combinations for the control of markets as criminal conspiracies, a reduction of interest rates on loans to no more than 8 per cent, and a system of local grain inspection.[4]

The 1886 platform also reflected an Alliance intention to court organized labor. The document was actually adopted by a joint convention of the Farmers Alliance and the Knights of Labor. On behalf of the Minnesota workingman it demanded, among other things, a state bureau of labor statistics; effective factory inspection; equal wages for men and women doing the same work; and a ban on child labor in mines, workshops, and factories.[5] Alliance espousal of labor's cause failed to establish an intimate co-operative relationship between agriculture and the unions, but it did popularize the notion that joint farmer-labor action was the reform movement's best hope.

Like the Minnesota Grange, the state Farmers Alliance at first operated as a pressure group rather than as an independent third party, and it persuaded the legislature, particularly in the 1885 and 1887 sessions, to adopt several of its demands. But the membership was not content with such limited success. In the late 1880s a conviction developed that a third party could accomplish more than pressure-group activity. Shortly before the campaign of 1890 got under way, the organization spawned an Alliance party which made a creditable showing in the November election. Parallel developments in other states accelerated the drive for a national third party, and in 1892 the People's party, more commonly known as the Populist party, was organized both nationally and in most of the western and southern states, including Minnesota.[6]

The twenty-two electoral votes cast for the national Populist ticket in 1892 encouraged third-party men to believe that Populism had a future, a conviction strengthened by election results in 1894. However, in 1896 the national Democratic party embraced free silver, which had become the chief plank in Populism's program, and nominated William Jennings Bryan for the presidency. Bryan's strong free-silver stance, his semi-Populist viewpoint on other issues, and the appeal of his style to the mass of Populist voters created a dilemma for the People's party. Fusion with the Bryan Democrats might advance favored causes, but only at the risk of sacrificing Populist identity.

The national Populist convention of 1896 responded to the problem by coupling an endorsement of Bryan with the nomination of Thomas E. Watson, the leader of southern Populism, for the vice-presidency. Bryan refused to acknowledge Watson as his running mate, and after the decisive defeat of the free silver cause in the 1896 election the Populist party rapidly declined — thanks largely to the return of prosperity beginning in 1897. Populism could perhaps claim that it had served as an educational force, but the American political arena remained under Republican-Democratic domination.[7]

In Minnesota Populism developed less strength than in the wheat-growing and silver-mining areas to the west. The People's parties of Kansas and Colorado captured control of their state governments. Minnesota, however, sent only two third-party men to congress, and by a wide margin rejected every Populist bid for state-wide office. While carrying the Great Plains and Rocky Mountain states in his race against Republican William McKinley, Bryan lost Minnesota by more than 60,000 votes. In the North Star State McKinley polled 193,503 to Bryan's 130,735.[8]

The weakness of free silver Populism in Minnesota was primarily attributable to the fact that by the 1890s the state was rapidly moving out of its frontier phase. Wheat still dominated the economy of the northwestern counties, as it would for several decades, but diversified agriculture had developed in the south, and the Twin Cities of St. Paul and Minneapolis had grown into a metropolitan center of more than 300,000 people. Free silver and Populism appealed powerfully to the depressed farmers of Minnesota's wheat belt. That area elected the state's two third-party congressmen and also returned a Bryan plurality in 1896. Elsewhere Populism attracted only minority support. Like the older agricultural areas of Wisconsin and Illinois, the diversified farming counties of southern Minnesota voted decisively against the People's party in 1892 and 1894 and rejected Bryan in 1896. And the voters of Minneapolis and St. Paul followed the national urban trend by spurning Populism both in its independent and Bryan-fusionist form.[9]

Notwithstanding its limited success at the polls, the Minnesota People's party helped maintain the continuity of the state's reform tradition. In addition, its pressure persuaded the Republican party to adopt a part of the Populist program, particularly during the administration of Governor Knute Nelson (1893–95). Lind ran his first race for governor in 1896 with the backing of a Democratic-Populist-Silver Republican coalition. Thus Populism was also a factor in pushing him into the forefront of state politics.[10]

Lind's political career, however, antedated his identification with the free silver movement, and his base of support included elements outside Bryan's following. He was born in Sweden in 1854, a circumstance that gave him considerable ethnic appeal. Thanks to persistent effort, he had acquired sufficient formal education to qualify for a teaching certificate at the age of sixteen, two years after he and his parents migrated to the United States. For the next few years he taught in rural schools and in 1875 enrolled in the University of Minnesota law school. The following year he was admitted to the bar, and he then set up a law practice at New Ulm, where before long he built up a substantial clientele. He also became involved in Republican politics. In 1886, at the age of thirty-two, he won election to the national House of Representatives.

In Washington Lind was "a sturdy supporter of Republican measures generally and did not fail to gather his share of plums for his . . . district."[11] He also managed to retain the confidence of constituents associated with the Farmers Alliance. Of the five Republican congressmen from Minnesota — the entire delegation — Lind alone survived the Democratic-Alliance sweep of 1890. Two years later he returned to his New Ulm law practice, choosing not to seek another congressional term.

Two developments in the mid-1890s — one related to state politics and the other national in scope — combined to alter the course of Lind's political career. In 1895 Governor Knute Nelson with the backing of ex-Governor William R. Merriam, the Minnesota Republican boss, defeated United States Senator William D. Washburn for re-election in a bitter contest that was to shatter the unity of the Republican party for many years to come. This episode deeply disturbed Lind, who distrusted Nelson, liked Washburn, resented the tactics of the Merriam machine, and possibly feared that Nelson's victory would adversely affect his own political advancement. One interpretation of Lind's career attributes his subsequent defection from the Republican party primarily to his chagrin at the outcome of the Washburn-Nelson contest.[12]

Whatever his private reasons, Lind left the Republican party in 1896 ostensibly because its national convention rejected free silver and embraced the gold standard. Shortly after announcing his apostasy, he accepted a Silver Republican-Democratic-Populist "draft" to run for governor. Thanks to Republican disunity, the unpopularity of Governor David M. Clough, who had the backing of the Merriam machine, and his own strong appeal,

Lind nearly won. In the final count he ran more than 30,000 votes ahead of Bryan and lost to Clough by only about 2,500 votes.[13]

A very different set of circumstances from those of 1896 dominated the Minnesota campaign of 1898. The return of prosperity reduced the intensity of the gold-silver controversy. American victory in the Spanish-American War raised the issue of imperialism: Should the United States retain the Philippines and other distant territories which had become available for the taking? Within Minnesota the issue of political bossism lost its cutting edge when the 1898 Republican state convention repudiated Governor Clough and nominated William Henry Eustis, former mayor of Minneapolis and a prominent leader of the antimachine faction of the Minnesota party. This, however, failed to unify the Republicans. The schism between the party's machine element and the Minneapolis-based "clean government" faction persisted throughout the campaign and contributed substantially to the defeat of Eustis.[14]

Encouraged by his impressive showing in the 1896 election, Lind in 1898 accepted a second fusionist invitation to run for governor. His strategy this time called for concentration on state issues. Free silver, said Lind in his acceptance speech, had no relevance to the contest for governor, although he did not retract his earlier stand on the currency question. He also minimized the significance of the imperialism issue without disavowing an earlier warning against permitting the "shimmer of a proposed imperial policy in distant lands to blind the eyes of the people to existing abuses at home" — a striking anticipation of the neutralist point of view during World War I.[15] The real issue, according to Lind, was of the opposition party's own making. During their forty-year tenure in office, he charged, Minnesota Republicans had been unduly generous to railroads, large lumber firms, telegraph companies, and other big corporations. A Lind administration, he promised, would proceed moderately in reversing this policy of favoritism, but it would be reversed.

Lind won the 1898 election by a margin of approximately 20,000 votes. This outcome must be viewed as a personal triumph, since the Republican party kept its top-heavy majority in both legislative houses, retained all the other state offices, and won every congressional race.[16]

Although Lind's policy recommendations won the governor warm praise, the 1899 legislature ignored most of them; the *Minneapolis Journal* calculated that only four out of twenty-one Lind proposals won legislative approval.[17] Partisanship largely explains this record. Many Republican legislators favored Lind's basic program, for at the turn of the century, the division between progressive and conservative by no means followed party lines. Nevertheless, a legislature dominated by one party was, as usual, reluctant to help an opposition governor create a presumption in favor of his own re-election.

Notwithstanding its immediate fate, the Lind program was important. It became a norm, a point of reference for the policy-making of succeeding administrations, although it was not strikingly original, and most of it had been advocated for years. Lind's achievement was to give reform added impetus and respectability, an achievement made possible by his ability to fraternize with the Populists and at the same time retain the confidence of middle-class citizens whose tolerance for radicalism was low.

In two other directions Lind wielded lasting influence. His cavalier attitude toward party affiliation helped sanctify what became a hallowed Minnesota progressive tenet: the independent voting ethic, the notion that the virtuous citizen should cast his ballot for the man rather than the party. When Lind left the Republican party in 1896 he did not align himself with any other single group. In 1898 he described himself as a "political orphan," meaning that he acknowledged no partisan identification. After becoming governor he professed a loose allegiance to the Democratic party which did not preclude his support of opposition candidates if they seemed more worthy than their Democratic rivals. This stance Lind maintained for the rest of his life.[18]

Secondly, his strictures against imperialism articulated a suspicion held by many midwesterners that a venturesome foreign policy might be a planned diversion by Wall Street to block the advancement of domestic reform. Debate over retention of the Philippines subsided soon after 1900, and popular interest in foreign affairs correspondingly declined until the outbreak of World War I urgently raised the issue of America's relationship to Europe. Then many of Lind's old followers refurbished the 1898 case against imperialism and used it to defend American neutrality against the threat of involvement in the European conflict.[19]

Lind lost his bid for re-election in 1900 by a narrow margin of less than 2,500 votes. Few observers interpreted this as a rejection of his program. Samuel R. Van Sant, the new governor, did not propose to reverse the policies of the preceding administration. On the contrary, he promised more of the same, and during his two terms the reform tempo in Minnesota accelerated. For this the governor could claim some credit. Van Sant's flair for flamboyant patriotic oratory and his eloquent defense of values which no one disputed, coupled with a reputation for rectitude, invested his stands on public issues with an aura of morality. But his managerial talents were limited, and he failed to gain undisputed control of the Minnesota Republican party.[20]

In November, 1901, two months after Theodore Roosevelt became president, Minnesota progressivism—and, incidentally, Van Sant—found an issue of extraordinary potency. This was the so-called railroad merger.[21] For several years James J. Hill, president of the Great Northern Railroad, and Edward H. Harriman, head of the Union Pacific, had battled for control of the Chicago, Burlington and Quincy, a road that provided access to Chicago as well as to the rich markets of Iowa. The entry of Kuhn, Loeb and Company on the side of Harriman and of J. Pierpont Morgan on the side of Hill escalated the conflict. The Hill-Morgan group won an important round in the spring of 1901 when it apparently secured control of the Burlington.

This coup was not final, however. Due to complex interlocking stock arrangements, the key to permanent and full control of the Burlington was vested in the Northern Pacific, a road over which the Hill-Morgan combination had operating control without holding a majority of the stock. Presently a titanic struggle to secure control of the Northern Pacific developed between the two groups. When it became clear that neither side could win a conclusive victory, negotiations were opened. Ultimately these created the Northern Securities Company, founded on November 12, 1901, and incorporated in New Jersey. This move in effect consolidated the Great Northern, the Northern Pacific, and the Burlington into a single system under the joint control of the two groups.

Announcement that the Northern Securities Company had been formed produced an intensely angry reaction in Minnesota and throughout the Midwest. In 1901 the automobile was in its infancy, and airlines, trucks, and motor buses had not appeared. The railroads enjoyed a virtual monopoly in the carrying of goods and passengers at a time when government regulation was rudimentary and ineffective. Under the circumstances, therefore, concentration of railroad control in a single group of powerful financiers seemed intolerable.

Hill's reputation as the great benefactor of the Northwest and the theory that his leadership would dominate the new railroad combine scarcely softened the blow. Like one editorial writer for the *St. Paul Pioneer Press*, many Minnesotans may have wondered what would happen when the aging Empire Builder passed from the scene. Then Midwest transportation might

In the early twentieth century Minnesota progressives found a potent issue in railroad monopoly. Governor Samuel R. Van Sant stoutly opposed a proposed merger of the Great Northern, Northern Pacific, and Burlington railroads which was later invalidated by the U.S. Supreme Court in the famous Northern Securities case. This cartoon entitled "Blocking the Ball," was first published in the Minneapolis Journal of November 20, 1901.

be, as Hill himself suggested, at the mercy of "other great systems south of Minnesota and the Dakotas whose controlling interests would lead them to build up that region at the expense of the Northwest." Other papers were less charitable to Hill. The *Rock County Herald*, published by former state senator Herbert J. Miller, a prominent leader in Republican politics, anticipated successful legal action against the Great Northern president, declaring, "The laws of this state will be upheld and enforced, and for once and at last James J. Hill will bow to the will of the people he has so contemptuously and haughtily defied."[22]

Van Sant responded to the Northern Securities announcement with a speed and vigor that won him an enviable reputation as a champion in the battle against mergers. First he issued a protest declaring that a Minnesota law prohibiting the consolidation of parallel lines within the state had been violated. Next he invited governors of the states traversed by the railroads within the combine to a conference. The conference, which met at Helena, Montana, passed a resolution condemning the consolidation and endorsing any court action which the affected states might institute. Finally, Van Sant directed the Minnesota attorney general to start legal action against the Northern Securities Company on the grounds that its formation violated state law.[23]

The court proceedings undertaken at the governor's behest ended in a blind alley. Federal action was required to down a giant like Northern Securities. This was instituted by President Roosevelt in February, 1902, and culminated two years later in a United States Supreme Court decision invalidating the projected merger on the grounds that it violated the Sherman Antitrust act. Nevertheless, the governor's apparently courageous stand against railroad monopoly paid rich political dividends; he won re-election in 1902 by an overwhelming majority.[24] For the next few years Minnesota politicians found "antimergerism" as useful politically as a later generation of office seekers would find anti-Communism.

Van Sant's standing as a reform governor did not rest solely on his antimerger zeal. His legislatures passed several important reform measures, some of which he had recommended and all of which he signed into law. The direct primary, which the 1899 session had applied to Hennepin County, was in 1901 extended to all county offices, state legislative races, and congressional contests, but the state-wide offices were left under the convention system. Lind's recommendation that state institutions be placed under a board of control was adopted. And most important, the 1901 legislature, after a stormy debate, raised the railroad gross earnings tax from 3 to 4 per cent, a measure that railroad lobbyists had managed to block for more than a decade.[25]

Van Sant enjoyed less success with comprehensive tax reform. A special legislative session which met in 1902 rejected the basic recommendations of a special tax commission set up in 1901 at the governor's request. But consideration and discussion of the tax commission's report laid the groundwork for a constitutional amendment which liberated the legislature's taxing power from the onerous restrictions written into Minnesota's original constitution. This amendment was finally approved by the voters in the 1906 election.

As the campaign of 1904 approached, Van Sant did not disavow interest in a third term. Merger litigation was still pending, and his standing with the people of the state seemed to assure his re-election. But the professionals in his own party had other ideas. Unfortunately for Republican unity, they failed to agree on who the nominee for governor should be. A spirited contest developed between Robert C. Dunn, state auditor and editor of the *Princeton Union*, and Loren W. Collins of St. Cloud, who had served as associate justice of the Minnesota Supreme Court since 1887. Although Collins seemed a more convinced antimerger man than Dunn, neither candidate "was champion of any particular measure."[26] Collins, the older of the two, had the support of the Grand Army of the Republic and of Van Sant, himself a Civil War veteran. The party's younger element, restive under the prolonged control of the GAR faction, tended to favor Dunn.

Despite Van Sant's support of Collins, Dunn won the nomination. But the bitterness of the preconvention race prevented full Republican support of the victor. Van Sant refused to work for Dunn, and a number of Collins men publicly endorsed John A. Johnson, the Democratic candidate, whose agreeable qualities made him acceptable to disaffected Republicans. Notwithstanding President Theodore Roosevelt's four-to-one sweep of the state, Johnson won the governorship by a narrow margin.[27]

The Johnson administration, which gained re-election in 1906 and 1908 and ended with the governor's untimely death in September, 1909, significantly expanded the Lind-Van Sant policies.[28] It recommended and got voter approval of the "wide-open" tax amendment in 1906 which in turn opened the door for further reforms, including a strong permanent tax commission and an effective inheritance levy. At the governor's recommendation the 1907 legislature passed several statutes tightening railroad regulation. One of these prohibited the issuing of free passes, another fixed passenger rates at two cents a mile, and a third set up a classification of commodities and prescribed maximum rates for their carriage.

The most important accomplishment of Governor Johnson lay in the area of insurance regulation. An investigation conducted shortly after he took office disclosed that a leading Minneapolis insurance firm was in a deplorable financial state due to gross mismanagement. The governor used his influence to effect a reorganization of the company and followed this up by recommending a thorough restructuring of the Minnesota insurance code. The legislatures of 1905 and 1907 acted favorably on his proposals.

The productive sessions of the Johnson years also effected important reforms in a number of other fields. To the satisfaction of conservationists, the legislature of 1905 tightened the code governing the sale of timber on state lands. The 1907 session enlarged the authority of the bureau of labor, making activities like factory inspection more effective. Another law passed in 1907 conferred on municipalities the power to own and operate such public utilities as street railways, telephones, gas works, and electric light plants. Two years later the legislature passed a law setting up a department of banking; hitherto the public examiner had been responsible for the inspection of bank accounts.

This record coupled with Johnson's skill as a verbal exponent of progressivism won for him the reputation of being a reformer *par excellence*. Following his unexpected death at the age of forty-eight, a Johnson legend developed in Minnesota, and many historians of the period rank him with Robert M. La Follette of Wisconsin as an outstanding progressive governor. In one sense this reputation is deserved. The Johnson administration did make an impressive record, and his personal leadership was an important factor in establishing it.

On the other hand, the reformer stereotype fails to define the essential Johnson. At this point the contrast with La Follette is instructive. Unlike his Wisconsin contemporary, Johnson did not dedicate his political career to a series of crusades for righteous causes. Instead, from the time he became editor of the *St. Peter Herald* at the age of twenty-six, Johnson consistently adjusted to his surroundings, using to good political effect an uncanny ability to sense and define the hopes and anxieties of his contemporaries. Along with this he had a capacity for establishing friendly rapport with all kinds of people without, apparently, arousing serious suspicions of his sincerity. His commitment to the drive against political bossism, for example, did not preclude amicable and confidential relations with Richard T. O'Connor and Daniel W. Lawler, the conservative leaders of the St. Paul Democratic organization. Nor did his Democratic affiliation prevent effective co-operation with Republican-controlled legislatures. Johnson, in short, was a conciliator, a leader who avoided going beyond the consensus of his time.[29]

It is significant that the harshest criticism of Johnson's administration came not from conservatives but from a group of radical progressives who accused the governor of lacking vigor in dealing with the railroads. Late in the summer of 1906 the Railroad and Warehouse Commission instituted an investigation of freight rates. As the hearings proceeded, the militance of James Manahan, a zealous Bryan Democrat who was serving as legal counsel for the Minnesota Shippers' Association, produced a political storm. Manahan eventually succeeded in pressuring the commission into issuing a subpoena to James J. Hill, but when Hill appeared it was so arranged that Attorney General Edward T. Young examined all witnesses. Deprived of a long-awaited opportunity to question Hill, Manahan contemptuously characterized the hearing as a "polite affair." The commission responded by debarring Manahan from practicing before it, whereupon the lawyer appealed to the governor, who refused to reverse the commission's action. Thereafter Manahan became a determined leader of those who opposed Johnson.[30]

Lacking a candidate of sufficient stature, the Manahan Democrats did not challenge Johnson's renomination in 1908. But they vigorously fought the selection of a delegation to the Democratic national convention pledged to support him as a candidate for the presidency. Although state pride worked for the governor and the Johnson men won this round, the Manahan camp managed to underscore the essentially conservative orientation of the Johnson-for-president movement. Outside of Minnesota Johnson's principal supporters were anti-Bryan Democrats in search of a counterpoise to the party's long-time leader. At the national convention Bryan won an easy victory on the first ballot. In addition to the votes of the Minnesota delegation, Johnson received only scattered support from Connecticut, Maryland, New Hampshire, Pennsylvania, Rhode Island, Georgia, and Maine.[31]

A year later Johnson further antagonized the Manahan faction of his party and compromised his standing with other progressives as well by vetoing a tonnage tax bill calling for a levy of from two to five cents on every ton of iron ore taken from Minnesota mines. The veto message argued, among other things, that the proposed tax was inequitable and possibly unconstitutional, since it subjected the mining companies to double taxation.[32] The governor's reasoning may have been sound; the legislature of 1921 decided that the state constitution had to be amended before a tonnage tax could be enacted. However, the unpopularity of the United States Steel Corporation and its affiliated companies encouraged some progressives to suspect that Johnson had sold out to big business.

Other issues also were beginning to challenge Johnson's noncommittal posture on highly controversial questions. County option—the proposal that the voters of each county should determine whether liquor licenses should be issued within its precincts—was becoming particularly troublesome. Proponents of this measure developed impressive strength within the 1909 legislature. Had they succeeded in passing a county option bill, Johnson would have faced a decision comparable to the one posed by the tonnage tax.[33]

Death resolved these difficulties. On September 15, 1909, Johnson, who had never enjoyed robust health, underwent surgery to correct a chronic ailment. Six days later he died. The outpouring of public grief that followed swept away resentment and stabilized Johnson's reputation on a level of greatness. In commenting on the standing of another popular governor, Floyd B. Olson, who died in office in 1936 at the age of forty-five, Professor George H. Mayer wrote: "Olson's faults were forgotten and his achievements took on legendary proportions."[34] Although the two governors were in many respects dissimilar, the same could be said of Johnson.

CHAPTER THREE

The Dynamics of
Minnesota Progressive Politics

WHEN A POLITICAL LEADER of Johnson's style and temperament became a reformer, it could only mean that the reform spirit had captured public opinion. The behavior of the governor's partisan opposition confirms this premise. In challenging Johnson for re-election in 1906 and 1908, Minnesota Republicans did not accuse his administration of being irresponsibly radical or fostering policies detrimental to investment within the state. Rather, they implied that Johnson had failed to carry reform far enough, and they promised better performance under a Republican administration.[1] At the same time, spokesmen for all groups within Minnesota adapted progressive rhetoric to the promotion of their particular interests. Precisely what policies deserved to be called progressive became a moot question, but nearly everyone claimed the label.

The main push came from the nonurban middle class. Small-town Minnesota supplied most of progressivism's visible power structure. Before becoming governor, John Lind practiced law at New Ulm. Samuel R. Van Sant operated a river transport business out of Winona. Jacob F. Jacobson, the Minnesota GOP's major progressive leader and Johnson's opponent in 1908, managed a hardware and implement firm at Madison in Lac qui Parle County.[2] William E. Lee, who led the progressives to victory in the 1914 Republican primary, was a banker at Long Prairie. Like Johnson, a number of influential progressives were practicing journalists. Gunnar B. Bjornson, who organized Lee's 1914 victory, edited the *Minneota Mascot*, a highly respected weekly often quoted by other papers. Frank A. Day of the *Fairmont Sentinel*, who served as Governor Johnson's secretary, was another prominent member of progressivism's ruling fraternity. A few so-called dirt farmers also achieved leadership, the most striking example being state senator Ole O. Sageng of Otter Tail County.

Fear of a completely industrialized and urbanized United States largely explains the enthusiastic response to progressivism in small-town and rural Minnesota. If giant enterprises dominated the economy, what would happen to the small merchant? Would lawyers, too, be obliged to sacrifice professional independence and become paid servants of large corporations? And what would be the fate of individualistic journalism if a few metropolitan chains established monopolies in the newspaper field?[3]

A general dislike of the large city reinforced these apprehensions. For many years main street had reacted negatively to the rapid growth of Minneapolis and St. Paul. To small-town spokesmen, the large urban centers threatened not only the economic status of rural Minnesota, but also the system of values supporting the American way of life. Moreover, these spokesmen believed that preferential freight rates, not strategic location or superior enterprise, had stimulated the growth of the Twin Cities. As early as 1890 Joel P. Heatwole, editor of the *Northfield News* and a prominent Republican politician who later served several terms in congress, stated the small-town case against the Twin Cities in unambiguous terms: "Year after year the wealth of these two large municipal cormorants grows and expands under the bright rays of the sun of railroad discrimination and political bossism, while the Country Districts . . . are retrograding in wealth and importance. . . . The interests of the Cities and the Country are as identical as . . . those of the Wolf and lamb."[4]

In his presidential address to the 1904 convention of the Minnesota Municipal and Commercial League, Leonard A. Rosing, a Cannon Falls businessman, complained that while the railroads transported coarse grain from Minneapolis to Chicago for seven and a half cents per hundredweight, the rate from Cannon Falls to Chicago was fifteen cents, even though the distance from Cannon Falls to Chicago was forty miles less than from Minneapolis. The welfare of nonmetropolitan centers, said Rosing, dictated a distance tariff law which, by requiring uniform rates per ton-mile within each freight classification, would place small towns on the same basis as Minneapolis. He pointed out that Iowa had operated under such a law for years, and that Iowa was blissfully free of large urban concentrations.[5] In supporting this measure, which had been advocated by Ignatius Donnelly in earlier years, Rosing was not only speaking for himself. During the next decade the distance tariff became an important progressive goal.

Small-town Minnesota also viewed the national banking system with considerable suspicion. The most serious complaint related to Wall Street's tight control of the country's monetary and credit resources, including capital originating in the Midwest. Prevailing rules required national banks to maintain 15 per cent of their deposits as a protective reserve, three-fifths of

which had to be placed with banks in designated "reserve cities" or "central
reserve cities," a classification that included New York, Chicago, and
St. Louis.[6] This arrangement, coupled with restrictions on the lending power
of national banks (farm mortgages, for example, were an excluded category),
encouraged a flow of deposits from the interior region to large seaboard
institutions, thereby augmenting the funds on hand for stock market speculation and reducing those available to finance smaller local business ventures.[7]
Writing to Senator Nelson in 1908, E. W. Davies, a veteran southwest
Minnesota banker, illustrated the problem with an interesting case study:

> Until about five years ago, the First National Bank of Jasper,
> Minn. was a State Bank and kept its reserve with [Pipestone
> County Bank] and the average deposit from said bank was
> about fifteen thousand. When we changed the charter from state
> to national, the bank at Jasper was obliged to withdraw its
> deposit from [Pipestone] and place it in a bank in a reserve
> city, which is Minneapolis. Minneapolis, of course, could not
> deposit that money back into the interior and have it counted
> as a reserve, but was obliged by law to forward it to Chicago
> and New York. The result was that we had to reduce our business
> to that extent and withdraw that much money from circulation
> in this county.[8]

The panic of 1907 pointed up the essential weaknesses of the national
banking system and in the process laid bare its inequities. One accompaniment of the panic that particularly infuriated main street was the temporary
suspension of payments by leading New York banks, a step that froze
the reserves on deposit in these banks. In a widely quoted Senate speech
that elicited warm approval from many constituents, Nelson described the
economic impact of this move:

> Prior to the suspension and tie-up in New York, we had
> been moving all our crops with western money. . . . Our country
> banks were well supplied with currency, and they were devoting
> that currency to the movement of our crops and to commercial
> purposes, for be it known that our country banks in the West
> do not have any of these call loans on stock collaterals. It
> was not until the panic started in New York and until the banks
> of New York and Chicago tied up over $30,000,000 of the
> funds of our national banks in Minnesota that our banks in
> the Twin Cities were forced to follow suit.

Nelson also suggested that a double standard dominated banking.

> If the First National Bank of Alexandria, my own home, had
> suspended during that panic and refused to pay, as it did not
> do, the Comptroller of the Currency would have . . . put it
> in the hands of a receiver and wound it up. But when these
> great city banks all in a body resorted to this system . . . no
> action was taken.[9]

Small-town complaints against railroads and the credit system articulated
two long-standing discontents of Minnesota farmers. Stringency of credit
distressed agriculture even more than it did the bankers, and the belief
that railroads habitually discriminated against small shippers had commanded
agrarian acceptance ever since the 1870s. In addition, populism had conditioned many farmers to the rhetoric of progressivism. The two movements
were not identical — progressivism had a broader social and economic base
of support and was less regional in its appeal — but they shared a conviction
that a conspiracy of wealth threatened the republic. Although agriculture
had recovered from the dismal depression that spawned populism in the
1890s, farm prices remained uncertain, and many farmers still felt excluded
from the amenities of American life.[10]

Ambivalence marked the relationship of the Twin Cities business community to progressivism. While the progressive approach to some issues,
notably tariff protection, coincided with vital St. Paul and Minneapolis
interests, progressivism's hostility to large cities in general and the fears
of the metropolitan business community that overly enthusiastic reform
might create a climate unfavorable to commerce and industry, discouraged
full Twin Cities identification with the movement. This tendency to carry
water on both shoulders is illustrated in a 1907 editorial statement appearing
in the *Commercial West*, which was an authoritative voice of the Twin
Cities business community. "The Harriman type of frenzied stock jobbing
is of no benefit to the country," it commented, but "On the other hand
no cure will be effected by treatments of frenzied reform."[11]

The progressive drive against political machines, however, struck a responsive chord in Minneapolis. The defeat of Senator Washburn in 1895
by the Merriam organization had not only deprived the city of a United
States senator but had deeply wounded its pride. Following Washburn's
defeat, Minneapolis opinion makers began to advocate legislation limiting

the use of money in politics and other measures designed to curb bossism. One tangible accomplishment of this activity was establishment of the direct primary in Hennepin County by the 1899 legislature, a step taken at the initiative of Minneapolis leaders. Ironically, the first mayor produced by this reform was Albert Alonzo Ames under whom a series of unprecedented scandals developed. The Ames episode, however, did not discredit the primary as much as it reinforced the drive against machine politics.[12]

In the post-Ames period a Minneapolis Voters' League, whose leadership roster included such prominent names as Carpenter and Washburn, agitated the cause of urban reform. Its periodic addresses to the electorate of Minneapolis forcefully stressed shortcomings in municipal government without advocating radical change in the city's political structure. The one issued in 1906 perceived a corrupt alliance between political machines and public service corporations. The city council, it charged, included too many "drones, deadweights and gangsters." The Minneapolis Street Railway Company was "the original corrupting influence in our city council" and was continuing "its persuasive attentions to aldermen." Another utility, the Northwestern Telephone Company, also granted "far too many favors" to council members, while the city clerk's office served as "a social center for contractors and lobbyists."[13]

The modest reform proposals advanced by the Voters' League assigned higher priority to efficiency and economy than to an extension of city services. The league's most important recommendations were substitution of day labor for the contract system in the area of public works, conversion of the post of city clerk from an appointive to an elective office, and transfer of authority over public works from the city council to the city engineer. In addition, the voters were urged to retire a number of influential aldermen.[14]

Tangible self-interest led the Twin Cities business community to support another cause which midwestern progressivism generally favored. This was tariff reform, meaning a reduction of import duties. Since the American market could not absorb all the flour and grain produced in the country, the prosperity of those engaged in any aspect of the grain business depended in part on foreign outlets. An excessively high protective tariff threatened these outlets in two ways. If other countries were unable to sell their products in the United States, they could not earn the exchange required to purchase American goods; and high American tariffs encouraged foreign governments to levy retaliatory rates against American exports. It followed that a reduction of the high level of American tariff protection commanded strong support in Minnesota and neighboring states.[15]

Most Minnesota progressives favored tariff reform and reduced import duties. They believed that a high protective tariff promoted monopoly. This point of view was reflected in a cartoon entitled "Thin Ice," which was published in the Minneapolis Journal *of November 18, 1901.*

Grain traders and millers also favored Canadian reciprocity. An exchange of tariff concessions between the United States and its northern neighbor under which Canada would reduce its tariff on American manufactures in return for a more liberal admission of Canadian raw products into the American market promised a flow of Canadian wheat into Minneapolis for marketing and processing. "Suppose," dreamed the *Commercial West*, "reciprocity with Canada should be made broad and sweeping. Minneapolis and St. Paul would then have an opportunity to grow as they never have, because they would be a natural distributing center for the great northwest territory." Spokesmen for agriculture, who feared the competition of Canada's fertile wheat fields, were scarcely enthralled at the prospect. Consequently President William Howard Taft's proposed reciprocity agreement with Canada, advanced in 1911, met a decidedly mixed response in Minnesota. The Twin Cities business community enthusiastically supported it while farm leaders organized a strong antireciprocity campaign.[16]

General tariff reduction, however, was another matter. On this question millers, grain traders, farmers, and small-town merchants were in substantial accord. Milling industry spokesmen as well as informed farmers realized that the sale of their products abroad depended in part on the willingness of the United States to admit foreign products into the American market. Farm spokesmen also believed that high protective tariffs encouraged monopoly by shielding American industry from healthy overseas competition. As early as 1902 one of Senator Nelson's constituents expressed this widespread conviction, saying that people he knew were "getting awfully sick of all kinds of Trusts, and especially those which are protected by any tariff, and they would welcome reductions in the tariff on all articles dealt in by Trusts."[17] The reality that farmers had to sell in a highly competitive and unstable market and purchase necessities in a protected one increased agriculture's suspicion of the tariff.

Nationally the pressure for tariff reduction became intense during the first decade of the new century. President Theodore Roosevelt, who appreciated the divisive potentialities of the issue, managed to evade these pressures until he left the White House on March 4, 1909. His successor was less fortunate. The Republican platform of 1908 pledged the administration of William Howard Taft to tariff reform. The plank in question did not explicitly promise a downward revision, but many Taft supporters, particularly in the Midwest, understood it to mean that.

After taking office Taft called congress into special session for the purpose of honoring the tariff reform pledge. Before long the Republican leadership produced the Payne-Aldrich bill, a highly protectionist measure. Most Midwest Republicans felt betrayed and outraged. A sizable number of them joined the virtually solid Democratic opposition to the bill. On the final count this coalition fell short of success. The Payne-Aldrich measure passed both houses of congress and President Taft signed it into law.[18]

During the Senate's consideration of the tariff bill Minnesota's two senators, Nelson and Moses E. Clapp, joined an opposition bloc consisting of ten midwestern Republicans including, among others, La Follette of Wisconsin, Albert J. Beveridge of Indiana, and the two senators from Iowa, Albert B. Cummins and Jonathan P. Dolliver. Eight members of the nine-man Minnesota delegation in the lower house, seven of them Republicans and one a Democrat, voted against the bill on final passage. Accusations that such a stand was disloyal to the Republican party created few political risks in Minnesota. When editorializing on the Payne-Aldrich measure even the ultraconservative *Commercial West* fully adopted the progressive idiom, lauding insurgency and condemning House Speaker Joseph G. Cannon and Senator Nelson W. Aldrich, the two national symbols of stand-pat Republicanism.[19]

Unlike tariff revision, railroad regulation did not command the united support of the Twin Cities business community. To be sure, both large and small shippers in Minneapolis and St. Paul frequently accused the railroads of malpractice. Early in the century the complaints of flour millers about rate discrimination were particularly loud, and the outcry in the Twin Cities against the Northern Securities merger rivaled the rural reaction in stridency. However, the proposition to grant the Interstate Commerce Commission full rate-making authority raised the familiar specter of the distance tariff, which Twin Cities spokesmen feared a strengthened ICC would adopt. Given this danger, means other than government control seemed preferable in attacking the railroad problem. *Commercial West* suggested in 1905 that "superior diplomacy" and "counter moves on the part of railroads whose chief interests are in this locality" had ameliorated the basic transportation complaints.[20]

Along with rural and small-town enthusiasm for the distance tariff, traditional agricultural hostility to the Minneapolis Chamber of Commerce — the older name of the Minneapolis Grain Exchange — complicated the position of Twin Cities interests within the progressive coalition. In the early 1900s this front was relatively quiet; full-scale hostilities between grain grower and grain trader did not erupt until after 1912. But there were rumblings. The American Society of Equity, a militant co-operative movement which proposed to establish control by farmers over the commodity markets, had by 1905 started an educational and organizational campaign among Minnesota and North Dakota producers. At the same time farm journals kept alive the notion that the so-called middleman — primarily the grain trader and food processor — was appropriating an excessive share of the consumer's dollar.[21]

The goals of organized labor also worried Twin Cities businessmen, particularly those in Minneapolis. Spokesmen for industry argued that the narrow profit margin in enterprises like flour milling precluded excessive wages, an evil which unionism theoretically encouraged. Whatever the truth of this claim, Minneapolis became known as an open shop town shortly after the turn of the century. Following a period of industrial strife, including a prolonged strike against the flour mills, Minneapolis employers in 1903 organized the Citizens' Alliance, which for more than a generation blocked effective unionization within the city. A similar organization in St. Paul failed to develop the strength of its Minneapolis counterpart.[22]

This determination of employers in the state's largest city to block any union advance was one of several handicaps which crippled the Minnesota labor movement and kept it from effective co-operation with middle-class progressivism. As in the nation at large, the state's trade unions were divided. The Minnesota Federation of Labor, like the American Federation of Labor with which it affiliated, was led by moderate unionists who were attuned to the cautious policies of AFL president Samuel Gompers. But within the MFL (as within the AFL) a militant socialist minority challenged the moderate leadership.

Although an AFL-affiliated labor movement existed in Duluth, the miners on the neighboring iron ranges remained unorganized. In part, this was due not only to the rigid antiunion vigilance of the steel companies, but also to the reluctance of the MFL to push the formation of industrial unions. Radical union activity moved into the breach. The Western Federation of Miners, which affiliated with the revolutionary Industrial Workers of the World from 1905 to 1907 but returned to the AFL in 1911, began organizing the miners in 1905. This effort culminated in the disastrous 1907 strike, which not only failed to achieve its immediate goals but also resulted in the liquidation of the local unions which the WFM had established. Thereafter the IWW, the dreaded "Wobblies," became active on the ranges, largely under Finnish-American leadership. Circumstances made it impossible, however, for the Wobblies to work for immediate unionization. Thus their primary goal was educational — that is, arousing the class consciousness of the predominantly foreign-born miners.[23]

Despite the inability of many citizens to distinguish between the AFL and IWW, the Minnesota labor movement did establish a limited rapport with the state's progressives. Annual MFL conventions ratified many of the standard progressive demands, including those calling for direct government. Progressives in the state legislature supported a few of labor's minimum goals. In the 1913 session, for example, they set up a workmen's compensation system. Few trade unionists won election to office, but William McEwen, editor of the Duluth *Labor World* and for many years a leader in the MFL, became one of Governor Johnson's closest and most influential advisors.[24]

Johnson's policy during the 1907 range strike epitomized at its best the response of humanitarian middle-class progressivism to labor's problems. When violence threatened, the governor refused, without entirely foreclosing, demands by management that state troops be sent to the mines. Instead he went to the scene in person on a mission of conciliation which put him in touch with employer representatives, union leaders, and rank-and-file miners. From one point of view his mission succeeded. His persuasive kindliness reduced tension and helped avert violence. In the end no troops were required. By treating "the miners as respectable and responsible citizens," the governor gained popularity and trust among the strikers — a lesson which management might have heeded. Moreover, personal contact with the strike situation broadened Johnson's outlook. The conditions in the mines appalled him and "led him to give careful thought to the demands of labor."[25]

In the final analysis, however, Johnson's intervention did nothing to shape the outcome of the strike, which utterly failed to achieve any of its objectives. The governor could not — or at any rate did not — exert pressure on the companies to meet the demands of the strikers, even though these demands seemed reasonable and moderate. And he sternly forbade the WMF to block the replacement of strikers by outside workers. To the people of Eveleth he affirmed the right of miners to organize, to strike, and to persuade others to strike, but he reduced the significance of these concessions by asserting that "if a man wants to work and he and his employer agree that he shall work, he has a right to work, and no one has any right to stop him."[26] The presumption that this stricture precluded even the most peaceful picketing is strengthened by the governor's warning to the miners against trespassing upon private mining property or attempting to keep anyone from working in the mines.

Law and precedent may have obliged Johnson to take this position, but there is no evidence that he acted contrary to his convictions. However greatly humanitarian progressives of his type sympathized with the plight of the wage earner, they could not concede the propriety of union interference with a laborer's presumed right to work or an employer's right to hire him. Labor spokesmen, on the other hand, contended that such restrictions on union activity virtually assured the failure of every strike effort.[27]

A developing alliance between progressivism and the antiliquor cause further embarrassed the movement's relationship with organized labor. By 1908 most Minnesota progressives had embraced the concept of county option, which would permit the voters of each county to decide whether liquor establishments should be licensed within it. Enthusiasm for this measure did not rest solely on the presumption that it would reduce drinking. The brewery-distillery complex seemed to embody most of the evils against which progressivism was contending. Allegedly it built and maintained corrupt political machines, bought and sold legislators, and conspired with other interests against the general welfare. Why not give the people an opportunity to vote against such a monstrous evil?[28]

Apart from the great end it was designed to serve, county option had a further charm. It preserved the home rule principle which Minnesota progressives were fond of extolling, and it concretely applied the initiative and referendum concepts. As a first step, a prescribed number of voters had to sign a petition requesting an election on whether to license or not to license; that done, the election would be held, with a simple majority determining the future of saloons within the county.[29]

Although organized labor consistently supported the initiative and referendum, only a minority of trade unionists joined the county option crusade. Annual MFL conventions consistently opposed the measure by large majorities, and the labor press editorialized against it. Economic considerations were in part responsible, for the liquor industry employed a large working force which saw its future employment prospects clouded by county option. In addition, the breweries, seeking allies to combat the mounting dry crusade, cultivated the reputation of being more friendly to organized labor than most other employers. Social and ethnic considerations reinforced the economic factors. Many wage earners regarded the saloon as a kind of workingman's club and resented the campaign of middle-class reformers to close it. And a considerable number of trade-union members were recent immigrants whose traditions predisposed them against so-called sumptuary laws.[30]

As a force shaping Minnesota politics, the ethnic factor operated beyond the confines of the labor movement. In the early twentieth century immigrants and their progeny dominated the state's population. The 1905 Minnesota census contained a table setting forth the nativity of the fathers of persons enumerated, a useful classification since it embraced both first- and second-generation Americans. According to this table, more than two-thirds of the state's nearly two million inhabitants were the children of foreign-born fathers. Within this group those of German origin ranked first with 361,099. Those of Norwegian parentage totaled 260,938, followed by those with Swedish-born fathers who numbered 253,885. These three groups accounted for more than 40 percent of the total population in 1905. A wide gap separated the Swedes from the next most numerous category, the Canadians, who numbered 80,814. Irish, Danes, English, Finns, Austrians, Bohemians, and Poles followed in that order. It should be noted that the Minnesota ethnic pattern was not fully stabilized in 1905. The substantial immigration of the next decade brought in a large number of eastern Europeans, particularly from Montenegro, Serbia, and the Slavic provinces of Austria-Hungary.[31]

Diversities of interest and outlook within this large foreign-born population prevented the organization of a solid immigrant voting bloc. Only a strong nativist crusade could have overcome the differences which separated Protestant from Catholic and "Nordic" Europeans from Latins and Slavs. On basic issues which touched firm ethnic values — public education and temperance legislation, for example — Scandinavian-Americans developed a stronger community of interest with New Englanders than with other immigrant groups.

Ethnic voting patterns in the nineteenth century clearly reflect the political heterogeneity of the foreign-born in Minnesota. Before 1890 the supremacy of the Republican party in state politics rested in part on a coalition of native Americans and Scandinavians. Republican majorities were predictable in counties like Hennepin (the Minneapolis area), where a substantial number of native Americans coexisted with many Scandinavians; Kandiyohi (the Willmar area); Polk (Crookston); and Chisago — all counties heavily settled by Scandinavians. The Democratic party, on the other hand, depended heavily on the non-Scandinavian immigrant element. Its principal centers of strength included Ramsey County (St. Paul), which had a substantial German-American and Irish-American population, and Stearns County, a center of German-American Catholic settlement.[32]

To some extent the power of mutual repulsion helped to create and sustain this partisan pattern. The stereotype of the Democratic party as the champion of "Rum, Romanism, and Rebellion," underscored by the dominance of Irish-American leaders like St. Paul's Michael Doran in Minnesota Democratic politics, reinforced the Republican allegiance of Protestant Scandinavians. At the same time Democratic spokesmen kept alive the image of Republican "blue-nose," "puritan" reform, which threatened the statute books with sumptuary legislation and challenged parental rights in education. Daniel W. Lawler, the Democratic candidate for governor in 1892 and for many years thereafter an influential leader of his party, ingratiated himself with German-American audiences by eloquently defending — in German — the "personal liberty" philosophy, which he affirmed the Republicans were determined to undermine.[33]

By the turn of the century, however, ethnic-based partisanship was beginning to disintegrate. A generation of third-party reform agitation, beginning with the Anti-Monopolists of the 1870s and culminating with the Populist party of the early 1890s, had pried many Scandinavians loose from their traditional allegiance to the Republican party. This was particularly true in the Red River Valley and to some extent in the Twin Cities. Although these apostates tended to return to the Republican party after the demise of populism in the late 1890s, their loyalty was less dependable than before. The wearing of the Democratic label by respected Scandinavians like John Lind and John A. Johnson, whose parents were Swedish born, strengthened these insurgent tendencies.[34]

Following the depression of 1893, which shattered President Grover Cleveland's second administration, the loyalty of the ethnic element in the Democratic party also began to weaken. St. Paul, for example, ceased to be as consistently Democratic as it had been in former years. While the capital city's Democratic machine continued to win local elections, St. Paul voters decisively rejected the presidential bid of William Jennings Bryan in 1896 and successively re-elected Frederick C. Stevens, a Republican, to congress from 1896 to 1912. The traditionally Democratic Minnesota Valley, which had a large German-American population, behaved similarly. Counties like Le Sueur generally cast heavy Republican majorities in congressional elections while sending Democrats to the state legislature.[35]

The movement of foreign-born voters out of traditional partisan patterns conformed to the progressive exhortation to defy the machine by voting for the man rather than the party. Since this trend antedated the turn of the century, the progressives could scarcely claim full credit for starting it, but their influence no doubt strengthened it. Perhaps the rhetoric of progressivism also strengthened the determination of immigrants to join the mainstream of American life, a factor which cannot be measured.

The progressive program, however, did not appeal with equal force to all ethnic groups. The German-American community, although divided within itself on many political issues, strongly disliked county option and other varieties of dry legislation. This fact, in turn, influenced the German-American relationship to progressivism. Since the drive for county option came to be closely allied with the campaign for utility regulation and direct government, opposition to one of these measures encouraged the formation of a common front against all of them. It is therefore not surprising that Lynn Haines, a reform-minded journalist and political commentator, who was later to gain prominence as executive secretary of the National Voters' League, found that the records of state legislators representing German-American areas were often reactionary.[36]

The impact of county option on the Scandinavian relationship to progressivism was entirely different. For many years spokesmen for this group had crusaded on behalf of temperance. Scandinavian Lutheran church leaders disagreed on questions of doctrine and theology, but most of them had joined the campaign against the saloon long before the turn of the century. A number of Norwegian- and Swedish-language reform papers combined advocacy of dry legislation with demands for other reforms. The evils of alcohol provided Norwegian-American fiction with one of its favorite themes, and temperance societies played an important role in Scandinavian-American social and cultural life. The drive against the demon rum, in short, enlisted strong support among Scandinavians.[37]

An attitude of hostility toward established political and religious authority which many Norwegians brought with them from the old country further reinforced the inclination toward progressivism. So did the education received by Norwegian-American farmers in the Red River Valley from the populist movement with which many of them had affiliated. And in Minneapolis, Scandinavian-Americans had long voiced a familiar immigrant complaint: that the leaders of the community discriminated against the foreign-born. An official of the Viking Republican League of Minneapolis wrote in 1899 that the time might soon come to strike "one tremendous blow and teach the silk stocking blue-blood Yankees that the Scandinavians are not descendants from the lower creations in nature."[38]

Two forces worked against the centrifugal tendencies that threatened from the beginning to disrupt the Minnesota progressive coalition. The first was an idealistic mood, vague but widespread, which ripened into a conviction that the promise of American life was not being realized and that a renewal effort should be made. The *Minneapolis Journal* attempted to define this mood in an editorial of April 18, 1903:

> We seem as a people to be getting ready to shake off the slouchiness which has naturally fastened itself upon us with the huge task . . . of occupying and utilizing a wilderness. . . . We have been in such a hurry to build houses to live and do business in that we have ignored the litter at the door. We have been so busy dealing with the large-looming essential physical elements of life that we have not cared for its refinements.

The second cohesive force was a sense of regional injury, shared to some degree by all classes within the state and clearly articulated during the Payne-Aldrich tariff debate. Minnesota and Midwest progressive rhetoric frequently extolled the creative influence of the American frontier and complained that the virtuous Mississippi Valley was suffering intolerable discrimination at the hands of eastern interests. With his happy faculty for sensing the climate of his time, Governor Johnson on February 18, 1905, succinctly summarized the Midwest grievance before an audience of Chicago businessmen:

> New York, with its vice, and New England, with its virtue to balance the ledger, to-day control the economic policy of the nation. The time has come to transfer the seat of empire across the Adirondacks, to Illinois, Indiana, Michigan, Ohio, Kentucky, Iowa, Minnesota, Wisconsin, Kansas, Nebraska, Missouri and the Dakotas. The best brain and the surest brawn of the nation is found here ̔and it should be organized into one mighty moral, material and patriotic force to overthrow paternalism and plunder, and regenerate politics and the Republic.
>
> As Americans we are proud of the fact that the bank clearings of New York are to-day one-half greater than those of London. . . . But the location of the counting-house in Wall Street does not justify the transfer of the power of the ballot there. . . . The Republic rests on men, not money. This central West of ours . . . is settled by the best class of inhabitants the world has ever brought together . . . and to them must come sooner or later that power for good which is the nation's hope.[39]

For more than a decade and a half this combination of idealistic discontent and regional frustration contained — but did not overcome — the tensions which stood between grain trader and farmer, employer and worker, main street and the open countryside, and, less visibly, between native American and recent immigrant. These tensions, however, continued to simmer below the surface of state politics. After 1914 they would break through and shatter the progressive coalition.

The shape of this future could not be foreseen on September 21, 1909, the day Governor Johnson died. At that point in time many basic progressive goals remained unfulfilled. On the national level an unreformed tariff, the trust issue, the banking and currency question, and the complexities of railroad regulation still challenged American statecraft. In Minnesota, county option, the state-wide primary, and effective control of utilities had not been achieved. The emotional outpouring sustaining Theodore Roosevelt's 1912 Bull Moose campaign was also to demonstrate that a vast reserve of idealism was still untapped. Far from having reached its peak, Minnesota progressivism in 1909 stood on the threshold of a period when its influence would be even more pervasive than it had been during the Johnson era.

CHAPTER FOUR

The Progressive Tide Rises, 1909–1912

LIEUTENANT GOVERNOR ADOLPH OLSON EBERHART was thirty-nine years old in 1909 when the death of John A. Johnson elevated him to the governorship of Minnesota. A Republican and a native of Sweden, Eberhart had practiced law in Mankato for more than a decade. His experience in public life covered a span of seven years, beginning with election to the state Senate in 1902. At the expiration of his term in 1906, he was elected lieutenant governor despite Johnson's decisive victory and he was re-elected in 1908.[1]

When he became governor, Eberhart did not hold the esteem of Minnesota progressives, and as the months passed their opinion of him declined even further. Their most frequent initial complaint related to the manner in which he had operated as presiding officer of the Senate, a responsibility constitutionally vested in the lieutenant governor, which in Eberhart's time included the power to appoint Senate committees. Advocates of county option and direct government often charged that Eberhart had discriminated against their cause by packing the strategic committees with opponents of reform legislation.[2]

The new governor also failed to create an impression of masterful leadership. According to Charles B. Cheney, political correspondent of the *Minneapolis Journal* over a period of many years, "Eberhart was a clever, personable chap, but that is about all one could say for him." His technique of evading commitment on controversial issues by throwing responsibility for their solution on the legislature prompted John Lind to remark that "The people do not pay a governor $7,000 a year for his autograph."[3]

It might seem that the strong reform tide which swept over Minnesota during the Taft years should have carried a governor of Eberhart's modest capacities along with it. To some extent it did: the state-wide primary law of 1912, for example, is a legacy of his administration. But the influences around Eberhart fortified his powers of resistance. The most important of these was a revived Republican state machine presided over by Edward E. Smith, a Minneapolis attorney, who, according to Cheney, "came as near the definition of a boss as any one ever did in Minnesota."[4]

The image of Smith and his organization developed by Minnesota progressives embodied the classic features of political bossism. Smith even looked like a boss. Cheney remembered him as "a big, lazy-looking chap with a friendly manner and a great sense of humor." Lynn Haines called him "a princely fellow" and added "Were he not so likeable he could never have become . . . the biggest personal power in Minnesota politics."[5]

Smith also preferred to work behind the scenes. He did serve in the lower house of the legislature from 1894 to 1898 and in the Senate from 1898 to 1906, but these were apprenticeship years. The period of his greatest influence came after his retirement from the Senate. Then, to use a Haines metaphor, he functioned as one of the "Alumni Coaches" who amiably but effectively directed the play of legislators willing to serve on their teams. His influential position within the state Republican organization further broadened the base upon which his power rested.[6]

There is little doubt that a complex of motives, including a love of the political game for its own sake, the gratification of a strong will to power, and even a sincere conviction that his policy positions served the public interest impelled Smith to set up a political empire. His progressive adversaries, however, could see only one purpose — serving the "plunderbund." This fearsome term described what progressives believed to be a tightly organized combine of "brewers and allied liquor forces. . . . The United States Steel Corporation. . . . The transportation trust . . . [and] a long list of such corporations as the Twin City Rapid Transit Company." According to the progressive thesis, these interests had secured the services of the Smith machine to protect the unwarranted privileges that had been granted them in the past and, if possible, to gain new ones in the future.[7]

It followed that deposing Eberhart and Smith soon became the primary goal of progressive political action in Minnesota. This, however, turned out to be extraordinarily difficult. Eberhart had his limitations, but, in addition to the managerial skill of the Smith machine, several forces worked for him. One of these was ethnic appeal. As a Swedish-American he enjoyed a measure of consistent support from within his own group. Also his obvious coolness to county option endeared him to many German-American voters.

Finally, he profited from the inability of his opposition to unite behind a single candidate.

The election of 1910 provided the progressives with their first opportunity to down Eberhart. Before the campaign got under way, however, it became clear that defeating him would have to be a Democratic responsibility. When the Republican state convention met in June, the Smith organization had the situation under sufficient control to dispel any doubt as to the outcome; Jacob F. Jacobson of Madison, Republican candidate for governor in 1908 and the major spokesman for the progressive faction of the party, refused even to attend the convention. As expected, Eberhart was nominated.[8]

Before the Democratic state convention assembled in Minneapolis on July 28, a strong Lind-for-governor movement developed both within the party and among disenchanted Republicans. The convention actually named Lind, who at the moment was on his way to Alaska, even though at the same time it voted down a county option plank which the nominee strongly favored. Lind refused the nonimation, probably because he doubted the commitment of the state's Democratic organization to progressive principles, and perhaps also because he felt that though winning the governorship again might be a personal triumph, it would be a hollow victory without commensurate progressive strength in the legislature. Thereupon the Democratic central committee turned to James Gray of Minneapolis who accepted the nomination with the understanding that he supported county option and would explicitly campaign for it.[9]

The Gray campaign met with disaster. Eberhart carried every county in the state, an unprecedented electoral feat, although the numerical size of the plurality he piled up had been topped before. A combination of adverse circumstances worked against Gray. Democrats opposed to county option voted heavily against him. The ethnic factor also may have handicapped him. Eberhart's two-and-a-half-to-one margin in Chisago County suggests that many dry Swedish-Americans overcame their scruples about liquor to vote for a candidate of their own nationality. Moreover, Gray's associations marked him as a big-city man, for he had at various times served on the editorial staffs of the *Minneapolis Times* and the *Minneapolis Journal*, and his political experience included one term as mayor of Minneapolis.[10]

Results of the 1910 state legislative election were more reassuring to Minnesota progressives than the outcome of the race for governor. Lynn Haines asserted that the voters had "eliminated practically all the remaining members of the old stand-pat machine." However, stalemate and deadlock prevented the 1911 legislative session from accomplishing anything significant. Progressive efforts to push through county option, the state-wide primary, a tonnage tax on iron ore, and the distance tariff publicized their reform program but failed to inscribe any of it on the statute books.[11]

Meanwhile frustrations on the state level were finding an outlet in national issues. The National Conservation Congress, which met in the Twin Cities in September, 1910, focused attention on the Pinchot-Ballinger dispute and related questions. This controversy grew out of accusations by Gifford Pinchot, director of the Bureau of Forestry and a close friend of Theodore Roosevelt, that Richard A. Ballinger, Taft's secretary of the interior, was reversing the Roosevelt conservation policies and failing to protect the public domain against predatory interests. After the charges became public, Taft backed Ballinger and dismissed Pinchot from his post. The president's stand angered the progressive element in the Republican party and further widened the developing rift between the so-called insurgents and regulars.[12]

Experienced observers who covered the Conservation Congress were sure that it measurably strengthened progressivism in Minnesota and neighboring states. Roosevelt and Taft, who still maintained a surface cordiality, addressed separate sessions of the congress. Roosevelt's impact was by far the greater. According to a headline in the *St. Paul Pioneer Press* of September 7, crowds along the parade routes "Cheered Taft, But Howled for Teddy." On the question of whether conservation and resource development should be a national responsibility or a state, local, and private one, proponents of federal authority — the Roosevelt position — clearly prevailed, as did champions of the anti-Ballinger point of view. Division of opinion on related issues followed a similar pattern. A *Pioneer Press* editorial evaluating the proceedings found it impossible to overestimate "the tremendous impetus . . . given in the last few days to the progressive movement, not only in conservation but in politics and economic thought."[13]

The conservation gathering also focused attention on the race for the Republican congressional nomination in the first district, the most important political contest of the year in Minnesota. The incumbent, Representative James A. Tawney of Winona, who had served since 1892, was a high-ranking member of Cannon's ruling circle and an outstanding symbol of "regular" Republicanism. If this separated him from the main drift of midwestern

*On a visit to Minnesota in September, 1909, President
William H. Taft praised the newly passed Payne-
Aldrich tariff bill in a speech at Winona. This cartoon
in the* St. Paul Dispatch *of September 18, 1909, called
attention to the visit and to Taft's identification with
standpat Republicanism on the Ballinger-Pinchot and
the tariff issues.*

political development, a number of countervailing factors — the prestige conferred by national leadership, respect for his acknowledged ability, a belief
that his seniority and status were convertible into tangible benefits for south-
eastern Minnesota, and the first district's strong Republican orientation — had helped beat back several previous challenges to his renomination
and re-election.[14]

Tawney's opponent, Sydney Anderson of Lanesboro, was a thirty-year-old
country lawyer with no political experience. Most observers foresaw another
Tawney victory, but they underestimated the degree to which the congressman's identification with ''Cannonism'' had undermined his prospects.

Memories of a Taft indiscretion inflicted further damage. On a swing through the country in September, 1909, the president had delivered an address at Winona that, among other things, praised the recently enacted Payne-Aldrich bill, lauded Tawney — the only Minnesota congressman supporting the measure — and pointedly omitted any reference to the nine Republican members of the delegation who were on record against the tariff. Editorial reaction indicated that Taft had committed a major political blunder. "Western sentiment, Western interest, Western influence in the settlement of this great question [the tariff] receives slight consideration from the president," commented the St. Paul Dispatch, hitherto a staunchly Republican paper.[15]

To the relief of regular Minnesota Republicans, Taft avoided offending insurgent sensibilities when he addressed the Conservation Congress nearly a year after his unfortunate Winona performance. However, spokesmen for Republican progressivism exercised no such restraint. While en route to the conservation gathering, Gifford Pinchot stopped at Rochester, in the heart of the first district, where he delivered a speech on behalf of Anderson that underscored the incumbent's vices rather than the challenger's virtues. "For several years," Pinchot declared, "I have believed . . . that Mr. Tawney is the most dangerous opponent of the public welfare in the house of representatives." In his course of address, Roosevelt, who resented Tawney's role in reducing appropriations for various conservation activities, also vigorously assailed the first district congressman.[16]

Political writers tended to minimize the probable consequences of the Roosevelt-Pinchot attack on Tawney. Some even hinted that Tawney might have gained the allegiance of voters who disliked high-level interference with Minnesota's electoral process. If so, the backlash was insufficient to rescue the veteran incumbent. Anderson won the September 20 primary by a margin of nearly 3,000 votes, an outcome interpreted by newspapers throughout the nation as a stunning defeat for standpat Republicanism. Notwithstanding the defection of some Tawney support to the Democratic candidate — although Tawney himself perfunctorily endorsed his successful rival — Anderson also triumphed in the fall election.[17]

The defeat of Tawney completed the transformation of Minnesota's congressional delegation from a predominantly standpat into an overwhelmingly insurgent body. Prior to 1906 five of the nine House members were generally classified as "regular" Republicans: Tawney; James T. McCleary of the second district (southwestern Minnesota); Loren Fletcher of the fifth (Minneapolis); Clarence B. Buckman of the sixth (central Minnesota); and J. Adam Bede of the eighth (Duluth and the iron range). Fletcher declined to run for re-election in 1906; his successor, Frank M. Nye, who served until 1912, generally supported insurgent positions. Also in 1906 Buckman lost his bid for renomination to Charles A. Lindbergh and McCleary was defeated in the final election by Winfield S. Hammond, the Democratic contender. In 1908 Clarence B. Miller, a thirty-six-year-old attorney whose background and image resembled those of Sydney Anderson, successfully challenged Bede's renomination and went on to win election.[18]

Like the Tawney-Anderson race, the Buckman-Lindbergh, McCleary-Hammond, and Bede-Miller contests were ostensibly waged on the issue of "Cannonism," a term denoting an unholy alliance between Wall Street and machine politics. To be sure, other factors, including the personalities of individual candidates, played a role, but "Cannonism" dominated campaign rhetoric. The response of Buckman and McCleary to charges that they were inextricably identified with standpat Republicanism is also interesting. Instead of acknowledging the identification and defending Cannon, they sought to create the impression of being in basic agreement with the goals and values of the insurgents.[19]

In January, 1911, President Taft presented to congress a reciprocity arrangement that he had negotiated with Canadian officials. This was not a formal treaty, but an agreement designed to go into effect after being approved by both houses and by the Canadian parliament. The president's recommendation was highly controversial; in fact it generated a debate comparable to the Payne-Aldrich issue. However, a very different alignment of forces emerged. The free trade Democrats, who had overwhelmingly opposed Payne-Aldrich, generally backed the reciprocity proposition, which in effect extended the free trade principle to Canadian agricultural imports. A number of protectionist senators and congressmen who had voted for the Payne-Aldrich bill maintained a consistent protectionist stand in opposing reciprocity. They were joined by a bloc of midwestern Republicans — Senators La Follette, Nelson, and Clapp among others — who had crusaded against Payne-Aldrich protection to industry but sought to preserve tariff barriers for agriculture.[20]

Democratic assistance coupled with a strong appeal to Republican loyalty by the administration pushed the reciprocity measure through both houses of congress in July, 1911. Unfortunately for Taft, a developing reaction against the agreement north of the border, nourished in part by American statements that reciprocity presaged annexation of Canada to the United States, defeated it in the Canadian parliament. Like most initiatives taken by William Howard Taft, reciprocity with Canada created more liabilities than assets for his administration.

On balance, this fiasco alienated Minnesota still further from Taft Republicanism. Temporarily, the president improved his standing with the Twin Cities business and industrial community. Millers, grain traders, and railroad executives had for many years desired access to Canadian wheat, and jobbers as well as wholesalers placed a high value on the potential of western Canada's consumer market. Because the reciprocity agreement promised to make these opportunities available, Twin Cities spokesmen enthusiastically supported it. If it had been ratified they would have been deeply grateful to the administration. But it was not, leaving Taft's administration to be judged mainly on the basis of his Payne-Aldrich performance.[21]

Rural and small-town Minnesota were not ready even to credit Taft with good intentions. On the contrary, men and women within these sectors of society saw Canadian reciprocity as an ominous threat to their vital interests. Because Canadian wheat fields had been opened for cropping more recently than those of the upper Midwest and hence were more productive, grain farmers south of the border adamantly demanded tariff protection as a shield against ruinous competition. Allied groups whose capital and aspirations were committed to the development of northern and western Minnesota seconded this demand. The lure of Canada, it was feared, would depopulate Minnesota farms, deflate land values, and reduce whole communities to a state of permanent depression. An ungrammatical letter to Senator Nelson illuminates the problem as it was viewed by residents of the affected area. Nelson's correspondent, who had recently toured the north country on both sides of the international boundary, "Found many old farmers on the boarder counties leaving for Canada . . . principal reasons, are poor or no roads, and s[e]cond it is so expensive work clearing the land. Have always agitated against Canada, but from my trip there I can not blame them as Canada are more liberal with settlers than the State of Minnesota."[22]

Given such a perception of the Canadian threat, it is not suprising that public sentiment in northern and western Minnesota took strong exception to the reciprocity agreement. In the spring and summer of 1911 spokesmen for the region collected signatures for monster antireciprocity petitions, organized tours to Washington in an effort to influence congress directly, and encouraged a flood of letters to senators and members of the lower house. Canadian rejection of the agreement allayed immediate anxiety but, as the campaign of 1912 would demonstrate, the reciprocity issue still retained a sharp cutting edge. There seemed to be no binding guarantee against ultimate ratification of the pact — indeed, to nervous opponents its revival appeared probable in early 1912 — and in any case they felt elected officials identified with the project deserved chastisement.[23]

An irritating discordance is evident between the rhetoric of the antireciprocity campaign and the substantive issue, an observation equally applicable to the Payne-Aldrich controversy. Why, one may ask, was it "progressive" to resist tariff reduction on Canadian wheat while demanding a lowering of rates on manufactured products? Similarly, most Minnesota objection to the Payne-Aldrich bill was not grounded on principled commitment to free trade, but rather on the premise that its schedules were relatively too high. Yet opposition to both measures was articulated in language suggesting a crusade for the liberation of oppressed humanity.

The discrepancy is explicable in terms of upper Midwest priorities and perceptions as well as the American proclivity for inflated rhetoric. A deep anxiety concerning the area's economic future permeated the polemics against both Canadian reciprocity and the Payne-Aldrich tariff. Adjustment to changing circumstances, some potentially adverse, on the part of farmers, millers, middlemen, merchants, and bankers appeared to be the price of survival. Among other problems, movement of the grain-growing frontier into Canada threatened Minnesota farmers with unequal competition and obliged the milling industry to seek access to Canadian wheat. If the Canadian challenge separated metropolitan and rural Minnesota from each other on a particular issue, both wanted a national policy that encouraged rather than restricted opportunities to dispose of the region's exportable surpluses in the world market. During the Payne-Aldrich battle *Commercial West* remarked that "The manufacturers of this country should be getting into the big game, — the control of the markets of the world, — and not spending all their spare time in holding up the home buyer by means of high tariff duties."[24]

For many years upper midwesterners had nourished a conviction that the national Republican party, personified by such leaders as Aldrich and Cannon, was indifferent if not hostile to the vital interests of the region. The main drift of Taft's policy reinforced this conviction. An initial editorial reaction by the *Pioneer Press* to the Payne-Aldrich measure defined a regional consensus. According to this paper, the whole program of Payne and Aldrich was "outrageous effrontery and chicane. . . . The West is sick of the domination of Cannon and Aldrich. . . . It would take very little leadership, if able and sincere, to detach the entire West from the Republican party. . . . The West is not Republican for the sake of the label. The Republican party has no mortgage on this section." *Commercial West*, which quoted

from the *Pioneer Press* blast, added its own comment: "This is straight
from the shoulder talk, and coming from a journal that has never failed to
support the Republican party and protection, is most encouraging. . . .
The absolute control of the dominant wing of the Republican party by
the protected industries . . . has always been recognized and never more
clearly than at this time."[25]

CHAPTER FIVE

The Campaign of 1912

WHILE CANADIAN RECIPROCITY was being debated, the presidential campaign of 1912 got under way. A group of insurgent Republican senators founded the Progressive Republican League in January, 1911, primarily to advance the candidacy of Senator La Follette. Before long a number of anti-Taft Republicans announced their support of the Wisconsin senator. However, his campaign failed to gain the required momentum. Some progressives doubted his temperamental fitness to be president, and the possibility that Theodore Roosevelt might enter the race inhibited others from joining the La Follette movement. Throughout 1911 the only certainty seemed to be that Taft faced a formidable battle for renomination.[1]

The situation became clearer in February, 1912, when Roosevelt announced his availability. A spirited contest for delegates developed between his supporters and the backers of President Taft, with the La Follette men in a minor role. When the national convention met in June, Taft won renomination, but before formal ratification of his victory a considerable number of Roosevelt delegates walked out, claiming that the nomination had been stolen. This laid the foundation for Roosevelt's famous 1912 bolt. At an emotional gathering held in Chicago in August, his followers created the short-lived Progressive — or Bull Moose — party which backed his presidential candidacy. In the meantime the Democrats had nominated Governor Woodrow Wilson of New Jersey.[2]

The Republican preconvention contest stirred considerable activity and interest in Minnesota. The issue there was not between Taft and Roosevelt, but between Roosevelt and La Follette. A combination of Payne-Aldrich, Pinchot-Ballinger, Canadian reciprocity, Roosevelt charisma, and La Follette appeal had reduced administration support to a few officeholders and a hard core of Republican regulars. Cheney recalled that when the selection of delegates got under way, "The Taft men were swamped in the party caucuses."[3] In some cases experienced Republican professionals found it impossible even to hold their own precincts for the president. At the same time elected Republican officials hesitated to court their own defeat by identifying with Taft.

As between Roosevelt and La Follette, Roosevelt prevailed. The delegation chosen to represent the Minnesota Republican party at the Chicago convention — which included, among others, Senator Clapp, Jacob Jacobson, and Walter Newton, the future fifth district congressman — was firmly committed to Roosevelt. La Follette influence, however, continued to be a force. The Minnesota branch of the Progressive Republican League maintained its organizational existence until after the election, ostensibly to help candidates representing the La Follette point of view. A few league adherents joined the Bull Moose campaign, and a greater number rallied to Wilson, but the organization as such took a neutral stand in the presidential race.[4]

When the Republican state convention met in mid-May to select delegates-at-large to the national convention, it became clear that the spirited presidential contest had revitalized the Republican party at the grass roots. Voters who never before had attended a precinct caucus did so in 1912 either because they hated Taft, venerated Roosevelt, or admired La Follette. The reformist mood of the May convention dispelled any illusions that Eberhart-Smith control of the Republican organization could be taken for granted. In fact, it seemed a certainty that Eberhart would be dumped when the Republicans reconvened a few weeks later to nominate for state-wide offices.[5]

An artful coup — for which Smith regretfully admitted full responsibility several years later — saved Eberhart. Following adjournment of the May convention, he called the legislature into special session and requested that it enact a state-wide primary law together with several other reforms, including an improved corrupt practices act. The governor's opponents soon recognized the strategy dictating this move. It appeared that Eberhart was dramatizing a sudden conversion to progressivism in order to strengthen his bid for re-election. An even more important consideration, however, was the fact that his renomination in a primary was more probable than in a convention controlled by his adversaries. A primary contest entailed risk, but it was likely that a number of candidates claiming the progressive label would file for the governorship, and in such a race Eberhart could — and probably would — prevail over a divided opposition.[6]

Although anti-Eberhart legislators hesitated to improve the governor's prospects of re-election, they could scarcely reject measures that many of them had championed for years. Consequently, the special session became a kind of competition between Eberhart and his opposition to demonstrate whose progressivism was the most thoroughgoing. The results were impressive. The *Minneapolis Journal* commented that "In many ways the session was the most memorable in the history of the state. In thirteen days the legislature completely revolutionized the state's present political system."[7]

Consistent with the chief purpose of the special session, the legislature passed a state-wide direct primary law to go into effect in 1912, with the first election scheduled for September 17. It also passed a stringent corrupt practices law which imposed strict limitations on the use of money in political campaigns. In addition it ratified two amendments to the federal constitution: the sixteenth, which authorized the national government to levy taxes on income; and the seventeenth, which provided for the direct election of United States senators. Finally, for good measure, the session strengthened the existing Minnesota child labor law and raised the railroad gross earnings tax from 4 to 5 per cent.[8]

The gubernatorial contest soon developed as expected. Five candidates filed against Eberhart. Three of them had respectable followings: Lieutenant Governor Sam Y. Gordon, former Attorney General Edward T. Young, and former House Speaker William E. Lee. On September 17 Eberhart polled about 22,000 votes more than Lee, his nearest opponent, but the Eberhart total of 62,402 fell far short of a majority of the 164,067 votes cast in the Republican primary. Following his triumph, the governor reappointed Smith as Republican state chairman. Whatever happened in the fall election, the machine would control the Minnesota Republican organization for another two years.[9]

The Bull Moose bolt had in the meantime thrown the Minnesota Republican party into disarray. When the break between the Taft and Roosevelt forces came at the national convention, the Minnesota delegation joined the majority of Roosevelt men in walking out. After the party split had taken place a few Minnesota Roosevelt partisans advocated entering their man on the ballot as the nominee of the Republican party. The Republican presidential electors selected at the May state convention were all for Roosevelt, and the claim that the Taft forces had stolen the nomination added plausibility to this solution of the problem.[10]

The more moderate Roosevelt men, however, balked at making Taft run as a third-party candidate in Minnesota; somehow this seemed to violate accepted rules of fair play. Doubts concerning the legality of such a move quickly laid it to rest, and Roosevelt backers faced the fact that officially and formally they would have to launch a non-Republican effort in support of their presidential candidate.[11]

The question then arose whether the organization created to back Roosevelt should be a permanent third party or a temporary structure that would — or might — pass out of existence after the election. As elsewhere in the nation, the Roosevelt following in Minnesota disagreed on this fundamental issue. Pro-Roosevelt Republican officeholders in particular hesitated to renounce their party once and for all; many hoped that the outcome of the September 17 primary would make it possible to convert the Republican state organization into a pro-Roosevelt force even though it was necessary to run him for the presidency under third-party auspices. Other Roosevelt enthusiasts had caught the vision of a permanent Progressive party that would renovate the nation; they were ready for a complete and final break with Republicanism.[12]

From the start the Bull Moose leaders in Minnesota equivocated on this troublesome issue, and in the end they never resolved it. The official call convoking a mass meeting in the St. Paul Auditorium on July 30 for the purpose of selecting delegates to the national Progressive convention avoided affirming that a new party was being founded.[13] So did the July 30 convention itself. In effect it postponed the issue until after the September primary by passing a resolution formally introduced by Franklin F. Ellsworth of Mankato. The Ellsworth resolution instructed Jacobson, chairman of the July 30 convention and virtual chieftain of the Minnesota Roosevelt forces, to appoint a committee of fifty, five from each of the nine congressional districts and five from the state at large. Following the September primary, this committee was to "assist in selecting . . . by petition" candidates for state office whenever two-thirds of the committee membership judged the regular nominees for a particular post to be unsatisfactory from a Bull Moose standpoint.[14]

The Committee of 50 held an organizational meeting on September 3 and chose St. Paul attorney Hugh T. Halbert as chairman.[15] The next meeting, the first session held after the primary election, obliged the committee to determine its role and revealed fundamental discord. One faction interpreted the Ellsworth resolution to mean that a full Progressive state ticket was mandatory and that no Republican could receive official Progressive backing unless two-thirds of the committee specifically approved him. An opposing faction advanced a very different interpretation: that two-thirds of the committee had to find the GOP ticket unsatisfactory before an independent candidate could be entered by petition under Progressive auspices. Obviously the first group leaned toward a permanent third party and the other wanted to remain with the Republicans. The committee overruled the latter group. But it also approved a resolution which reduced the required vote for endorsement from two-thirds to a simple majority. This greatly increased the probability that only a partial Progressive slate could enter the field, since the nominees on the Republican state ticket, Eberhart excepted, had many friends on the Committee of 50.[16]

Under this arrangement candidates wearing the Progressive label filed by petition for governor, secretary of state, and railroad and warehouse commissioner. All three polled an exceedingly modest vote. Had Jacobson consented to run for governor the outcome might have been different. But he emphatically refused the endorsement — a stand that may have indicated his determination to remain within the Republican party, although he gave business reasons for his refusal. Thereupon the Committee of 50 named Paul V. Collins, editor of the *Northwestern Agriculturist*, as its choice for governor. As a leader in the fight against reciprocity with Canada, which he had pushed vigorously in the columns of his paper, Collins had to some extent developed a state-wide reputation. But he lacked political experience, a deficiency that showed up in the conduct of his campaign.[17]

Two Progressive candidates also filed for congress: Hugh Halbert in the fourth district, and Thomas D. Schall in the fifth. Proportionately they polled a larger vote than Collins, but neither came close to victory. Two years later, however, Schall, again running as a Progressive, won in the new tenth district. He was the only candidate to win major office in Minnesota on the Bull Moose Progressive ticket.[18]

The Committee of 50 specifically endorsed several Republican nominees for state-wide office: Lyndon A. Smith for attorney general; Walter J. Smith for state treasurer; and Joseph A. A. Burnquist for lieutenant governor. Burnquist also received backing from the La Follette-oriented Progressive Republican League. Thus triply fortified, he won a magnificent victory in the fall election.[19]

James Manahan, who became a bitter Burnquist adversary six years later, enjoyed the same triple backing in his successful race for congressman-at-large, a post created by the failure of the 1911 legislature to incorporate into the congressional district network the new seat awarded Minnesota after the census of 1910. The Manahan campaign was the outstanding anomaly of an anomalous election year. Known primarily as an attorney for small shippers and a Bryan Democrat, Manahan had become associated with George S. Loftus, who in 1912 assumed leadership of the Equity Co-operative Exchange, a grain growers' association which three years later helped spawn the Nonpartisan League.[20]

Manahan recalled that one day in the summer of 1912 Loftus urged him to file for the Republican congressman-at-large nomination. After brief hesitation Manahan consented to do so. Perhaps the thought that Loftus' high position in the La Follette-oriented Progressive Republican League promised a substantial bloc of votes influenced his decision. A divided opposition in the primary helped him to victory, and following the primary, the Committee of 50 gave his candidacy an additional boost by endorsing him.[21]

This endorsement was in itself anomalous. Tension existed between Loftus and the PRL on the one hand and the Bull Moose movement on the other, largely because the PRL refused to endorse Roosevelt. The explanation for the committee's support of Manahan probably lay in the Canadian reciprocity issue. Manahan's alignment with the Equity movement placed him with the Roosevelt men in the antireciprocity camp. Be that as it may, the Committee of 50 action deepened the enigma of the Manahan campaign, an enigma admirably capsuled by a 1912 "political paragrapher": "We find it hard to classify this man, Manahan. He is running as a regular Republican, his sympathies are for the Bull Moose; and as a matter of fact he is a radical Democrat, and he is talking socialism."[22]

The race for United States senator, occasioned by the expiration of Knute Nelson's third term, created an enigma of a different sort for the Roosevelt men in Minnesota. Nelson, who was running for re-election, defied placement on the insurgent-standpat scale. Throughout his long career he had cultivated rapport with all major factions without identifying so firmly with any of them that his standing with the others was seriously prejudiced. At the same time he placed high value on formal party loyalty. In the early stages of the 1912 campaign Nelson refrained from publicizing his preference for President Taft, but he firmly resisted the pressure of Roosevelt supporters to join them. Late in October he issued a statement announcing his allegiance to Taft.[23]

The Nelson record, however, did not type the senator as a consistent administration supporter. It will be recalled that he vigorously opposed the Payne-Aldrich bill, and rural progressives found his stand on Canadian reciprocity to be supremely "right." On the other hand he had chaired a Senate investigation that allegedly "whitewashed" Ballinger, and Nelson's relationship with Senator La Follette was far from cordial. In short, no one could unambiguously classify Nelson as either insurgent or standpatter;

and this tempted both groups to let his prestige—which theoretically benefited Minnesota—tip the balance in favor of supporting his re-election.[24]

James A. Peterson, a Minneapolis attorney and member of the PRL crowd, filed against Nelson in the primary. With the La Follette men in his corner, Peterson assiduously courted the Bull Moose group. This effort failed, for Nelson had too many friends within the Roosevelt camp. Although Peterson's campaign developed a note of stridency which may have helped his opponent, in the final count he polled a fairly respectable vote. Nelson won renomination on September 17 by approximately a four-to-three margin.[25]

The final election phase of the senatorial contest developed a new pattern. Daniel Lawler, who emerged from the Democratic primary as Nelson's opponent, had fewer claims to progressive support than Peterson. "As between Nelson and Lawler," wrote one Peterson manager after the primary, "there is now no opposition to Nelson."[26] However, Nelson's refusal to support Roosevelt — and the knowledge that he probably would announce for Taft late in the campaign — precluded formal endorsement by the Committee of 50. The Roosevelt men met their dilemma by refraining from entering a senatorial candidate by petition — presumably a violation of the letter of the Ellsworth resolution — while unofficially backing Nelson. As expected, the senator won re-election by an impressive margin. He outpolled Lawler by more than three to two, even carrying Ramsey County, Lawler's home base.[27]

While Roosevelt managers in Minnesota wrestled with insoluble problems on the state level, the Bull Moose presidential campaign developed powerful momentum. Two priceless assets animated the Roosevelt cause: a charismatic candidate and an emotionally charged issue. If anything, Roosevelt's personal popularity in Minnesota ranked above the national average; many voters recalled him as the champion who had slain the Northern Securities dragon. Reaction to him during his visit to the state in September created an impression that his hold on the people of Minnesota was as secure as ever.[28]

Although Roosevelt's announced opposition to Canadian reciprocity did not endear him to the Twin Cities business community, it gave him the status of a hero in the rural areas. His supporters in the state had contrived to get him committed to antireciprocity early in the campaign. An important Roosevelt address at the Minnesota State Fair in early September dealt at length with the issue. In it the ex-president conceded what could not be denied — that initially he had supported Canadian reciprocity. However, investigation of the question had disclosed to him that the Taft administration

had worked out "a jug-handled arrangement, under which the farmer paid
all the freight." He went on to condemn with equal fervor both the alleged
Democratic proclivity for free trade and what he called excessive Republican
protection of special interests. He then proposed a scientific investigation
of the tariff question so that congress could write tariff laws protecting
everyone — particularly wage earners and farmers.[29]

The Democratic presidential campaign also worked up a head of steam
in the state. The major address of Woodrow Wilson's Minnesota tour,
delivered in Minneapolis before a crowd of 8,000 on September 18, elicited
more enthusiastic audience response than had his earlier efforts in Iowa
and South Dakota. At one point Wilson uncharacteristically remarked, "Let
Roosevelt tell it to the Marines," and he further asserted that "Rats"
was the best reply to Bull Moose trust-control proposals.[30]

Wilson might have made more of the trust issue in Minnesota, for here

On the day following Democratic candidate Woodrow Wilson's visit to Minneapolis, the Minneapolis Journal *of September 19, 1912, pointed up various issues in the presidential campaign in a cartoon captioned simply "If?"*

the Democratic position agreed more fundamentally with that of La Follette and midwestern progressivism than did the stand taken by Roosevelt. Basically Wilson advocated strengthening the antitrust laws to a point where competition would become the major counterforce to monopoly. Scorning this position as a manifestation of "rural toryism," Roosevelt called for virtual abandonment of the antitrust laws in favor of a powerful federal agency endowed with sufficient authority to hold the giant corporations in line without limiting their size. Disagreement with the Roosevelt preference for regulated monopoly may have been one reason for the friendly disposition of the La Follette faction to the Wilson campaign.[31]

A few experienced observers expected Wilson to carry Minnesota. This prediction was not completely off the mark, for on election day Roosevelt topped Wilson by less than 20,000 votes. But Wilson could not match Roosevelt's immense personal popularity. Other handicaps also worked against him. The nearly solid Democratic vote for Canadian reciprocity in 1911 identified him with an unpopular cause. In addition, factional disturbances within the Minnesota Democratic organization inhibited effective mobilization for the presidential campaign.[32]

Virtually no one predicted a Taft victory in Minnesota. Most Republican candidates for state and congressional office either supported Roosevelt or remained silent on their presidential preference. Eberhart, who came out for Taft in mid-July, and Nelson, who did so in late October, were the major exceptions. The principal Twin Cities dailies, including the *Minneapolis Journal*, backed the president, but in a perfunctory way that did little to raise the morale of the Taft effort. An atmosphere of dismal hopelessness settled over Taft headquarters throughout the state. One prominent Duluth Republican reported on October 1 that he and his associates would "do the best we can up here but no one can tell how it will come out on Taft."[33]

The election returns fully vindicated the pessimism of the Taft men. The Bull Moose vote of 125,856 gave Roosevelt a margin of nearly two to one over Taft's 64,334. Wilson polled 106,426 votes and Eugene V. Debs, the Socialist contender, 27,505 — twice the number cast for him in 1908.[34] If the premise that Roosevelt, Wilson, and Debs represented varying brands of progressivism is accepted, and if the Taft candidacy is interpreted as standing for conservatism, the progressive tide was indeed overwhelming in 1912, at least on the presidential level.

The Roosevelt appeal extended to all corners of the state; in terms of simple plurality, he carried sixty-two of the eighty-six counties. As expected, he polled a very large vote in the Red River Valley and adjoining counties where antireciprocity was a popular cause. He also swept Republican areas in southern Minnesota where historically support for third-party radicalism had been slight. He ran third in Hennepin County, where Wilson prevailed over Taft by about 1,000 votes. Roosevelt carried St. Paul, though he lost Ramsey County to Wilson by a half-dozen votes.[35]

Taft failed to carry a single county. Most of the twenty-three registering a Wilson plurality had in the past shown Democratic proclivities — Dakota, Scott, Stearns, Wabasha, and Winona, for example. Debs carried Beltrami County in the far north and ran well ahead of Taft in several neighboring counties.[36]

To the dismay of many progressives Eberhart survived the 1912 deluge. As he had in the primary, he again prevailed over a divided opposition; his proportion of the total vote for governor was about 40 per cent. Obviously no one candidate could have mobilized the other 60 per cent, but if Peter M. Ringdal, the Democratic contender, could have captured one-third of the nearly 100,000 votes cast for various third-party candidates, he would have defeated Eberhart.[37]

Ringdal, a former Populist state senator from Polk County and more recently a member of the State Board of Control, affiliated with the anti-Lawler progressive faction of the Minnesota Democratic party. Like James Gray in 1910, he cultivated support from non-Democratic progressives, but unlike Gray, he deferred to German-American Democrats by avoiding commitment to county option. To some extent his strategy of attracting progressive support while holding on to the so-called wet Democratic vote succeeded. Stearns County, for example, returned a substantial Ringdal majority; and the old Populist counties, where progressive sentiment ran strong, gave Ringdal a vote exceeding that cast for the remainder of the Democratic ticket.[38]

Eberhart, however, apparently captured part of the Democratic vote that opposed county option. At one stage of the campaign the friends of Senator Nelson worried about a rumored Lawler-Eberhart antidry combination. This did not become a major factor in the contests for governor and senator, but Eberhart carried Ramsey County by a substantial plurality, and elsewhere there are evidences of Democratic defection from Ringdal.[39]

Ringdal also lost support from the dry Democrats. The Minnesota Prohibition party polled the largest vote of its history in the 1912 election:

nearly 30,000, approximately 10 per cent of the total vote for governor. In part this reflected a rise in sentiment favoring a total ban on the manufacture, transportation, and sale of liquor, a more drastic proposition than county option. However, the Prohibitionist appeal went beyond the issue which gave the party its name. Lynn Haines characterized the four Prohibitionist lower house members of the 1911 legislature as "active, conscientious progressives" who "stood with the insurgent representatives of the other parties on all vital questions — temperance and otherwise." As if to reinforce this reputation, the 1912 Prohibitionist state platform demanded enactment of all the standard progressive reforms.[40]

Engebret E. Løbeck of Alexandria, the Prohibitionist nominee for governor in 1912, was a strong candidate by third-party standards. A fervent crusader whose colorful eloquence charmed a whole generation of midwestern Norwegian-Americans, Løbeck had attracted a flock of admirers, many of whom cast their votes for him in the 1912 election. He ran strong in Scandinavian-American areas, carrying his own county of Douglas where he and Senator Nelson coexisted as neighbors, sometimes uneasily. During the World War I period Løbeck and a contingent of fellow Prohibitionists showed their concern for reforms other than the dry cause by allying with the Nonpartisan League. This alliance teamed them with German-Americans, trade unionists, and others who, to say the least, did not share Løbeck's enthusiasm for the antiliquor crusade.[41]

David Morgan, the Socialist candidate for governor, ran slightly behind Debs in the presidential race, polling 25,769 votes. His support, like that of the other Socialist contenders in 1912, was largely concentrated in a few identifiable regions, including some of the old Populist strongholds in the Red River Valley, marginal economic areas in north-central Minnesota, Finnish-American communities on the iron range and its periphery, and the labor wards of the Twin Cities. In a few cases — Beltrami County, the ninth ward in south Minneapolis, and the township of Wuori in St. Louis County, for example — the Socialist ticket carried individual precincts. And two Socialist candidates for congress, M. A. Brattland in the ninth district (northwestern Minnesota) and Thomas E. Latimer in the fifth, polled a respectable vote.[42]

Paul V. Collins, the Bull Moose candidate for governor, polled 33,455 votes, a slightly larger total than Løbeck or Morgan. This vote, too, may have helped Eberhart by cutting into the Ringdal potential, although an opposite interpretation is possible.[43] The most striking fact about the Collins showing, however, is the wide discrepancy between his vote and that polled by Roosevelt. Minnesotans emphatically liked "TR," but enthusiasm for the Progressive party was no greater among the voters than among progressive Republican politicians.

The Eberhart campaign benefited not only from a divided opposition but from the efficiency of the Smith organization. The size of the Eberhart vote — 129,688 against Ringdal's 99,659 — exceeded Roosevelt's by about 4,000 and topped Taft's by about two to one. The machine apparently concentrated on getting Eberhart re-elected. Officially it backed Taft, but because his cause seemed hopeless it exerted a minimum effort for the national Republican ticket.[44]

At the same time the Smith organization avoided recriminations against the many Republican nominees for state and congressional office who implicitly or explicitly bolted Taft. It extended little or no assistance to these candidates, but since the congressmen had their own campaign establishments, and most candidates for state-wide office were fortified by Committee of 50 endorsement, they scarcely needed machine help. The voters, for their part, seemingly tolerated this anomalous situation. Many of them had come to place a low value on strict party loyalty.

This combination of circumstances minimized the damage to progressive Republican careers wrought by Bull Moose apostasy. The returns effected only two changes in the congressional delegation, neither of them an upset: the addition of Manahan as congressman-at-large, and the replacement of the fifth district Republican congressman, Frank M. Nye, who retired voluntarily, by Republican George R. Smith. The remaining eight congressmen — seven Republicans and one Democrat — won re-election. The Republican candidates for state-wide office who held Committee of 50 endorsement also triumphed, and by a margin considerably larger than the Eberhart plurality.

Nationally the impact of the Bull Moose bolt on progressive Republicanism contrasted sharply with what happened in Minnesota. Generally speaking, the progressive Republicans who followed Roosevelt's third-party venture suffered either defeat or diminution of influence within the GOP. This in turn tipped the balance within the Republican party in favor of conservatism. As Professor George E. Mowry puts it, "Now sapped of its reforming element, the party of Lincoln was overwhelmingly conservative and was destined to remain so for years."[45]

In the long run the Minnesota Republican party could hardly escape this unintended consequence of the Bull Moose movement. For the time being, however, the capacity of the party's progressive faction to battle for control of the state organization remained unimpaired.

CHAPTER SIX

Progressivism Triumphant

IN TERMS of their basic objectives, Minnesota progressives had solid cause for satisfaction following the election of 1912. The voting patterns registered on November 5 proved beyond doubt that they had captured the mind of the state. A broad progressive consensus permeated the editorial policy of most Minnesota newspapers, including the Minneapolis and St. Paul dailies. Even *Commercial West*, equivalent to a regional *Wall Street Journal*, hailed the advent of Wilson's New Freedom, particularly its pledge to end all forms of special privilege, as an improvement over the policies of the outgoing administration.[1] On most issues the congressional delegation affiliated with the progressive coalition in Washington. The state legislature, too, was responding to reform pressure — or so the special session of 1912 seemed to indicate.

Only the governorship remained in unfriendly hands. Rescuing this office from the clutches of Smith's machine remained a high-priority goal, but for better or worse, Eberhart would continue as chief executive at least until January, 1915. From a strictly partisan viewpoint his prospects appeared favorable. Technically the Republicans widened their lopsided majority in the state House of Representatives by nine seats, reflecting a drop in the Democratic delegation from twenty-six to twenty, and a reduction of the Prohibitionist contingent from four to one.[2] The senators were not up for election. However, since most Republican legislators were of the Roosevelt or La Follette variety, this outcome scarcely strengthened Eberhart's position. The 1913 session proved the opposite to be true.

The deadlock between governor and legislature that had stymied action in 1911 and that election year exigencies had broken during the special session of 1912, resumed after the 1913 legislature went to work. County option failed for want of sufficient support within the legislature itself. So did the tonnage tax on iron ore. Hostility between the executive and legislative branches impeded even measures on which the two agreed in principle. Among these was legislation to regulate utilities. The governor recommended the creation of an appointive state utilities commission. Although this conformed to the revered La Follette model in Wisconsin, the legislature refused to act on it, largely because the progressives lacked confidence in the appointments the governor would make. They favored instead vesting local units of government with authority to regulate utilities. Insofar as more state regulation was essential, the progressives called for expanding the power of the elected Railroad and Warehouse Commission. Both houses passed a bill placing telephone companies under this agency, but Eberhart interposed his veto. Streamlining the administrative structure of state government also ranked as an important progressive goal. Nevertheless Eberhart failed to get action on his proposals along this line. As Cheney later commented: "The legislature was pretty much anti-Eberhart in that 1913 session, on general principles."[3]

A few reforms overcame the impasse. The Cashman distance tariff bill — a measure that outlawed preferential freight rates by requiring uniform ton rates per mile for each class of freight — became law. But the 1913 United States Supreme Court decision in the Minnesota rate cases, which severely limited state authority over railroad transportation, considerably reduced the importance of this statute. Two items of social legislation were of greater long-range significance. One of these set up a workmen's compensation system — that is, compulsory insurance against industrial accidents. The other created a minimum wage commission endowed with authority to establish and enforce minimum wage scales for women and minors.[4]

Neither the governor nor any action in the legislature deliberately planned enactment of the measure that in a sense immortalized the 1913 session. This was the abolition of formal party designation for legislators. The drama began with the introduction in the Senate of a bill removing party designation for county officials — auditors, surveyors, coroners, and the like. The author of this bill evidently acted in good faith when he placed it in the senatorial hopper; many progressives favored limiting party designation to policy-making offices as one means of restricting the potential influence of political machines.[5]

During Senate consideration of the bill an opponent of the measure resorted to the old stratagem of amending an unwanted proposal to the point where not even its firmest supporters will vote for it. The amendment in question extended the ban on party designation to state legislators, a proposition no one had seriously advocated. To the surprise and probable dismay of the author, this amendment picked up sufficient support to survive the entire legislative process of Senate and House action, conference committee deliberation, and approval by the governor.

A number of motives built this support. Some members who worried about the recent increase in the Socialist party vote fancied that a nonpartisan primary election would eliminate legislative candidates of that party before they could contest the final election. Others expected a continuation of the troublesome conflict between their Republican and Bull Moose loyalties and saw nonpartisan elections as an escape from this dilemma. Still others hesitated to assume the heavy burden. of local party responsibility which nonpartisan election of county officials would place on legislative shoulders. A number welcomed the provision in the final bill that moved the date of the primary election from September to June. And a few thought that a nonpartisan legislature might be an interesting experiment, although debate on the measure hardly touched on its intrinsic merits.

The bill also became entangled with the county option issue. Following introduction of the amendment, representatives of the liquor industry conceived that a nonpartisan legislature might serve their cause. They reasoned that the Republican party would soon become a powerful force on the side of county option; it followed that eliminating party designation might blunt direct Republican influence on the legislative process, thereby reducing the probability that county option would triumph. Brewery and distillery spokesmen could not publicly proclaim this theory. Possibly they confided it to trusted retainers, but for the record they subtly suggested that the liquor interests favored retention of party designation in the legislature. Apparently a number of drys — but by no means the entire county option contingent — accepted the proffered bait and voted for the measure. Whatever the liquor industry opposed, some drys automatically supported.

The passing of time soon dissolved or invalidated the complex of short-range considerations that propelled the bill into law. Before long, however, a new set of interests, including the personal political advantage that legislators perceived in the absence of partisan commitment, raised barriers to the restoration of party designation. Informally and unofficially the legislature in time restored a form of party division; but formally the legislature remains "nonpartisan" more than half a century after 1913.[6]

On January 9, 1914, the *Minneota Mascot*, a southwestern Minnesota weekly edited by Gunnar Bjornson, a state legislator and prominent progres-

sive Republican, outlined a plan of action to defeat the Smith machine.
Recognizing that a multiplicity of progressive candidacies had assured
Eberhart's renomination in 1912, the *Mascot* suggested that "a body of
representative men" from all over the state should meet to build a united
progressive front for the coming primary battle. The Bjornson plan aroused
enthusiastic response. In February a number of progressive Republican
leaders issued a call for a Republican state conference to be made up of
delegates chosen by mass meetings on the county level.[7]

Eberhart supporters also reacted to the Bjornson proposal. They charged
that it violated the spirit of the primary law, that in principle it re-established
the old convention system. This accusation drew blood. Bjornson's paper
heatedly denied that the forthcoming conference was a convention in the
usual sense. It was rather "a monster conference for the purpose of helping
the people to secure, through the primary law, that which the primary
law was designed to give them — control of the nominations for all offices."[8]

Perhaps the *Mascot* made a point. The proposed conference no doubt
offered wider opportunity for voter participation than a Smith-controlled
convention; and its decisions were subject to voter ratification in the primary.
Nevertheless when the conference met on March 19 it discharged the basic
responsibilities of a traditional convention. It created an organization for
the forthcoming campaign, endorsed William E. Lee of Long Prairie for
governor, and approved a platform featuring county option.[9]

After the March 19 gathering adjourned, doubts about its success in
achieving progressive Republican unity lingered for a few weeks. Most
of Lee's potential rivals for the governorship rallied to him, but a remnant
of the 1912 Committee of 50 led by Hugh T. Halbert of St. Paul refused
to give up the permanent Bull Moose party dream. The slight promise
of this venture depended on the kind of candidates for high office Halbert
and his associates could recruit. Had their efforts to persuade state Senator
Ole Sageng to accept a Progressive party nomination succeeded, they might
have made a showing. Sageng, a prominent champion of county option,
woman suffrage, and related reforms, had a substantial following throughout
the state. He was, in fact, a kind of progressive folk hero, a practicing
farmer who personified the rural virtues and a political independent whose
use of the Populist label long after the demise of the People's party pointed
up his total aloofness from machine politics.[10]

About a month after the March 19 conference Sageng declined the Halbert
invitation. In effect his action dissipated the Bull Moose dream in Minnesota.
It also reassured the Lee men by removing a potential threat to progressive
unity. The Halbert faction, however, persisted in pushing the forlorn hope

The Minneapolis Journal *of May 18, 1914, published this cartoon entitled "Tramp, Tramp, Tramp, the Boys Are Marching," in a pointed reference to Governor Adolph O. Eberhart's associations with machine politics and the spoils system in the state.*

with Halbert himself as the Progressive party candidate for governor. The final election merely confirmed what experienced political observers knew: Halbert polled only 3,553 votes, about 1 per cent of the total cast in 1914.[11]

After refusing the Bull Moose tender, Sageng enlisted in the Lee campaign, not as a Republican— an identification he did not yet acknowledge— but as a friend of good government. The Lee managers, who knew that a Sageng contribution would give their campaign the desired style, assigned him a heavy schedule of speaking engagements that took him to all parts of the state. An address delivered on April 27 at Detroit, Minnesota, typified the senator's line of argument and in effect keynoted the Lee campaign. "Minnesota is today one of the worst interest-ridden states in the union,'' asserted Sageng. He then went on to place responsibility for this allegedly dismal situation: ''I know Adolph O. Eberhart pretty well. I served with him in the senate when he presided over that body. I know his attitude. . . . He packed every important committee . . . in the senate. I make this statement knowingly and deliberately, knowing full well the gravity of the charge — that Adolph O. Eberhart packed the railroad committee, the tax committee and the temperance committee against the people.''[12]

The intensity of the Lee campaign, maintained in approximately equal measure by speakers like Sageng, a large sector of the small-town press, and the influential *Minneapolis Journal*, diverted public attention from Democratic politics. As it had in 1910 and 1912, a kind of floating factionalism disturbed the inner harmony of the Minnesota Democratic party. Two groups struggled for mastery of the state organization, while a third, the diehard Bryan supporters, stood on the sidelines. The one headed by national committeeman Frederick B. Lynch, a personal friend of President Woodrow Wilson and dispenser of federal patronage in Minnesota, was the more progressive of the two major factions. The other followed the lead of Lawler, who had opposed the nomination of Wilson in the 1912 preconvention campaign and who personified old-line Democratic conservatism of the Grover Cleveland variety.[13]

Like the progressive Republicans, the Democrats held a gathering in March, which out of deference to antimachine sentiment they called a conference rather than a convention. Factional disturbances erupted immediately. Two separate sets of delegates, one pro-Lawler and the other partial to Lynch, claimed the right to represent Hennepin and Ramsey counties. The conference leadership proposed a compromise that would have seated both sets of delegates, with the proviso that each be given half of the assigned Ramsey-Hennepin vote. After rejecting this proposition the Lawler men walked out. The conference then transacted its main business. It endorsed Congressman Winfield S. Hammond of the second district for governor. It also approved a policy statement that lauded President Wilson and included the standard progressive demands, county option and woman suffrage excepted. When the conference adjourned, the most troublesome question seemed to be, what would Lawler do?[14]

The veteran St. Paul Democratic leader soon answered this question by filing against Hammond in the primary. The assumption that Lawler had a substantial following, coupled with Hammond's reluctance to leave Washington for a Minnesota speaking tour, led Democratic leaders to fear that the challenger would overcome the endorsed candidate in the primary.

This nearly happened. So close was the Hammond-Lawler vote that the outcome could not be determined until nearly all the precincts had reported. In the final count Hammond won by a margin of less than 1,000 votes.[15]

Lee defeated Eberhart by a plurality exceeding 16,000. As might be expected, the Lee men were jubilant. Bjornson, who would soon replace Smith as Republican state chairman, proclaimed in his paper that "the day of machine domination is gone" and predicted that "brewery influence and the public utility interests" would no longer control Minnesota politics.[16]

This exuberant optimism was in one sense justified. The Smith machine had been smashed and the progressives were in control of the Republican state organization. The nomination of Hammond was also a victory, conferring on the Minnesota Democratic party an opportunity to renew itself and guaranteeing a progressive governor no matter which party prevailed in November. Much of the progressive program had been enacted and the way apparently lay open for realization of the rest. In terms of its immediate and explicit goals, progressivism was triumphant.

What progressives in the innocence of the prewar world did not see was that successful adaptation to the challenges of the twentieth century required more than the liquidation of political machines, county option, local control of utilities, and direct government. They grossly exaggerated the efficacy of their policies. Tensions between capital and labor and the rising demands of grain farmers for a thoroughgoing reform of their marketing system were acquiring high visibility. Issues such as these would presently subject the Minnesota progressive coalition to an intolerable strain. Problems relating to American foreign policy also would confuse and divide the movement, for the assassination on June 28, 1914, of Archduke Franz Ferdinand, heir to the Austro-Hungarian throne, by a pro-Serbian nationalist set off a chain of events that within five weeks plunged Europe into World War I.

CHAPTER SEVEN

Minnesota's Initial Response
To World War I

MENTALLY, PSYCHOLOGICALLY, AND SPIRITUALLY, the American people were totally unprepared for the outbreak of World War I. For more than a decade progressivism had encouraged preoccupation with domestic affairs. To be sure, the outside world had occasionally demanded attention. Instability in Latin America and the Far East at times appeared to require some kind of response from the United States government, and a few influential Americans like Theodore Roosevelt firmly believed that foreign policy had a vital role in shaping the country's future. But the vast majority regarded foreign affairs as an unwelcome intrusion that diverted attention from more important concerns, while even highly educated people knew little about international politics. Woodrow Wilson, who had earned a doctorate in history and government, keenly felt his own inadequacy in this area. Shortly before taking office he remarked to a Princeton friend: "It would be the irony of fate if my administration had to deal chiefly with foreign affairs."[1]

The view of the world held by most Americans, particularly those who affiliated with progressivism, heightened their psychological and spiritual unpreparedness. A few avant-garde intellectuals may have begun to doubt human rationality and the basic orderliness of the cosmos, but the American people as a whole firmly believed in the capacity of humanity to control its own destiny. For all their violent denunciations of the status quo, the progressives were convinced optimists who expected their reform program to guarantee realization of the American dream. As the popular historian Walter Lord put it, the years before 1914 "were good because, whatever the trouble, people were sure they could fix it."[2]

It followed that few Americans could comprehend the intransigence of the diplomatic crisis that led to the outbreak of war in the early days of August, 1914. As Europe passed over the brink, a lingering disbelief in the possibility of war gave way to a shocked horror and then to an agitated search for explanations of the catastrophe.[3] One which seems to have commanded widespread popular acceptance held that European depravity — from which the American people had happily escaped — had brought on the conflict. Dr. Frank Crane, a popular syndicated columnist, developed this notion in a piece entitled "War Dialogue" which appeared in the newspapers about two weeks after the outbreak of the war:

Europe: We are drawing the sword to show our enemies how to respect us.

U.S.A.   - We adopt such a policy that we have no enemies. Even the weaker nations we seek to conciliate. We are proposing to indemnify Colombia for a questionable wrong. . . .

Europe: We are preparing to trample the grain fields, burn houses, blow up granaries and butcher the workers, to maintain our monarchies.

U.S.A.   - To maintain our PEOPLE (we have no thrones to fight over) we are moving a record crop. . . .

Europe: The glory of the houses of Romanoff, Hohenzollern, Hapsburg, Piedmont, and Wettin must be made to shine.

U.S.A.   - Nothing doing in that line, and glory be to God for it.

Europe: We are playing the grandest wargame in history.

U.S.A.   - You are playing hell. We are playing baseball. . . .

Europe: Our states are separate empires, each prepared to whip any or all of the others.

U.S.A.   - Our states are united. They have no armies. All our soldiers are for the United States. Why don't you organize the United States of Europe.

Europe: We are true to the glorious traditions of the past.

U.S.A.   -That's what ails you. We are true to the glorious principles of the future.

Europe: Think of our ancestors!

U.S.A.   - Think of our posterity!

Europe: We will soon have some more ruins for your tourists
to visit.

U.S.A.   - And, as soon as they get a chance, your workers,
your real red blood, will begin to come here to live,
come as in the past at the rate of thousands a day.[4]

This image of the war and of Europe obviously encouraged neutralism throughout the United States. True, degrees of partiality for the various belligerents soon developed. The predominant sentiment unquestionably favored the British, the French, and particularly the Belgians, whose land was overrun by the German army in the early days of the war. But a substantial minority, augmented by the country's large German-American and Irish-American blocs, leaned toward the Central Powers, Germany and Austria-Hungary. Neither side, however, placed itself outside the neutralist context. A solid popular consensus backed President Wilson's proclaimed determination to keep the nation out of the European war.[5]

In Minnesota the initial response to the war conformed to the national pattern. Undoubtedly the forces working for neutrality were stronger within the state than in the country at large. In size and influence the Minnesota German-American community ranked above the national average, and the tradition that associated a venturesome foreign policy with the wicked designs of Wall Street held a stronger sway in the Midwest than along the Eastern Seaboard. In time these factors would produce a pronounced regional division on foreign policy issues. However, the strong neutralist wave that swept the nation in early August, 1914, largely obscured the existing differences in the degree of noninterventionist sentiment. Even Theodore Roosevelt, who soon would become the country's foremost pro-Ally advocate, made a statement on August 5 that contained "not the faintest touch of partisanship for either side of the struggle."[6]

Like their counterparts elsewhere, Minnesota editors had voiced the general reluctance to believe that armed conflict among the so-called civilized nations could actually develop in the twentieth century. On July 27, when the European diplomatic crisis had reached an advanced stage, the *Minneapolis Journal* thought that "War between the Great Powers . . . is improbable . . . because either the Triple Entente or the Triple Alliance is pretty sure to flinch." Four days later, on the eve of the German declaration of war on Russia, the *Minneapolis Tribune* still hoped that full-scale conflict might be averted. Incredulous horror followed the final dashing of this hope. The *Red Wing Daily Republican* found it "difficult . . . to adjust our minds to the magnitude of this awful tragedy." The *St. Paul Pioneer*

Press called the outbreak of war "inexplicable and unpardonable . . . the greatest crime of modern times."[7]

Most Minnesota newspapers blamed the war on the European political system, which editorial writers apparently believed vested absolute authority in monarchs, aristocrats, and militarists. According to the *Blue Earth County Enterprise*, "the masses do not want war, but a few of the aristocrats want to show their power and supremacy and under the guise of patriotism drive the common soldiers to their shackles like cattle."[8] Jens K. Grondahl, editor of the *Red Wing Republican*, articulated the same theory in a poetic work entitled "The Madness of the Monarchs," which occupied the front page of his paper on August 5:

> Tis the Madness of the Monarchs 'neath whose
>   lash the nations groan!
> And humanity, obedient, rushes on to slay its
>   own —
> Marches on, in servile millions, to appease
>   the royal wrath —
> Oh, what feast awaits the vultures in that
>   dark and bloody path! . . .
>
> Tis the Madness of the Monarchs bound by some
>   Satanic spell,
> That invokes the help of Heaven to perform the
>   deeds of Hell —
> That implores the Prince of Peace and cries,
>   "Thy will be done, not mine,"
> While the Madness grasps the saber to destroy
>   by "right divine."

In the early months of the war the disposition to blame it on general monarchical "madness" predominated over the inclination to hold Kaiser Wilhelm of Germany responsible for its outbreak. Late in August the *Minneapolis Tribune* refused to place "the heavier blame" on either group of belligerents. Rather, it said, "The blame is rooted in a false conception of national power, the existence of armed forces without occupation, a failure to realize the glory of moral strength, a lack of leadership earnestly consecrated in love for humanity."[9]

Occasionally, it is true, Germany and Wilhelm II were singled out for hostile comment. On August 3 the *Pioneer Press* affirmed that the nations east of the Rhine wanted war, an indictment that included Russia, but placed Britain and France in a more favorable light than Germany and Austria-Hungary. "The kaiser has taken the attitude that he can master the world," asserted the *Red Wing Republican* on August 5. A few days later, however, the *Republican* retreated to a more neutral editorial line, and its weekly edition began carrying a regular German-language feature on the progress of the war prepared by a German-American news service. Other weekly papers with a substantial German-American readership also introduced this feature. At the same time several editorials warned readers against the kind of intemperate street-corner discussion of the war that could stir up ethnic differences.[10]

Such counsel followed President Wilson's injunction to be neutral in thought as well as in deed. It also showed deference to the large German-American population in the region. On August 5 several Minnesota German-American organizations directed to the press an appeal that pointed out the difficulty of obtaining war news from any but Allied sources. The appeal went on to request suspension of judgment "until authentic reports . . . are available." In addition it protested "the careless handling of unconfirmed, biased and sensational news" and called attention to the "liberal support" given American newspapers by German-Americans. It did "not ask that any partiality be shown Germany or Austro-Hungary" but requested "fair treatment."[11]

In the meantime German-American spokesmen were formulating their own interpretation of the war. A widely circulated editorial from the *Illinois Staats-Zeitung* asserted that Germany stood as a mighty fortress guarding Europe against the Russian menace: "while France fights to regain her German provinces, while England fights to regain her maritime and commercial supremacy, Germany defends herself against them with the one hand, and with the other fights to preserve not only herself but France and England and the civilization of all western Europe from Slavic domination."[12]

The exalted German mission, continued the *Staats-Zeitung*, placed a heavy obligation on German-Americans. They "should take the necessary action to make the situation clear to their American fellow citizens; there should be organization and propaganda; and American sympathy for the brave fellows who rush forts in close order, American help for those who fall wounded and helpless, American moral support when peace is negotiated will be the result."

German-American travelers returning from Europe also gave testimony favorable to Germany which country editors, suspicious of "distorted" eastern press accounts of the war, gladly published. A New Ulm Catholic nun returning in November told of Belgian cruelties to the Germans who, she said, did not seek the conquest of Belgium but merely the use of its territory as a highway to France. Belgian women, she testified, actually cut off fingers of wounded German soldiers. She reported that "In one instance . . . a German officer asked a small Belgian girl for a drink, which she willingly offered. . . . As she handed the wine to the officer with one hand she leveled a revolver at him with the other and killed him instantly."[13]

A mass meeting in New Ulm on September 14 at which "Standing room was offered at a premium" organized community support for the German-Austro-Hungarian Red Cross — a cause that continued to receive substantial German-American support throughout the country until the American declaration of war on Germany two and a half years later. Several speakers coupled a defense of Germany's cause with pleas that the United States maintain strict neutrality. Before adjourning, the meeting endorsed the selection of a committee to supervise systematic solicitation for the German-Austrian Red Cross. Response to the project delighted its organizers.[14]

In 1914 public opinion magnanimously tolerated this German-American campaign. Politicians were loathe to alienate a large group of voters, and newspapers as well as other business enterprises valued German-American patronage. Activity of ethnic groups on behalf of a besieged homeland was a familiar if not wholly accepted practice; Scandinavian-Americans also were sensitive to the impact of the war on Norway, Sweden, and Denmark.[15] Moreover, the avowed German-American goal was not involvement of the United States on the side of the Central Powers, but strict American neutrality, a policy that commanded almost universal public support.

Despite their strong determination to stay clear of the European conflict, the people of Minnesota soon discovered that the war was raising many troublesome issues, some of which conceivably imperiled American neutrality. The most urgent were economic. The first impact of war deranged existing commercial relationships and created alarm in the business community. Heavy liquidation of European investment precipitated panic on the New York Stock Exchange, which closed its doors temporarily on July 31. For a few days business spokesmen seemed uncertain as to what kind of counsel would restore a climate of confidence.[16]

They soon discovered an effective spur in the idea that a Europe at war would need American raw materials and manufactured products. In early August James J. Hill confidently proclaimed: "The European war has not injured the financial soundness of this country . . . conditions are good. . . . It will be only a few days until means are devised to carry on trade relations with Europe. What we have to sell Europe needs and must buy and will be delivered."[17]

The same reassurance came from other quarters. A Minneapolis furniture store inserted a paid advertisement in the *Journal* that called attention to Europe's need for "our grain, flour and manufactured products," expressed confidence "that Uncle Sam will arrange in some fashion to see that they are shipped and delivered," and advised "improving every opportunity for advantage which may present itself." The *Blue Earth County Enterprise* perceived advantages for agriculture. "With war raging in Europe," the journal advised, "it beho[o]ves the American farmer to make plans for the best crop possible next year."[18]

The national administration did not disappoint those who hoped the war would broaden American economic opportunities. Although Secretary of State Bryan initially discouraged loans to belligerent governments — a policy which Washington reversed a few months later — the president decided at the outset to insist on the right of Americans to trade with all nations, subject only to the customary restrictions of international law. Theoretically this position was compatible with American neutrality, but serious differences with Britain developed almost immediately over interpretation of international law.[19]

Americans took strong exception to the British practice of conducting "visit and search" of Germany-bound vessels within British ports, because taking the ships into port necessarily delayed arrival at their ultimate destination. The British justified this modification of international law by asserting that lurking submarines made searches on the high seas excessively perilous. The progressive lengthening of British contraband lists on the grounds that the nature of modern warfare required a redefinition of contraband (goods which cannot be supplied to one belligerent without risk of seizure by the other) aroused even more resentment in the United States. This move had the effect of subjecting an increasing number of American exports to capture by the British fleet, thereby limiting the trading opportunities of the United States.

An exchange of notes, some of them in forceful language, between Washington and London followed, and Anglophobic tendencies within the United States were reinforced. The two nations did not, however, reach the point of severing diplomatic relations. The British government avoided pushing its blockade practices beyond the limits of American tolerance, and the United States was apparently intent on laying a basis for a postwar settlement similar to the one negotiated after the Civil War, when London indemnified this country for losses suffered as a consequence of British action.

Relations between the United States and Germany remained relatively calm until February, 1915, when the imperial government's announcement of unrestricted submarine warfare produced a major diplomatic crisis. Earlier, however, the partisans of Germany had begun to complain that the American stance toward the war was not neutral. American goods, they argued, should be available to all belligerents, and all overseas markets should be open to American exporters, subject only to the restrictions of international law. The British blockade, which by degrees effectively cut contact between the Central Powers and overseas countries, precluded this. Some German-American editors soon called upon the administration to display more vigor in pressuring Britain to bring its blockade policies into line with international law, thereby redressing the imbalance between Allied and German accessibility to American markets.[20]

By the end of 1914 it had become clear that the economic fruits of the European war could be garnered only at the expense of endless diplomatic complications. The risk to American neutrality at this point, however, was still not large. So long as most Americans regarded the war as an unseemly monarchical brawl involving no basic American values and posing no fundamental threat to national security, economic complaints by themselves could hardly provide a popular demand for American intervention.

The situation would change when idealism and morality became entangled in the American relationship to the war. The possibility of such entanglement may have seemed remote in 1914, but potentialities along this line were close to the surface. The plight of "violated" Belgium stirred American emotions and reinforced an undercurrent of hostility to Germany that had been developing since the Spanish-American War. Added to this was an American tendency to attach moral significance to the nation's policies, both domestic and foreign. When protesting against the German submarine policy announced in February, 1915, President Wilson invoked not only the abstractions of international law but also the "rights of humanity."

There were even a few comments appearing in August, 1914, that foreshadowed the transformation of the war into a crusade for the liberation of mankind. The *Dawson Sentinel*, edited by Theodore Christianson, predicted that the conflict would doom monarchy and thus assure a brighter

European future. "The blood which is being spilled," commented the
Sentinel, "is the price the Old World pays for democracy."[21] And Grondahl's "The Madness of the Monarchs" closed on a note that anticipated
the "war to end all wars" and the effort "to make the world safe for
democracy":

> From the funeral pyre of nations, from the drenched
>   and reeking sod,
> There shall rise the soul of freedom to proclaim
>   "One king, one God;"
> But the king no maddened monarch of the crowned and
>   sceptered birth —
> Nay — that king shall be the Manhood and the Womanhood of
>   Earth. . . .
>
> Then the weak and strong shall prosper and the warrior
>   earn his bread,
> For the sword shall turn to plowshare when the dynasties
>   are dead;
> Then the olive branch and dove of peace together shall
>   be seen
> On the coat-of-arms of nations that profess the Nazarene.

Grondahl's messianic vision was an authentic expression of a midwestern
tendency to look with favor on wars of liberation. With at least as much
enthusiasm as other Americans, the people of the Mississippi Valley expected
the ultimate triumph of the democratic idea everywhere in the world and
vaguely accepted a degree of American responsibility for the realization
of this dream. An interior geographic location may have inhibited their
understanding of American dependence on the world balance of power,
but it did not prevent the development of a naïve, idealistic internationalism
within the region.

Early in the 1850s Louis Kossuth, the Hungarian patriot whose revolution
had recently been suppressed, received a tumultuous welcome west of the
Alleghenies; and more than forty years later the Midwest reacted to the
cries of the Cuban rebels by stridently demanding the chastisement of Spain.
In 1892 Ignatius Donnelly, the philosopher of Populism, had written a
tract on the money question, thinly disguised as a novel. At the book's
close Donnelly, speaking through the character of a prophetic angel, told
his readers: "Within the next twenty-five years America will have to lift
up Europe, by wiping out the kings and aristocracies, or go down to ruin
under the feet of armed mobs, driven to desperation by wretchedness. The

world has got to be . . . 'all free or all slave.' There is an irrepressible conflict that takes in the planet.'' The words — uncanny in their accuracy as to time — rang like a mandate of support for Wilson's great crusade after the American declaration of war on Germany.[22]

The possibility that the European war would become a crusade for a better world seemed extremely remote in 1914, however — too remote to justify American entanglement on any level. What most Americans thought they saw in Europe was a conflict between two unprincipled power blocs, neither of which had a sufficient moral edge to warrant risking American neutrality.

Other factors further reinforced midwestern determination to keep the nation out of war. The debate between the so-called imperialists and anti-imperialists following the Spanish-American War had conditioned Bryan supporters, ex-Populists, and others to dislike a venturesome foreign policy. Such a policy, agrarian reformers suspected, might be a planned diversion to block domestic change. Many old Lind followers in Minnesota may well have remembered their leader's 1898 injunction against permitting the "shimmer of a proposed imperial policy in distant lands to blind the eyes of the people to existing abuses at home."[23] Midwestern progressives also detested a large military establishment, an inescapable accompaniment of a vigorous overseas policy. This attitude was based in part on the traditional American aversion for standing armies, and also on a conviction that the manufacture of armaments augmented the ill-gotten wealth of Wall Street. In addition, an awareness of the heterogeneous nature of the population of Minnesota created a fear that American departure from a policy of strict neutrality would promote domestic discord.

A neutrality rally held in the Minneapolis Auditorium on September 22, 1914, revealed the depth of antiwar feeling in the region seven weeks after the outbreak of the European conflict. The roster of speakers included prominent business, political, educational, and ecclesiastical leaders, and an overflow audience responded approvingly to eloquent pleas for neutralist restraint. Allen D. Albert of the *Minneapolis Tribune* defined the consensus of the meeting when he asserted:

> God has put us in a country of peace. We, too, have a war party that tells us we must mount the same horse they are riding in Europe. We are met in this meeting that you and I may be prepared to meet that argument when it is presented. . . .
>
> Here in the Northwest we have representatives of all the nations at war. We have 400,000 Germans, a greater number

of Scandinavians, and large numbers of other nationalities. Here
we are brothers, neighbors. Across the sea they are fighting.
It is necessary that we should so act as not to disturb this
feeling of brotherhood.[24]

With exhortations like this echoing in their ears, the people of Minnesota
returned to pursuits which the outbreak of war had momentarily interrupted.
Much of the initial shock was waning by late September. The near panic
precipitated by the disruption of peacetime commercial relationships had
passed, and the American economy was adjusting to the European war.
Stalemate was settling over the military fronts in western Europe. Seven
weeks of battle headlines had impressed on newspaper readers the fact
that a bloody conflict was raging in the Old World, although the printed
page could scarcely convey the cruel realities. At home the forthcoming
World Series engaged the interest of millions of Americans, and in a number
of states, including Minnesota, hotly contested fall election campaigns were
getting under way.

CHAPTER EIGHT

Progressivism Crests

"THE PRESENT EUROPEAN WAR has almost put politics in the discard," remarked the *New Ulm Review* on September 23, 1914. Two weeks later the *Sherburne County Star-News* delivered essentially the same verdict: "The political campaign is . . . tame this year. . . . It is hard to interest the public and nobody seems to care much who is elected."[1]

As October wore on, however, the gubernatorial contest developed a high degree of intensity. The total vote cast for governor in November, 1914, exceeded that of 1912 by almost 25,000. In fact, the 1914 vote set a record for nonpresidential years and nearly so for all elections; only in 1908, a presidential year, had a larger vote been recorded.[2]

County option rather than progressivism *per se* was the chief issue in 1914. Strongly emotional commitments on both sides of the wet-dry issue had elevated this question to top significance in state politics. The people favoring county option saw it as an important reform that would promote temperance and strike at an influential sector of the "plunderbund." Those who opposed it also appealed to high moral principle. They argued the right of private property — including jobs — to protection and objected to legislation that invoked the coercive power of the state to establish codes of personal conduct based on moral and religious values not shared by the entire community. County option, to be sure, stopped short of total prohibition, but the practical difference would not be great in areas where a number of neighboring counties were expected to vote dry. Moreover, its opponents feared (and the more exuberant drys proclaimed) that enactment of county option would be a long step toward the final triumph of complete prohibition.

As the 1914 campaign got under way, it became clear that county option would make a stronger bid than in preceding elections. The Lee victory in the June primary had officially committed the Republican party to the cause. In addition, the Minnesota branch of the Anti-Saloon League entered the fray in full force. It formally endorsed Lee and actively backed candidates in 95 of the 131 House contests and 48 of the 67 Senate races. Realistically, the leaders of the Anti-Saloon League did not expect to elect all these candidates. But they did indicate a determination to assure enactment of county option by winning at least 66 House and 34 Senate seats.[3] This they succeeded in doing, an achievement that determined the course of the 1915 legislature.

William E. Lee delivered his keynote address at Marshall in southwestern Minnesota on September 14.[4] As expected, he reiterated previous pledges to work for the enactment of county option. Implicitly, however, he avoided the impression of a single-issue campaign. Rather, he sought to make county option an integral part of a comprehensive reform program that included reorganization of state government "along modern business lines," the initiative and referendum, reclamation of state lands, curbs on pernicious forms of lobbying, and vesting local and municipal governments with the authority to regulate their own utilities. In addition, he declared himself "in full accord with the world movement to better protect the . . . welfare of the people by prohibiting excessive hours of labor . . . with rigid restrictions of hours and conditions of employment of women and children." Minimum wage and workmen's compensation laws, he said, were "movements in the right direction and should be so developed that exact justice will be done."

Lee also discussed the issue that would bring the North Dakota Nonpartisan League into existence a few months later. Without specifically mentioning the controversial Equity Exchange or the Minneapolis Chamber of Commerce, he noted that the people of Minnesota were "interested in free and open markets." He went on to say that "All fair-minded persons will agree that no unnecessary burden . . . should attach to the product of the farm, the factory, or the shop on its way from the producer to the consumer." However, he failed to indicate how he proposed to eliminate the "Unnecessary charges and profits" that burdened existing markets. Herein is a clue to the failure of prewar progressivism to hold the allegiance of discontented grain growers.

Hammond formally opened his campaign two weeks later at a rally in Red Wing.[5] Although his basic approach to state problems was similar to that taken by Lee, Hammond developed a more cautious campaign strategy. In the Red Wing address he began by noting the diminishing importance of party lines in Minnesota and remarked that as a result of the law passed in 1913 the next governor would have no party to lead in the legislature. This precluded the advocacy of a party program as such and meant that the chief executive would have to "confine himself more particularly to the things connected with the administration of the state government, *per se*, rather than economic, social or political problems.'' This observation created an opening for a statement on county option. Personally Hammond indicated a preference for local option, which was already on the statute books, but he declared he would leave resolution of the issue to the legislature. Although he refused to recommend county option, he promised to sign the proposed reform into law if the legislature on its own initiative passed a suitable county option bill. He went on to observe that the issue was being debated in the legislative campaign, and this would give the people an opportunity to decide whether county option should be adopted.

On other issues Hammond took a stand virtually indistinguishable from that of his opponent. He favored reorganization of state government along lines recommended by an Economy and Efficiency Commission appointed by Eberhart. He endorsed reclamation and reforestation. He alluded to woman suffrage without endorsing it, and he supported the initiative and referendum. He also noted Lee's charges that the breweries had dominated Minnesota politics for many years. If this were true, Hammond remarked, Lee must be indicting the Republican party, as the GOP had been in power most of the time since the achievement of statehood. Hammond identified his own stance on special interest politics with that taken by President Wilson, whose program he had supported while serving as a congressman.

The difference between Lee's explicit pledge to push county option and Hammond's promise to sign a county option bill if the legislature passed it became the principal issue of the gubernatorial campaign. It might seem that the forthright Lee position on this issue was more agreeable to majority opinion in the state than the equivocal stand taken by Hammond. The voters elected a legislature favorable to county option in 1914, and after the law went into effect in 1915, a preponderance of counties outlawed the saloon. In addition, the majority position of the Republican party presumably worked for Lee; everything else being equal, a Republican candidate for state-wide office in pre-World War I Minnesota could expect to triumph by a margin of approximately 50,000.

Hammond nevertheless won over Lee by a plurality of nearly 13,000.[6] This outcome vindicated the cautious strategy that had governed the Democratic campaign. Hammond's equivocation on county option had held his party together; his pledge to sign a county option bill no doubt displeased wet Democrats, but the Lee stand scarcely tempted them to bolt. The Democratic drys grumbled about Hammond's ingratitude to them for helping defeat Lawler in the primary, and a few defected to Lee. For the most part, however, Republican efforts to capture the support of progressive-dry Democrats by branding Hammond as a reactionary and the "whiskey candidate" failed. His record in congress clearly marked him as a progressive, and his promise to sign a county option bill reassured those Democratic drys who for other reasons wanted to support him.[7]

Minnesota wage earners, many of whom normally cast Democratic ballots and most of whom staunchly opposed county option, also voted for Hammond in large numbers. With this group the shade of difference between Lee and Hammond on county option apparently counted for more than Lee's espousal of advanced social legislation. Identification with President Wilson, whose standing with trade unionists was high in 1914, may also have assisted Hammond. In addition, the 1914 Democratic state platform explicitly called for legal curbs on the use of court injunctions in labor disputes, a proposal that AFL unionists valued more highly than demands for minimum wage legislation.[8]

Continuing dissension within the Minnesota Republican party yielded Hammond an additional bloc of votes. On October 2 Eberhart ended speculation about his role in the campaign by declaring that while he would "vote for Mr. Lee, he and his partisans have created a situation which makes it impossible for me to make speeches for him and maintain my self-respect." This statement protected the governor's record from the blight of an outright bolt, but political commentators interpreted it as part of a planned effort to encourage the Eberhart following to vote for Hammond. Be that as it may, Hammond polled a substantial vote in areas that had been Eberhart strongholds both in the 1914 primary and the 1912 election.[9]

In the contest of personalities that accompanies every political race Hammond undoubtedly held an edge over Lee. Republican spokesmen demonstrated anxiety on this point by frequently disputing Democratic claims that Hammond would give Minnesota leadership of the Wilsonian variety. From one point of view the Republicans made a case. The Hammond conception of executive leadership contrasted sharply with the precept and practice of Woodrow Wilson, who aggressively worked for congressional approval of his program. As an editorial writer for the *Minneapolis Journal* pointed out, Hammond most certainly did not propose to "Wilsonize" the legislature on the county option question.[10]

Nevertheless Hammond's personal appeal overshadowed that of the other candidate. Lee, a "self-made man" who frequently alluded to his early experience as a wage earner, was sixty-one in 1914 — a trifle old by Minnesota standards, which seem to dictate that a governor should be in his thirties or forties when he takes office. A native of Illinois, Lee migrated with his family to Minnesota in 1857. He ultimately settled in Long Prairie where he engaged in banking. His experience as an elected official consisted of one term as register of deeds of Todd County and membership in the lower house of the legislature during the sessions of 1885, 1887, and 1893. In 1893 he also served as speaker. Thereafter his involvement in politics was avocational. He became a prominent champion of county option after the turn of the century, and in 1912 he made an unsuccessful bid for the Republican gubernatorial nomination.[11]

Lee unquestionably possessed qualities of character and competence that impressed his contemporaries in the Minnesota progressive movement. But he lacked those personality traits which make good copy in political columns, and his physical appearance did not invite caricature by cartoonists. In other words, he blended too well into the small-town progressive landscape to command the notice on which political success in part depends.

Hammond was ten years younger than Lee. Born in 1863 in Massachusetts where his parental line had lived since the 1630s, he was reared and educated in New England, graduating from Dartmouth College in 1884. In the autumn of that year he became principal of the high school at Mankato, a post he relinquished in 1885 to accept appointment as superintendent of schools at nearby Madelia. This position he held for five years. Meanwhile he studied law during spare hours. Following his admission to the bar in 1891, he combined the practice of law — first at Madelia and after 1895 in neighboring St. James — with involvement in Democratic politics. His party nominated him to run for the second district congressional seat in 1892. Hammond lost this race to James Thompson McCleary, whose years of service as a teacher of history and civics in the Mankato Normal School (later Mankato State College) won for him the sobriquet, "schoolmaster politician." In 1906 Hammond decided to challenge McCleary again.[12]

The main feature of the 1906 contest was a series of debates in the Lincoln-Douglas tradition. These confrontations, which aroused considerable interest even beyond the boundaries of the second congressional district, focused mainly on the powers of House Speaker Joseph G. Cannon, and on the protective tariff, which McCleary defended eruditely and sometimes dogmatically. Observers disagreed as to who argued the more effective case, but the voters of the second district sent Hammond to congress.[13]

As a Democrat representing a Republican district, Hammond was compelled to establish an impressive record if he wanted to survive politically. This he managed to do with a fair degree of success. His votes against the Payne-Aldrich tariff and in favor of reducing the powers of Speaker Cannon reflected the sentiment in his district. He also secured appointment to the important ways and means committee, which inherited the responsibility of making committee assignments after Cannon was stripped of his authority. However, Hammond endangered his political future by voting for Canadian reciprocity. He barely won re-election in 1912, and some observers believed that pessimism about his 1914 congressional prospects encouraged him to accept progressive Democratic entreaties that he run for governor.[14]

Hammond's style might not have suited voters of the mid-twentieth century, but it met the standards of a generation that preferred decorous and solemn political leaders. Cheney recalled that Hammond "was not as dour as Lind, but quite as dignified, and in personal contacts . . . very reserved." Consistent with his background, Hammond also enjoyed the reputation of having a profound intellectual understanding of statecraft. In addition, he was an effective speaker. His address placing the name of John A. Johnson in nomination for the presidency at the 1908 Democratic convention won him considerable acclaim. And the *St. Paul Pioneer Press* reported that his opening speech of the 1914 campaign, the one delivered at Red Wing on September 28, aroused "Political enthusiasm unsurpassed in Minnesota since the day of John A. Johnson."[15]

Another Democratic contender who scored a surprise victory in the 1914 election was Carl C. Van Dyke, who defeated the veteran fourth district Republican congressman, Frederick C. Stevens. At the beginning of the campaign an easy Stevens triumph had been anticipated. Van Dyke, reported Cheney, was "not strong in the favor of his party organization." However, the St. Paul labor movement, which was becoming increasingly effective in local politics, strongly supported Van Dyke, a lawyer who had recently served as legal counsel for government employees in Washington, D.C. Other circumstances also encouraged the latent Democratic majority in St. Paul to assert itself. Hammond polled an immense vote in Ramsey County, thereby reinforcing other Democratic candidates. Van Dyke may also have profited from the prestige of President Wilson, an asset cherished by Democratic campaigners in 1914.[16]

There were two other congressional changes. The reapportionment law passed by the 1913 legislature deprived Congressman-at-large Manahan of his base, and Thomas D. Schall, who ran as a Bull Moose Progressive, won in the new tenth district, which included part of Hennepin County and a bloc of counties immediately north of Minneapolis. Franklin F. Ellsworth, the Republican who had given Hammond a close race in 1912, triumphed in the second district. As expected, the remaining seven congressmen, all Republicans, easily won re-election.[17]

On balance these results strengthened progressivism within the congressional delegation. Reformers of both parties interpreted the Van Dyke victory as a gain, for Stevens had compromised his standing by supporting Taft in 1912. The replacement of Hammond by Ellsworth substituted a progressive Republican for a Democrat of similar orientation. Many regretted the loss of Manahan, but Schall presumably defined his commitments by wearing the Bull Moose label. Of the re-elected incumbents, three were regarded as militant progressives: Sydney Anderson of the first district, whose primary victory over Tawney in 1910 had attracted nationwide attention; Charles Russell Davis, who had represented the third district since 1902; and Charles A. Lindbergh, Sr., who had held the sixth district post since 1906. The other four — George R. Smith of the fifth district, Andrew J. Volstead of the seventh, Clarence B. Miller of the eighth, and Halvor Steenerson of the ninth — had the reputation of being more moderate than Lindbergh or Davis, but their voting records generally commanded the approval of progressives.

Postelection comment in Minnesota newspapers concentrated on the implications of the Hammond victory over Lee. Disappointment at Lee's defeat led some progressive Republican organs to re-examine progressivism's negative attitude toward party organization and partisan loyalty. The *Minneapolis Journal* argued that liquidation of party responsibility had created unparalleled opportunities for special interests to dominate the legislative process. The "nonpartizan" legislature, charged the *Journal*, "was an excrescence grafted onto the nonpartizan system by the brewery element for its own purposes." In the absence of the discipline exercised by a responsible party ultimately accountable to the electorate, the writer reasoned, legislators and other public officials were more vulnerable than ever to pressures mounted by irresponsible private interests.[18]

The *Minneota Mascot*, whose editor had stood in the forefront of the antimachine crusade, also wondered whether the progressive effort to purify politics had not gone too far. "By entirely doing away with party," the *Mascot* asserted with more political perception than grammatical consistency, "the floodgates have been let down and the state is swept by fads and isms that befuddle the political mind and give every freak thinker an opportunity to air his pet scheme."[19]

Although these editorials were written under the emotional stress of a humiliating defeat, they made a point. By the end of 1914 the drive against political bossism had not only smashed the Smith machine; it had also largely undermined the foundations of party organization in Minnesota. The glorification of "independent voting" by "political orphans" like John Lind and Ole Sageng had persuaded many citizens that partisan loyalty was a vice rather than a virtue. The open primary had transferred the nomination of candidates — a traditional party function — from party conventions to the entire electorate with no checks against the voters of one party participating in the primary of the other. Strict corrupt practices legislation forbade many traditional campaign practices. Formally, though not always in reality, municipal and county offices along with the state legislature had been removed from the realm of party politics. In short, the significance of party organization in the political life of the state had been greatly reduced.

The merits of what the *Journal* called Minnesota's "nonpartizan system" are debatable. On the one hand this system deprived potential bosses of the leverage needed to operate and maintain strong political machines. Perhaps it stimulated the development of an "issue-oriented" style of politics (in contrast to the "job-oriented" variety) which one political scientist has seen as characteristic of Minnesota in the mid-twentieth century.[20] On the other hand, the weakness of party organization may have heightened political extremism in 1917 and 1918. During this period the vulnerability of an "unbossed" Republican party to Nonpartisan League capture impaired Republican ability to mount an orderly opposition to the league's radicalism. This in turn intensified the hysteria of those who felt menaced by the independent farmers' movement. At the same time, the incapacity of a faction-ridden Minnesota Democratic party to capitalize on the discontents of grain growers and wage earners obviously created an opening for the strident Nonpartisan League appeal.

Hammond, whose political success rested in part on the wreckage of party organization in Minnesota, disputed the contentions of those who affirmed a need to re-establish party responsibility in state politics. His inaugural message, which was delivered on January 5, 1915, opened with a discussion of the new nonpartisan legislature. Many people doubted "the expediency of this departure," said Hammond, but he asked that it be given "a fair trial."[21]

The new governor also lauded the direct primary. "The people believe in primaries," he asserted. Experience had uncovered defects in the present law, but retention of the primary was preferable to restoration of the convention system. The complaint that the existing system permitted voters of one party to invade the primary of the other did not impress Hammond. On the contrary, he suggested establishing what is known as the wide-open primary. "Should the Legislature see fit to amend the primary law so as to permit all electors to participate in each primary," he observed, "considerable criticism of the system would be avoided; no harm would be done, and on the whole, probably better nominations would be made."

A considerable portion of the Hammond message dealt with the modernization of state government. The governor requested the legislature to adopt the major proposals of Governor Eberhart's Economy and Efficiency Commission. These included comprehensive reorganization of state government, the establishment of a merit system in state employment, and an executive budget. Hammond anticipated (correctly) that the budget recommendation would pass but that reorganization and the merit system would encounter stout opposition.

The governor also honored other campaign promises. He recommended resubmission in modified form of a constitutional amendment providing for the initiative and referendum. The voters had failed to ratify this in 1914 — as they would again in 1916. In addition, he called upon the legislature to adopt an ambitious reclamation and reforestation program, at the same time suggesting a reduction in total appropriations. He pointed out that state expenditures had been mounting more rapidly than population and recommended the 1911 appropriation level rather than that of 1913 as the guiding norm.

In line with his pre-election pledge, Hammond left the county option question to legislative determination. "There are," he said, "numerous plans for the promotion of temperance, and every one is in favor of temperance legislation or claims to be." The immediate question was, "Shall there be county option in place of existing local option?" This question, Hammond noted, had generated "a bitterness entirely unwarranted by its importance from a temperance standpoint or from any other standpoint." He asked for early action "so that other matters of great importance" might be considered.

The legislature obviously placed greater weight on the county option issue than did the governor. In the absence of the formal Republican and Democratic caucuses of preceding sessions the issue provided the basis for legislative organization. House members committed to county option met on November 17, 1914, and nominated Sam Y. Gordon, Browns Valley newspaper publisher and former lieutenant governor, for speaker. The opposition bloc gathered under the banner of H. Howard Flowers of Le Sueur County, a Cleveland banker. Both sides claimed a majority: some House members, it seemed, had pledged their votes to both candidates. Actually the county optionists had a thin majority, but friction within their caucus enabled Flowers to win the speakership. Given the role of the speaker in the selection of committees and management of daily procedure, Flowers' election was an important victory for the wets.[22]

Meantime county option senators had met with Anti-Saloon League officials and Lieutenant Governor Burnquist, whose power to appoint Senate committees made him a key factor in the forthcoming battle. Burnquist's partiality to county option, coupled with a wider dry margin than in the lower house, virtually assured Senate passage of the measure. Senate temperance committee hearings on the bill began on January 27. On February 4, after the committee had given it a favorable report by a vote of six to three, the bill was made a special order. After brief debate the Senate passed it by a vote of 36 to 31.[23]

At this stage favorable House action on county option seemed doubtful. That body's temperance committee was known to oppose the bill by a margin of nine to six, and the exact division of the total House membership remained uncertain. However, adroit management by the Anti-Saloon League — including the recruitment of scores of enthusiastic drys to attend a crucial February 11 committee hearing — generated sufficient pressure to assure passage. The temperance committee discharged the bill without recommendation, a dry victory considering the committee's wet majority, and on February 24 the House passed it by a vote of 66 to 62. Within a few days Hammond ended speculation about his course by signing the bill into law.[24]

With county option on the statute books, legislative energies supposedly were freed for the "other matters of great importance" mentioned by Hammond. The drys, however, were determined to push their cause further. State-wide prohibition by statute — as distinguished from constitutional amendment — which if passed would have superseded county option, now became their goal. This effort attracted impressive support, but it failed. The roadhouse bill, a measure that banned licensed liquor establishments outside incorporated villages and cities, had more success. After a hard fight this passed both houses and received approval by the governor.[25]

Partly because preoccupation with temperance took a heavy toll of time and effort, the 1915 legislature established an essentially negative record in many other areas. As Hammond had feared, it rejected most of his proposals for the reorganization of state government. The executive budget alone survived. Following demonstrations by both prosuffrage and antisuffrage forces in the vicinity of the Capitol, the Senate by a one-vote margin defeated a state constitutional woman suffrage amendment. Several bills providing for the regulation of grain marketing and trading in commodity futures died in committee. Aside from minor amendments, the primary system remained unaltered.[26]

A few relatively important reforms won legislative and gubernatorial acceptance. Although the session left the problem of comprehensive utility regulation unresolved, it passed two measures in this field. One of these, the Minnette bill, which Eberhart had vetoed in 1913, placed telephone companies under the jurisdiction of the Railroad and Warehouse Commission. The other authorized the Minneapolis city council to institute franchise negotiations with the Twin City Rapid Transit Company. The existing charter was due to expire in 1923. Although this measure stopped short of giving the council full authority over the transit company, it embodied in a limited way the home-rule utility regulation principle which Minnesota progressives had long advocated.[27]

A number of other measures, none of them revolutionary in character, completed the 1915 legislative record. One statute set up a state-wide pension system for public school teachers. Another tightened state supervision of fire insurance companies. Amendments to the workmen's compensation act of 1913, formulated in negotiations between the Minnesota Federation of Labor and the Minnesota Employers' Association, liberalized the disability benefits available to injured wage earners.[28]

The passage of county option softened the disappointment occasioned by the otherwise bland record of the 1915 session. The *Minneapolis Journal* spoke for many progressives when it affirmed that "Much may be forgiven" a legislature that had enacted two such laws as county option and the antiroadhouse bill.[29] The *St. Paul Pioneer Press* was more critical, suggesting that more vigorous leadership on Hammond's part might have increased the session's productivity.

Following adjournment, middle-class reformers launched an energetic drive to force a showdown on the future of liquor throughout the state. The technicalities of the county option law were onerous: petitions bearing the signatures of 25 per cent of a county's registered voters had to be submitted before an election on the license issue could be held. Nevertheless, more than thirty counties held referendums before the middle of June. A month later the count was fifty-one, with forty-three in the dry column and eight remaining wet. At this point the county option crusade had nearly reached its peak; the saloon had been outlawed in forty-six counties when national prohibition went into effect on January 1, 1920.[30]

The early months of 1915 marked the crest of the progressive movement in Minnesota. Thereafter, to be sure, the causes that had given progressivism its dynamic force continued to influence state politics. The push for dry legislation moved from county option to total prohibition; the woman suffrage campaign gathered force; a child welfare commission was created and a comprehensive children's code enacted; the virtues and shortcomings of the direct primary were still debated; and the search for an approach to utility regulation went on. Increasingly, however, these issues had to compete with other concerns, some of which had festered beneath the surface of Minnesota politics for several years. The founding of the Farmers' Nonpartisan League of North Dakota in 1915 and the strong possibility that this organization would shortly move into Minnesota promised intensified conflict between the grain trade and Northwest wheat growers. The Minnesota labor movement also was becoming more militant, and on the iron range, many middle-class citizens were becoming more hostile to the steel companies and friendlier to the predominantly foreign-born miners.

The surfacing of these new concerns failed to elicit a unified reponse from men who had co-operated in support of the direct primary and county option and who had stood shoulder to shoulder against the trusts and special interests. Some progressives saw the founding of the Nonpartisan League and the demands of labor as a continuation of the reform movement that had started under Lind's administration. Others reacted against the radicalism of the wheat farmers and saw in trade-union aggressiveness a mounting threat of violence and anarchy. In short, internal strain was beginning to imperil the solidarity of the progressive coalition. Growing controversy on issues relating to the European war multiplied these inner tensions. Early in 1915 a spirited foreign-policy debate developed. The question at this stage was not whether the United States should go to war, but even the issue of what policies would most effectively guarantee American neutrality without damage to national honor was explosive enough to spread dissension within all political camps.

Minnesota progressivism also suffered a leadership loss at the close of the year. On December 30, 1915, Hammond died suddenly and unexpectedly. How he would have responded to the iron miners' strike of 1916, growing labor trouble in Minneapolis, the Nonpartisan League invasion of Minnesota, and the sharp controversy concerning the American relationship to the European war could be the subject of interesting but altogether futile speculation. Cheney's evaluation says all that reasonably can be affirmed: "Hammond was a good governor, but had little chance to make a record."[31]

CHAPTER NINE

Foreign Policy Becomes an Issue:
A Strain on Progressive Solidarity

BEFORE THE END of 1915 the question of the United States' relationship to the European war had become highly controversial. Three broad schools of opinion had developed. The interventionists and near interventionists, who were strongest on the Eastern Seaboard and led by Republicans of that region, frankly embraced the Allied cause, demanded an uncompromising defense of American rights, and called for a sizable increase in the nation's armed strength. The noninterventionists or neutralists were a loose, informal coalition of German- and Irish-Americans, midwestern progressives, pacifists, antimilitarists, and socialists. They championed scrupulous American neutrality, favored renunciation of such basic rights as travel on belligerent vessels in war zones, advocated restrictions on the American sale of munitions and the granting of credit to belligerents, and generally opposed drastic increases in the military establishment. A third group approved President Wilson's course of steering midway between the interventionist and neutralist extremes, both of which became highly critical of the administration.[1]

As is true with most administrations, Wilson's policy was largely shaped by the pressure of events. In meeting these pressures the president was guided by three broad objectives: First, he sincerely and passionately wanted the United States to remain neutral. Second, he was determined to maintain American rights. Third, he hoped to mediate the war, and he remained alert for opportunities to do so.

Aside from the war's upsetting effect on normal commercial and diplomatic relations, the president's first difficulties grew out of Britain's blockade policies. As we have seen, he met these by placing the American case on record through the medium of diplomatic notes. A more serious situation developed in February, 1915, when the German admiralty announced the institution of a submarine blockade which aimed to destroy all enemy ship-

89

ping within a specified zone. British misuse of neutral flags, said the announcement, made it impossible to guarantee the safety of nonbelligerent ships and their passengers. A submarine on strike against a merchant vessel had to do its work quickly or take unwarranted risks.

Rightly or wrongly, Wilson regarded the announced German policy as a more flagrant flaunting of international law and the "rights of humanity" than the blockade practices of the British. He dispatched a note to Berlin promising that the United States would hold the imperial government to "a strict accountability" for the destruction of life and property resulting from the announced policy.[2] Thus the stage was set for a hostile confrontation between the two governments.

On May 7, 1915, a German submarine sank the *Lusitania*, a large British passenger liner, and more than eleven hundred lives were lost, including those of 124 American citizens. Now Wilson had to decide what strict accountability meant in a specific situation. His note of May 13 in effect demanded that Germany abandon submarine warfare against unarmed merchantmen, but the absence of threat or bluster in the note and Wilson's speech on May 10, which asserted, "There is such a thing as a man being too proud to fight," softened the severity of the American position.[3] The Germans replied evasively, and Wilson then drafted and dispatched a second note which Secretary of State Bryan regarded as too strong, a conviction that led to his resignation. Again the Germans responded evasively, and the exchange of communications continued.

Gradually American pressure induced the Germans for a time to leash their submarines. On August 26 the imperial government ordered the cessation of unrestricted submarine warfare against all passenger ships. Serious difficulties remained, however. The status of merchantmen and armed ships, whether merchant or passenger, was still uncertain. Wilson tried to promote a tacit agreement—a *modus vivendi*—between Britain and Germany involving disarming of merchant vessels by the British in return for a German pledge to observe the rules of cruiser warfare in all its submarine operations. The effort not only failed but also created the impression both in the United States and in Germany that American policy was becoming pronouncedly pro-Ally.[4]

A new crisis developed in March, 1916, when a German submarine torpedoed without warning an unarmed French channel steamer, the *Sussex*, inflicting eighty casualties. Wilson responded by sending a note to Berlin threatening to sever diplomatic relations unless the German government abandoned its relentless use of the submarine.[5] The imperial government promised in a note dated May 4 that submarines would henceforth observe the rules of visit and search — that is, make provision for the safety of those aboard — before sinking merchant ships. This concession was made on the condition that the British modify their blockade practices to conform with the rules of international law.

Again Wilson had won a diplomatic victory, and from May, 1916, until January, 1917, when the Germans resumed unrestricted submarine warfare, relations between Germany and the United States were free of major crisis. This state of affairs made it possible for Wilson's supporters in the campaign of 1916 to claim that his policy had been remarkably successful. The country remained at peace and American rights had been maintained. The seeming plausibility of this claim contributed to his re-election.

By this time American opinion was deeply divided on issues relating to the war. The proposition that the United States should forego the defense of its traditional maritime rights commanded considerable support throughout the country. In March, 1916, congress debated the Gore-McLemore resolutions, which called upon American citizens to avoid taking passage on vessels bound for the war zones — a recommendation that the president regarded as an intolerable surrender of American rights. All the political skill the administration could muster was required to defeat these resolutions.[6]

Vigorous and sometimes acrimonious debate also developed on other questions. Neutralists advocated and interventionists opposed the imposition of bans on arms shipments and loans to the nations at war. The degree to which national safety required an increase in American armed strength became a burning issue. The threat to national unity from immigrants who identified with their homeland and kept cultural ties alive (a phenomenon that came to be known as "hyphenism") was heatedly discussed. Yet another argument that generated considerable emotion was whether starvation imposed by the British blockade violated the laws of humanity more flagrantly than unrestricted submarine warfare.

Wilson's policies did not fully satisfy either side. The neutralists disapproved of his vigorous defense of American rights and argued that American neutrality was one-sided. Many interventionists wanted a more explicit avowal of pro-Ally sympathy, and most of them did not feel "too proud to fight."

In 1914 Wilson had refused to be moved by agitation of the preparedness cause, but a year later he made preparedness one of "the keynotes of his Annual Message."[7] This led to the development of a preparedness program which pleased no one. On the issue of loans, noninterventionists had at first been reassured by Bryan's initial discouragement of credit to belligerent governments. There, too, the administration soon reversed itself.

In March, 1915, the State Department explicitly approved a commercial credit of $50,000,000 to the French government, and in the following months American bankers extended additional loans.

By the time of the 1916 election, it would seem on balance that the noninterventionists had more cause for complaint against Wilson than their adversaries. His administration opposed the Gore-McLemore resolutions, ignored demands for arms and loan embargoes, and changed course on preparedness. In addition, the president in 1915 had joined the crusade against hyphenism, a position which enraged German-Americans, who were already smarting under his strong moral condemnation of Germany's submarine policy. Nevertheless, in 1916 many noninterventionists voted for Wilson; Charles Evans Hughes, his Republican opponent, was even more closely identified with eastern interventionism.[8]

As the foreign policy debate of 1915 got under way, it soon became clear that neutralism held a strong grip on public opinion in Minnesota. Scientific polling lay in the future, but observers who professed to know the mind of the state almost invariably reported strong opposition to any policy that might risk involvement in the European conflict.[9] Elected officials studiously avoided the interventionist label. Even Senator Nelson, who in 1916 became an uncompromising advocate of firmness toward Germany, remained uncommitted through 1915.[10]

Neutralism did not, however, go unchallenged. Pronounced interventionism of the variety championed by Theodore Roosevelt enjoyed little favor, but a number of persuasive voices pleaded for a moderately pro-Ally course. Daily newspapers in the Twin Cities generally backed Wilson's submarine policy, editorialized against the arms embargo proposal, and supported preparedness.[11] Some prominent individuals seemed to be of a divided mind. Cyrus Northrop, the highly respected president emeritus of the University of Minnesota, held simultaneous memberships in a neutralist peace society and in the interventionist National Security League.[12] Nor did positions held early in 1915 necessarily remain fixed. Growing distrust of Germany, reinforced by revelations of German spy and propaganda plots, encouraged marginal neutralists to shift their stand.

In 1915 and 1916 moral concern rather than conceptions of national self-interest seemed to dominate most discussions of the European war. Was the calculated starving of civilians less reprehensible than the sinking of merchant ships without warning? Was German imperialism worse than the British variety, or did the one cancel out the other? Was the German occupation of Belgium more heavy-handed than the Russian occupation of Poland? Was it ethically justifiable for American investors and manufacturers of arms to profit from Europe's misery? The moral indignation generated on all sides of these issues was undoubtedly genuine enough. As might be expected, however, a high correlation between ethical passion and tangible economic, social, and ethnic interests is clearly visible.

Spokesmen for rural Minnesota generally took a neutralist position. This was consistent with the dictates of economic interest. Farmers and small-town businessmen believed that the prosperity stimulated by Allied purchases in the United States was not reaching them. "The only business that is prospering is the manufacture of war material for the allies," commented the *Park Region Echo* in July, 1915. More than a year later the *Blue Earth County Enterprise* rejected the notion that the misfortunes of Europe were a boon to the United States: "It would be nearer the truth to say that some of the munition factories of the United States are making money out of the war. Most everybody else is paying extortionate prices for life's necessities," asserted the paper.[13]

These complaints made a point. The cost of living rose steeply in 1915. Since Minnesota was not a manufacturing center, British and French arms orders were no direct spur to the state's economy. In addition, the farming areas suffered acutely from the credit stringency accompanying initial American adjustment to the war, and anti-Wall Street farmers could readily be persuaded that the appropriation of available capital by the munitions makers was a conspiracy against the welfare of agriculture. Grain prices reached a satisfactory level by 1916, but in that year crop yields in the Red River Valley fell off and remained abnormally low for the next three years. Farmers in that region who tried to build their prosperity on acreage expansion found themselves frustrated by high overhead and interest costs. Beginning in 1916, mortgage indebtedness in rural Minnesota — particularly in the northwest section of the state — rose rapidly.[14]

The Minnesota labor movement also embraced neutralism, and again, as in the case of agriculture, vital group interests were a significant factor. Military preparedness, one of the prime goals of the interventionists, was particularly offensive to organized labor. Henry L. Stimson, who later served as secretary of state in President Herbert C. Hoover's cabinet and as secretary of war under Franklin D. Roosevelt, regretfully observed in early 1916 that the American worker did not look upon "the militiaman as a citizen, training to perform his duty of defending the country in case of real war." Instead, said Stimson, the wage earner thought of the guardsman

"as a representative of capital, being trained as a policeman against labor."
Discussion at the 1915 and 1916 Minnesota Federation of Labor conventions,
resolutions passed by local labor bodies in the Twin Cities and Duluth,
and the editorial line of the state labor press underscored labor's fear that
preparedness was directed against trade unions rather than the country's
potential enemies. As might be expected, labor's antipreparedness attitude
reinforced distrust of the interventionist program in general. The Duluth
Labor World of June 26, 1915, estimated that a majority of trade unionists
were "peace at any price" men, a point of view with which the editor
disagreed.[15]

Noninterventionist feeling within the ranks of the Minnesota labor movement was strengthened by the conspicuous involvement of the metropolitan
business communities with preparedness and the pro-Ally cause. In the
late summer of 1915, a number of Minneapolis business leaders lent their
names and influence to the creation of a local branch of the National Security
League, an organization that had been founded on the Eastern Seaboard
a year before and had since become the nation's leading interventionist
pressure group. Edward W. Decker, president of the Northwestern National
Bank and head of the Minneapolis Security League chapter, defined the
organization's goals as being "to get at the farmers" and "to break up
the insularity of view and get the people thinking about the country as
a whole and its situation among the countries of the world." Shortly after
this group came into being, the business communities of St. Paul and Duluth
took the lead in establishing similar chapters in their cities.[16]

The labor press did not fail to note the involvement of big business
in the preparedness drive. In commenting on the creation of the Duluth
Security League chapter, the editor of *Labor World*, though himself a
moderate preparedness advocate, wanted to know who was "behind all
this propaganda for 'preparedness?' " Duluth, he reported, had just "entertained one of these itinerant, violent patriots this week, and about twenty
of our richest and most influential citizens met him, organized a Security
League, contributed some $500 toward his expenses, and were left with
the job of 'arousing' this particular section of the country to its 'danger.' "[17]

The premise that employers favored preparedness as a defense against
trade-union militance was in part correct. A number of business spokesmen
argued that a strengthened military establishment would insure against
domestic disorder which they believed radical unionism would instigate
whenever relations with Germany reached a crisis point. Other considerations
also reinforced pro-Ally and preparedness tendencies within the top echelons
of the business community. Midwest investors valued participation in the

huge American loans to Britain and France.[18] In addition, provincial business elites throughout the nation tended to be strongly influenced by Atlantic Seaboard opinion. According to Randolph S. Bourne, prominent liberal essayist of the World War I period:

> . . . war feeling centered . . . in the richer and older classes of the Atlantic seaboard, and was keenest where there were French or English and particularly social connections. The sentiment then spread over the country as a class-phenomenon, touching everywhere those upper-class elements in each section who identified themselves with this Eastern ruling group. . . . In every community it was the least liberal and least democratic elements among whom the preparedness and later the war sentiment was found.[19]

To some extent, Bourne overstated his case. Liberals and conservatives did not divide along neutralist-interventionist lines as sharply and neatly as he implied. Nevertheless, he correctly described a predominant tendency. Metropolitan chambers of commerce generally placed themselves on record in favor of preparedness and a firm stand toward Germany. Periodicals like *Commercial West* frequently reprinted the pro-Ally opinions of eastern newspapers and based their own editorial line on that of the seaboard press.[20]

The most vigorous advocacy of ethnic interest came from within the state's large German-American community. Perhaps the rise of popular feeling against the Central Powers in the spring of 1915 should have cautioned German-Americans to mute their sympathetic identification with the Fatherland. Unfortunately, Germany's deteriorating reputation seems to have had the opposite effect. Instead of detaching themselves from the Kaiser's cause, German-American spokesmen defended the imperial government with more stridency in late 1915 than they had at the outset of the war. Clearly they aimed not only to mobilize the political and economic power of their own constituency on the side of American neutrality, but also to reinforce the noninterventionist proclivities of other groups.[21]

The weapons available for the German-American neutrality crusade were formidable. The German-language press in Minnesota had an estimated circulation of 125,000, a total that did not include English-language papers under German-American control. In issue after issue these newspapers condemned the Wilson administration for allegedly tolerating the British "starvation blockade" while holding Germany to a "strict accountability." They also advocated the imposition of arms and loan embargoes, charged that a Wall Street conspiracy was steering the United States toward involvement in war with Germany, and accused the nation's leading newspapers of distorting Germany's case. As if to redress the alleged pro-Ally bias of the metropolitan press, German-American papers unabashedly editorialized in their news columns. Three days after the *Lusitania* sinking, headlines in the *St. Paul Volkszeitung*, a German-language daily, announced that: UNMOVED AS A ROCK IN THE OCEAN, GERMANY DEFIES THE WORLD. GERMAN PRESS REJOICES OVER SUCCESS OF SUBMARINE AND ANNOUNCES FURTHER ATTACKS BY THE GERMAN NAVY.[22]

Lecture tours by prominent German and German-American scholars supplemented the crusading zeal of German-American editors. In June and again in October, 1915, Eugene Kuehnemann, professor of German literature at Breslau University and onetime visiting professor at the University of Wisconsin, spoke in several Minnesota German-American centers. At New Ulm on June 28 he delivered a two-hour lecture — in German — on the topic of "Germany's Destiny." According to Kuehnemann, French, Russian, and British aspirations to crush Germany had led to the outbreak of the current war. He then treated his audience to a glowing account of the Fatherland's political development, purporting to show that William II was the heir of a tradition which fused the legacy of Frederick the Great's powerful leadership and the democratic ideals of 1848 rather than the "War Lord" of Allied propaganda. More than that, asserted Kuehnemann, William headed "the greatest democratic state in the world" wherein laws enacted by the people's representatives were enforced "by the authorities without fear or favor." Even the United States, Kuehnemann insisted, could learn lessons in practical democracy from Germany.[23]

Some pro-Ally spokesmen who deplored the exuberance of advocates like Kuehnemann comforted themselves with the thought that sympathy for Germany was a myth fostered by "professional German-Americans," that is, out-and-out propagandists in the service of the Berlin regime. This view is questionable. Carl Wittke, the distinguished German-American historian, does not minimize the importance of the propaganda effort sponsored by the German Information Service, but he also insists that "Most German-Americans . . . would have been in general agreement with the arguments presented by German propagandists" anyway.[24]

Kuehnemann did not address empty meeting halls. When he appeared in New Ulm, "Practically every seat in the theatre was occupied and the audience showed its appreciation by repeated applause during the two hours' discourse." Moreover, Minnesota German-Americans continued to support the German-Austrian Red Cross with generous donations. In addition, the membership of several German-American organizations endorsed an attempted boycott of financial institutions participating in the Allied loans of 1915. The boycott failed, but it aroused serious concern within banking circles.[25]

Elected politicians also felt the force of German-American pressure. In replying to an early 1916 "peace-at-any price" missive from a Swedish-American constituent, Senator Knute Nelson reported having "received a number of letters from German-Americans in the same tone as yours, but very few from Scandinavians."[26] These letters generally reflected the line taken by the German-American press, but they bore the marks of individual composition and apparently were not the product of an organized letter-writing campaign. A German-American farmer from Wells, for example, returned some garden seed which the senator's office had sent him with a suggestion that Nelson seek to have the money hitherto spent for such seed appropriated to assist the families of men killed by American-produced ammunition. He wrote:

> It is a shame that we have people in Washington that go to church on Sunday and pray for peace and the next day they are in favor to sell more ammunition to kill people. . . .
>
> I am an American Citizen since 1871 and I am willing to help protect the American coast if some foreign nation tries to land troops on our coast but I am not willing to work fight and get killed for John Bull.
>
> If two parties are fighting and the third one gives him a gun to shoot I think he is a bigger murderer than the two that are fighting and uncle Sam aloud [sic] it so far to send good many shiploads over to the warring nation.
>
> We german farmers like to have a free sea to send food of all kind to all foreign what have money to pay for it especially milk to the little babies and medicines for the sick people and all supplies for the Red Cross.[27]

There can be little doubt that the German-American neutrality crusade strengthened both sides of the growing foreign-policy controversy. On the one hand, it most certainly helped rally a powerful voting bloc on the side of nonintervention, a political reality which elected officials could not ignore.[28] Conceivably, too, it strengthened the neutralist tendencies of other groups. The line taken by German-American advocates meshed neatly with the anti-Wall Street, the antimilitarist, and the anti-British traditions, all of which enjoyed considerable standing throughout the Midwest.

On the other hand, a pronounced backlash against the German-American community developed in 1915. As suspicion of the Kaiser's regime grew throughout the United States, many people began to question whether retention of a residual loyalty to a European homeland could be squared with the obligations of American citizenship. Theodore Roosevelt launched a furious campaign against hyphenism and on behalf of what he called unadulterated 100 per cent Americanism. In a more moderate tone but nonetheless with sharpness, President Wilson in October, 1915, denounced those who professed patriotism but at the same time "spoke alien sympathies, which came from men who loved other countries better than they loved America." And a few months later Elihu Root, the eminent lawyer and diplomat, expressed a fear that the nation's recent immigrants, "with entirely different traditions, will change us unless we change them."[29]

To some extent, the drive against the hyphen found a sympathetic response in Minnesota. The Twin Cities dailies frequently editorialized on the need to discard Old World loyalties, and civic leaders organized "Americanization" rallies which they hoped would encourage the foreign-born to become thoroughgoing patriots. "Standing by the President" in times of crisis was a popular keynote of such occasions. Politicians generally avoided an issue as explosive as hyphenism, but several times in the summer and fall of 1915 Governor Hammond spoke out against the German-American Alliance, the leading German-American organization in Minnesota.[30]

In Minnesota as in the nation at large, German-Americans generally reacted to the rise of antihyphenism by intensifying their campaign for American neutrality and combining this with vigorous affirmations of loyalty to the United States and a spirited defense of the right of ethnic groups to retain their languages and cultures. "By German-Americans," asserted the *New Ulm Review*, "we mean American citizens of German blood, who are first for their country, America, but have a very great sympathy (and it is right they should have it) for the Fatherland." This strategy may not have been prudent, but it was understandable. The German-American neutralist effort was based not primarily on a commitment to the political aims of the German empire but on a drive for self-preservation. German-Americans sensed that war between Germany and the United States would generate pressures on them to abandon their language and cultural identity. The mounting crusade against the hyphen underscored this threat.[31]

Antihyphenism also stirred the apprehension of other ethnic groups that retained cultural ties with Europe. Worried editorials appeared in the Scandinavian-American press. Christian K. Preus, president of Luther College at Decorah, Iowa, thought that he detected signs of a hysterical, nativist "Knownothing" revival in the United States. Norwegian-Americans, said Preus, accepted the inevitability and desirability of assimilation into an American mainstream, but a process so complex required time. The American way of life was still amorphous, still unformed. It would take shape, he predicted, simultaneously with the assimilation of those who had recently arrived from Europe. Moreover, if assimilation was permitted to proceed on an unhurried course, all groups would have an opportunity to influence the final shape of American civilization.[32]

Although Preus did not touch on foreign policy, his analysis may in part have explained the neutralist proclivities of midwestern Scandinavian-Americans. If, indeed, American civilization had not yet taken shape, unhyphenated Americanism was an impossibility. It followed that the pure unadulterated Americanism of antihyphenist agitation must in reality be Anglo-Americanism — a conclusion supported by the pro-Ally orientation of most antihyphenists and their demand that all immigrant groups immediately adopt the English language. Thus, the crusade against the hyphen seemed to be in league with pro-Ally interventionism, and resentment of the former tended to discredit the latter. Emotionally charged outpourings in the letter columns of Minnesota newspapers associated interventionism with "Anglomaniac" efforts to disparage the culture and language of continental immigrants and establish British-Americans as an elite group.[33] Some of these letters may have been inspired by German propaganda managers; nonetheless, they articulated a resentment which in the absence of other ethnic interests (like the hope among some Slavic-Americans that Allied victory would liberate an occupied homeland) encouraged neutralism within the ranks of recent immigrants.

Other factors strengthened Scandinavian-American neutralism. Sweden's traditional distrust of Russia predisposed many Swedish-Americans against the Allies. In addition, Scandinavian-Americans generally were proud of the traditional neutrality of their homelands; to them the adoption of a similar policy by the United States seemed a good idea. Arguments insistently pressed by German-Americans that the British blockade was detrimental and unjust to Scandinavia also may have had an influence.[34]

As an organized group, the Irish-Americans of Minnesota registered a surprisingly slight impact on the foreign-policy controversy. Politicians seldom expressed anxiety about the Irish vote, and political writers hardly ever subjected the Irish-American position to analysis. If this seems curious, it should be remembered that the Minnesota Irish-American community was considerably smaller than either the Scandinavian-American or the German-American in size and voting power. Moreover, the precept and example of Archbishop John Ireland, who recommended avoidance of fixed positions on issues that might separate Irish-Americans from the rest of the community, may have discouraged a militant stance by Irish-American societies. Nevertheless, it is likely that most of this group in Minnesota favored neutralism. That was the predominant national Irish-American pattern, and one that received staunch support from Daniel Lawler, who in the minds of many people ranked as a spokesman for the Irish element. After the diplomatic break with Germany in February, 1917, the St. Paul Democrat became an enthusiastic advocate of the war, but in 1915 and 1916 he was a zealous noninterventionist.[35]

If the size and disposition of Minnesota's German, Scandinavian, and Irish communities fortified neutralism, there were still some countervailing ethnic influences. As we have seen, an anti-German backlash with antihyphenist and pro-Ally overtones developed in 1915. This reaction gained strong support from the progeny of the earlier and predominantly Anglo-Saxon immigration to North America — an element liberally represented within the power structure of the Twin Cities. A few prominent individuals of recent European origin also embraced the antihyphenist and pro-Ally causes. Minneapolis attorney John F. McGee, an Irish-American who later became the stormy petrel of the Minnesota Commission of Public Safety, was arguing the interventionist case with a superlative ardor in 1916. More circumspectly than McGee, Senator Knute Nelson, who was born in Norway, committed himself to a similar position early in the same year. As might be expected, spokesmen for Belgian-Americans residing in Minnesota also wanted the United States to follow a firm anti-German course. And as the war proceeded, it became increasingly clear that Allied victory would create the best prospect for realizing nationalist aspirations among the Czechs, Poles, Serbs, and southern Slavic peoples.[36] Nevertheless, German-American and Scandinavian-American voters dominated the Minnesota electorate. One informed calculation estimated that nearly two-thirds of the vote in the 1914 election had been cast by electors of German, Norwegian, Swedish, and Danish parentage. The state's pro-Ally ethnic groups tended to be either numerically small or politically unorganized, and they therefore wielded proportionately little influence in the final outcome.[37]

From a strictly short-range point of view, the rise of controversy over American foreign policy in 1915 and 1916 possibly strengthened Minnesota progressivism. The noninterventionist position was based on premises that enjoyed high standing among midwestern progressives — the notion that an active overseas policy was a calculated diversion from problems at home, the suspicion that only the wealthy stood to gain from American involvement, and a general distrust of militarism. In addition, the neutralist cause seemed to be a rallying point for agriculture, labor, and the small towns, groups that had coexisted rather uneasily within the progressive movement. It also laid the groundwork for rapport between antiwar progressives and German-Americans, whose enthusiasm for progressivism had hitherto been chilled by the county option issue. For years the German-American press had ridiculed William Jennings Bryan, one of midwestern progressivism's folk heroes, principally because of his conspicuous identification with the dry cause. This unflattering treatment changed abruptly following Bryan's resignation as secretary of state in June, 1915, and his subsequent emergence as the chief advocate of nonintervention. With a suddenness that startled editorial writers, German-American spokesmen discovered that Bryan possessed the qualities of a great statesman. The *St. Paul Volkszeitung* confessed that it had not hitherto admired him but now valued his effective opposition to Wilson's "dictatorial" policies. Expressions such as this caused the *Fairmont Daily Sentinel* to remark dryly: "The Germans have suddenly taken an awful liking to Billy Bryan, and that too in spite of the fact that he is heart and soul against booze in every form."[38]

In the long run, however, the foreign-policy dispute had a divisive rather than a unifying effect on the progressive movement. Most progressives were neutralists in a relative rather than an absolute sense, and the degree of their commitment to nonintervention varied widely. As crisis followed crisis, their susceptibility to pro-Ally, anti-German persuasion became increasingly clear. A movement that affirmed so strongly the inseparability of morality and public affairs could hardly ignore the plight of "violated" Belgium or remain indifferent when its own national leader, speaking from the presidency, invoked the "rights of humanity" in the submarine controversy. The claims of patriotism also exerted a strong pull on a generation that had been reared on spread-eagle Fourth-of-July oratory.

The rise of pro-Ally pressures in 1915 did not, however, produce a neat and clear-cut division between interventionist and noninterventionist progressives. Nonintervention continued to be the avowed position of Minnesota progressivism until February, 1917. On specific issues relating to foreign policy, however, neutralist solidarity broke down. Some progressives endorsed preparedness to a greater or lesser degree, while others opposed any increase in armed strength. A number supported Wilson's stand against unrestricted submarine warfare, but some argued that peace was more important than American maritime rights. Hyphenism also divided the movement as did issues like the propriety of banning loans and munitions sales. Some progressives were neutralist on one or two issues, but pro-Ally on others. The *Minneota Mascot* continued to advocate an embargo on loans and munitions as late as early 1917 while supporting administration submarine policy, deploring the Gore-McLemore resolutions, and moderately endorsing the campaign against the hyphen.[39]

Open disagreement on these issues became evident about five months after the outbreak of war. A committee claiming to represent the "neutral and belligerent nationalities" residing in the area organized a mass rally at the St. Paul Auditorium on January 12, 1915. The announced purpose of this meeting, which attracted a sizable crowd, was to launch a "nation-wide movement against the exportation of arms and munitions to the belligerents." After hearing speeches from such luminaries as ex-Governor Eberhart, Lawler, and Albert E. Pfaender of New Ulm, the rally voted approval of resolutions demanding an embargo similar to the one that had earlier blocked the flow of war materials to rival factions in the current Mexican civil war.[40]

A mixed reaction greeted the embargo proposal. Several influential country newspapers, including the *Red Wing Republican* and the *Fairmont Sentinel*, warmly supported it. So did local German-American organs. However, the *Minneapolis Journal*, a paper that progressives regarded highly because it had unambiguously supported county option and antibossism, editorialized against the embargo — albeit without questioning the good faith of the rally's sponsors.[41]

In February imperial Germany's announcement of unrestricted submarine warfare together with Wilson's response widened the area of controversy. The doctrine of strict accountability laid down by the president deeply offended the German-American community; before long political columnists were predicting that Wilson would lose most of Minnesota's normally Democratic German-American vote in 1916. Papers like the *Fairmont Sentinel* and the *Red Wing Republican* avoided explicit attacks on the administration but stepped up their crusades for an embargo, a proposition that Wilson had by this time rejected. The Twin Cities metropolitan dailies, on the other hand, supported the president both on strict accountability and maintenance of full trading relations with the Allies.[42]

The *Lusitania* sinking on May 7 produced alarmed excitement throughout Minnesota, as elsewhere. According to the *St. Paul Volkszeitung*, news of the disaster struck capital city residents "with the force of a bomb." People grabbed newspaper "extras" as avidly as they had in the early days of the war. Animated debates developed on street corners, and the paper reported sharp clashes of opinion: "At every new report of . . . the catastrophe . . . the many enemies of Germany in St. Paul spewed forth . . . poison and gall about the 'piracy' and demanded at the very least an immediate declaration of war against Germany while the . . . Germans, wherever they met, wore a revealing smile of quiet satisfaction."[43]

The *Volkszeitung* no doubt exaggerated the sense of crisis. Although street-corner orators in the full flush of excitement may have demanded forceful action against Germany, no responsible spokesmen, public or private, did so. The *Minneapolis Journal* severely condemned German "barbarism," but cautioned against rash action that might bring war. Cyrus Northrop called the sinking "horrible," adding, however, that "all war is horrible, and Germany had given warning that British vessels were in danger, owing to the state of war existing between the two nations." Within a few weeks the sense of crisis receded and concerns temporarily in eclipse resumed their sway.[44]

Nevertheless, the *Lusitania* affair left an indissoluble residue: a heightened distrust of Germany, a corresponding rise in pro-Ally feeling, and a barrier of suspicion between German-Americans and "peace at any price" men on the one hand and moderate neutralists on the other. Shortly after the sinking, the noninterventionist *Fairmont Sentinel* raised a disturbing question: "In case of war between Germany and the United States where will Martin county Germans be found?" A few weeks later, Day's paper reported that "outside of the Germans, the dominant sentiment in Martin county is unmistakably with the allies."[45]

An acrimonious exchange of views within the Minneapolis labor movement illustrates how tense relations between peace advocates and moderate neutralists became in the post-*Lusitania* period. At a regular meeting of the Minneapolis Trades and Labor Assembly early in the summer of 1915, a radical unionist declared labor's stake in American society was so slight that workingmen "could not be interested in the defense of this country, even were it invaded by a foreign foe." This remark brought a sharp rejoinder from the *Union Labor Bulletin*, the voice of Minneapolis labor's conservative wing, which rebuked the Trades and Labor Assembly "for the dissemination of disloyal sentiments" and asked: "Can the labor unions of this city afford to permit their representatives . . . to give utterance to disloyal and unpatriotic thoughts that are sure to be spread broadcast as representative of the sentiment of union men?"[46]

Through the last half of 1915, concern about hyphenism, preparedness, maritime rights, and balanced neutrality sustained a spirited foreign-policy debate. However, intensity of feeling apparently did not rise above the level established after the *Lusitania* crisis subsided. Whether neutralism lost substantial support cannot be determined. Zealous pro-Ally activity by groups like the National Security League possibly won converts, but it also stimulated "countereducation" by noninterventionists.

In February and March, 1916, congressional deliberation on the Gore-McLemore resolutions, which warned Americans against taking passage on belligerent ships bound for war zones, stirred public excitement to a pitch that anticipated the hysteria of 1917 and 1918. In the House, the entire Minnesota delegation voted against tabling the resolution, a vote generally interpreted as being for it. When the question came up in the Senate, Clapp voted negatively, and Nelson affirmatively: in other words, Clapp voted with his House colleagues and Nelson with a coalition made up predominantly of administration Democrats and eastern Republicans.[47]

Although the resolutions were tabled in both houses, the stand of the Minnesota contingent in congress aroused a storm. An angry *New York Times* editorial seriously questioned the quality of Minnesota patriotism:

> The Minnesota delegation in Congress consists of eleven
> Kaiserists and one American, and a mighty fine one, Senator
> Knute Nelson, born in Norway. Ten Minnesota Representatives
> in Congress, eight Republicans, one Democrat, one Progres-
> sive, and the other Minnesota Senator, Moses Clapp, voted
> against the President, against the upholding of American rights.
> The German-American Alliance of Minnesota urged or bullied
> these eleven weaklings to the course they followed. Knute Nel-
> son is the only man, the sole American, Minnesota has in
> Congress.[48]

Angry reaction also developed in Minnesota. The House of Representatives, observed the *Duluth Herald*, had voted 276 for Wilson and America, and 142 for Germany, but Minnesota's record was worse; it had favored Germany by a score of ten to zero. The *Le Sueur News* declared allegiance to "the United States, first and last" and blasted "officials who are with the enemies of this country." Robert C. Dunn's *Princeton Union* predicted a tough re-election fight for the entire delegation because of its "un-American votes on the McLemore resolution." The *Minneapolis Jour-*

nal took a similar line. "We still believe," it asserted, "that whenever the people of this State and City have an opportunity so to declare by their votes, there will not be enough hyphens in sight to intimidate even a Minnesota Congressman."[49]

A few weeks later the *Sussex* crisis, which terminated with Germany's conditional pledge to leash its submarines, cooled the furor, and for the next eight months the defense of American rights against German encroachment became less pressing. However, the calm was highly deceptive. Containment of the ugly passions that had erupted during discussion of the controversial resolutions depended entirely on maintenance of reasonably good relations with Germany, and since these relations rested on a pledge subject to recall on short notice, there was little ground for optimism.

CHAPTER TEN

Domestic Discord

WHILE CONTROVERSY over foreign policy was threatening progressive solidarity, a growing agrarian militance was straining the relationship between main street and the open countryside, two vital elements in the movement's supporting coalition. An episode at Fargo, North Dakota, on the evening of January 23, 1914, carried an intimation of the future.

Earlier in the day local businessmen had expressed hostility toward the Tri-State Grain Growers' Association which was holding its annual convention in the Civic Auditorium. When the delegates returned for an evening session, they found access to the building blocked by the county sheriff, city police, Fargo Chamber of Commerce officials, and the Auditorium Association president. Another group, these dignitaries announced, had made prior arrangements to use the facilities. Unimpressed with the good faith of the statement, the Tri-State men contested possession of the hall. In the scramble that followed, the sheriff was thrown off the platform three times and serious violence was threatened. The Tri-State Association's presiding officer calmed the situation, after which Fargo's police chief ordered the meeting dispersed. The farmers obeyed but refused to forget. Prolonged and ultimately futile litigation against the police chief followed.[1]

The Tri-State Grain Growers' Association, a body representing wheat farmers in Minnesota and the two Dakotas, was a subsidiary of the Equity movement which operated through a number of branches, some based on geography and others on specific agricultural commodities. Although Equity affiliates occasionally worked at cross purposes, all claimed descent from the American Society of Equity, founded in Indianapolis, Indiana, on December 24, 1902. James A. Everitt, Equity's prophet if not its undisputed founder, advocated market control as the solution of agriculture's problems. Farmers, he said, should organize commodity holding movements "to keep the market in a seeking condition," an approach that the National Farm Organization would adopt more than half a century later. An organizational

106

upheaval in 1907 deposed Everitt from Equity leadership. Important policy changes followed. The new leaders placed more emphasis than Everitt had done on orthodox co-operative marketing and buying, and Everitt's disposition to centralize authority gave way to greater local autonomy. However, much of the militant idealism infused into the movement by Everitt persisted.[2]

Experience had conditioned farmers in Minnesota and the Dakotas to accept the Equity message. From their point of view, existing marketing arrangements needed extensive improvement. Midwest agriculture, to be sure, had gained some advantages in its continuing war with so-called middlemen. By 1900 farmers' co-operatives were strongly entrenched on the local marketing level, and public regulation shielded agriculture from the grosser forms of exploitation. Nevertheless, many farmers, particularly grain growers, remained dissatisfied. Prices still fluctuated widely, and fixed marketing and transportation charges seemed excessive. Most of these grievances focused on terminal marketing. Co-operative elevators were obliged to dispose of their grain through commission firms holding seats on the Minneapolis Chamber of Commerce (the older name for the Minneapolis Grain Exchange) or the Duluth Board of Trade. Most farmers firmly believed that these institutions held tight monopolistic control over the grain market and that this control was exercised for the benefit of speculators in grain futures, commission merchants, and terminal elevator companies.[3]

Indirectly before 1907 and more directly thereafter, Equity agitation encouraged extension of agricultural co-operation from the local to the terminal level. If the farmers could dominate marketing up to the point where their products passed into the hands of flour millers, brewers, and the like, they would be in a position to threaten "monopolistic" grain exchanges with competition, if not extinction. On May 30, 1908, a group of Equity representatives, meeting in Minneapolis, organized the Equity Co-operative Exchange. The promoters of this enterprise hoped to make it a terminal grain marketing agency fed by a chain of local co-operative elevators. If their scheme succeeded, the Minneapolis Chamber of Commerce would lose all reason for being.[4]

In its first four years, the Equity Co-operative Exchange put on a feeble performance. It did not incorporate until 1911, and it disposed of most of its grain through the Minneapolis Chamber of Commerce. However, in 1912, when George S. Loftus became sales manager, growth rapidly accelerated. Loftus, a strident, idealistic, and uncompromising crusader against the financial interests, was "more a reformer than a business manager," but his skill as an agitator renewed the commitment of old Equity supporters and gained new adherents.[5]

The established grain trade, which had ignored the new exchange during its ineffective first four years, responded to Loftus' appointment with alarm. Almost immediately, John G. McHugh, the resourceful secretary of the Minneapolis Chamber of Commerce, organized a counterattack. Hostilities soon raged on several fronts: at conventions of elevator managers who had to choose between dealing with Equity or the Minneapolis Chamber; in the courts; in the public press; and in legislative halls, both state and national. Neither side gave, expected, nor accepted quarter. Loftus brutally characterized established grain exchanges as wicked monopolies engaged in a conspiracy to bilk the farmers. Hotly resenting these attacks, grain trade spokesmen questioned the basic honesty of the Equity Exchange. A *Commercial West* editorial characterized Loftus' enterprise as "a farce, and a most transparent one . . . an attempt at deception upon the Northwestern farmers and grain shippers. For such an outfit to presume to attack the integrity of the Chamber of Commerce was an exhibit of insincerity, like a rogue questioning the motives of an honest man."[6]

Although the Loftus-McHugh conflict was basically economic, political repercussions were inevitable. For one thing, small-town editors, merchants, lawyers, and bankers were called upon to choose between alliance with Equity or the grain trade, a choice that had implications for the relationship between main street and the farmers. In addition, the Equity program included demands for stringent regulation of grain marketing. James Manahan, a close friend of Loftus, pushed these demands in his successful race for congress in 1912. In the same year a number of Equity champions also won election to the Minnesota legislature.[7]

Neither Manahan nor the Equity bloc in the state legislature succeeded in getting action on regulatory laws, but both managed to initiate investigations of grain trade practices. In fact, the Minnesota legislature launched two investigations, a pro-Equity one in the House of Representatives, and a pro-Chamber one in the Senate. Committee findings conformed to expectations. The House report called attention to "conditions . . . which your committee considers unsatisfactory and tending to burden the producers." Senate investigators found "the Chamber of Commerce . . . an open, broad, competitive market."[8]

Loftus and McHugh made effective use of these findings, and their battle continued at high intensity. The immediate impact on state-wide politics was, however, minimal. Reform of the grain trade was scarcely mentioned in the 1914 state campaign. Governor Hammond failed to allude to it in his inaugural message, and the 1915 legislature buried Equity-sponsored bills. No state official in his right mind wanted to become entangled with a controversy as divisive as this one.

It was otherwise in North Dakota, where sheer numbers gave grain growers greater political influence than in Minnesota. For several years state ownership and operation of terminal elevators as one means of freeing North Dakota's economy from domination by the Minneapolis Chamber of Commerce had commanded enthusiastic support — and not from wheat farmers alone. By 1915 this project seemed on the point of realization. The voters had approved two constitutional amendments authorizing North Dakota to own and operate terminal elevators both within and outside the state. A tax to finance the enterprise was being levied, and the state Board of Control had been instructed to formulate plans for construction. A report from this body was awaited when the 1915 legislature went into session. Instead of presenting construction plans, however, the board argued against proceeding with the project. Its recommendations stunned elevator proponents. Constitutionally the Board of Control could not veto the elevator plan, but the report definitely fortified opposition to it and reduced the probability of final legislative approval.[9]

The North Dakota Union of the American Society of Equity held its 1915 convention in Bismarck while the legislature was in session. With the help of Farmers' Union representatives whom they had invited to attend, Equity leaders hoped to influence legislative deliberation on state elevators and other issues. Loftus addressed a rally the night before the crucial vote on the elevator bill was scheduled. In an impassioned speech he denounced not only the Board of Control and legislators who opposed the measure, but also those still undecided. The chagrin of the latter at this treatment may have helped defeat the bill; at any rate, the legislature turned it down.[10]

Thereafter the Equity convention became a focus of mass protest. Farmers demanded and often got hearings before legislators which usually turned into tumultuous debating sessions. At one of these a House member allegedly told his agrarian adversaries to "go home and slop the hogs," since running state government was beyond the ken of simple rustics. Very likely these words were never uttered — at least not in the represented context — but the contempt they carried aptly epitomized the farmer's feeling about the treatment he had long received from "old gang" politicians. So, apocryphal or not, the words helped ignite what one scholar called a "political prairie fire."[11]

Among the angry farmers attending the Equity convention was Arthur C. Townley, a thirty-five-year-old flax grower who had recently gone broke. Townley was not entirely unknown in the state. He had left his native Minnesota in 1904 at the age of twenty-four to seek new opportunities in the Beach, North Dakota, area, then being developed by land speculators. After a variety of experiments — farming in partnership with his brother Covert, serving for a year as an itinerant plasterer's helper, and attempting with a number of partners large-scale wheat farming in Colorado — he committed himself to flax growing, an enterprise which he and Covert pursued jointly. Immediate success followed, and railroad land agents hailed him as the "flax king of the Northwest" and "a sterling example of what a man could do in a few years" if he undertook to crop the virgin lands of western North Dakota.[12]

Thus encouraged, Townley in 1912 planted 8,000 acres to flax and purchased on credit enough machinery to handle the anticipated crop. Before marketing time, however, double disaster struck. Inclement weather reduced the yield to a fraction of normal, and instead of an anticipated three dollars a bushel, Townley got less than a dollar. The flax king of the Northwest found himself $80,000 in debt. After surveying the wreckage, Townley decided that a normal price for his less-than-normal crop would have preserved his solvency. As he put it years later, "We went broke because the flax didn't bring us any money."[13]

Brief meditation suggested a political solution. "I figured there ought to be a law of some kind," said Townley. An investigation of existing possible remedies did not reassure him. He found that "the same crowd that fixed the price of flax owned the Republican party," and "the same crowd that controlled the Republican party controlled the Democratic party." The only alternative was Socialism. "So for one year," Townley recalled in 1956, "I tried to use the Socialist party . . . but found during that year — that was in 1914 — that their program covered too much territory for me. They wanted to take over everything. So in the winter of 1915, I severed my association with the Socialist party. And I went out and organized the Nonpartisan League."[14]

Since the Townley of the 1950s was a crusader against left-wing causes, it is not surprising that he minimized the importance of his brief association with Socialism as preparation for his role in the Nonpartisan League. The Socialists, however, gave him a program which appealed powerfully to discontented North Dakota farmers. Socialist demands for state ownership not only of terminal elevators but also of rural credit facilities, mills, and insurance systems became the core planks in the Nonpartisan League platform. From the Socialist party Townley also learned effective organizational techniques. While working for it, he became familiar with the utility of Ford cars, signed pledges to support candidates, membership dues, and postdated checks in payment of dues from farmers short of cash — all techniques later used by the Nonpartisan League. Finally, he must have gained confidence in his own capacities as an organizer and agitator.[15]

Townley's later recollections also failed to describe the circumstances surrounding his brief association and his break with the North Dakota Socialist party. By 1914 the party had achieved modest success within the state, not because North Dakota farmers subscribed to the Marxist dialectic, but because the Socialists had developed a program which appealed to them. Ultimate Socialist victory in North Dakota, however, seemed highly improbable, since the party's label repelled many farmers who liked its state platform. To overcome this difficulty the party's state committee set up an "organization department" which non-Socialists who liked the program could join without signing the red card. The requirements for membership on this limited basis included a signed pledge to work and vote for candidates committed to the state program and the payment of one dollar a month into a fund which supported campaign and educational activities. The department employed Townley in the position of organizer. Under him the enterprise succeeded beyond expectations. Soon the organization department nearly equaled the parent party in membership and promised to overshadow it in influence — a development that worried North Dakota Socialist leaders, who saw a threat of the proverbial tail wagging the dog. So the 1915 Socialist party state convention, meeting in January, discontinued the department, terminating Townley's formal association with Socialism.[16]

Shortly after he was undercut by the Socialists, Townley attended the Equity convention described above. "What he saw and heard there convinced him that the farmers were ready for organization," and presently he conceived "the idea of nonpartisan political action through control of the primaries." He discussed his ideas with friends and gained several promises of assistance. Before winter yielded to spring the Farmers' Nonpartisan Political League of North Dakota was an organizational reality.[17]

The avowed goal of the new organization was breathtaking. It proposed to capture the entire state government — executive, legislative, and judicial — for the purpose of enacting a program which combined North Dakota Socialist party proposals with Equity demands. As the first step in its bid for power, the Nonpartisan League intended to gain control of the dominant party by means of the primary election. This accomplished, it would work for the election of its endorsed candidates, who would appear on the ballot as the nominees of the established party. After the election the league would watch the officials selected with its help to see that they carried out the program.[18]

Since discontented grain farmers constituted a healthy fraction of North Dakota's electorate, this audacious scheme was not completely mad. Its success would depend on large numbers of farmers becoming active, zealous, participating members of the Nonpartisan League. Unity was also essential. Internal dissension could, and later did, reduce the movement to ineffectiveness.

Townley proved equal to the challenge. Since he personally shared the discontent he sought to mobilize, he understood it as few men of leadership caliber could. He also had the capacity to articulate the discontent both in conversation and on the platform. A contemporary observed that when Townley "commences to talk he appears to be about 'five foot ten'; when he finishes he seems to be about 'ten foot five.' " In addition, he had a keen awareness of his movement's organizational needs. He entrusted these details to competent associates, while retaining close personal supervision over such important matters as the briefing of organizers on how to recruit farmers into the movement.[19]

The well-organized North Dakota Nonpartisan League made its first bid for power in 1916. All league members were eligible to participate in precinct meetings, which elected delegates to various district conventions. These, in turn, selected delegates for a state convention which met in Fargo on March 29 and 30, 1916. The state group named a slate of candidates who, with one exception, filed in the Republican primaries. It also generated reserves of enthusiasm which sustained the cause throughout the campaign. The Nonpartisan slate was spectacularly successful in a vigorous contest, virtually sweeping the primaries on state and local levels. Success also crowned the league's efforts in the fall campaign. Its candidates failed to win only one state race — that for state treasurer, which the league-endorsed candidate entered on the Democratic ticket— and they filled 81 of the 113 seats in the lower house. In November, 1916, North Dakota stood on the threshold of a new era.[20]

The Nonpartisan League had by this time invaded Minnesota also. Townley's organizers held their first meeting east of the Red River early in July, 1916, on the farm of one Arne Grundysen some eight miles south of East Grand Forks. During the next few weeks, the league's missionaries

SAMUEL R. VAN SANT, *an ex-steamboatman with a flair for patriotic oratory, served as governor of Minnesota from 1901 to 1905.*

JOHN LIND, *governor from 1899 to 1901, initially defined progressivism's goals on the state level.*

MOSES E. CLAPP, *an insurgent Republican, served as U.S. Senator from 1901 to 1917.*

JOHN A. JOHNSON, *an amiable anti-Bryan Democrat, gained the reputation of being one of the nation's outstanding reform governors.*

JACOB F. JACOBSON, *an unpolished man of the people and a militant reform legislator, was* Johnson's *GOP opponent in 1908.*

GOVERNOR JOHNSON *(left), Presidential Candidate William J. Bryan, and Frank A. Day (right) during Bryan's visit to Minnesota in 1908. Day, who served as Johnson's secretary, had earlier led a drive to win the Democratic presidential nomination for Johnson.*

GOVERNOR WINFIELD S. HAMMOND *at his desk in the Minnesota Capitol in 1915.*
A native of Massachusetts and a graduate of Dartmouth, Hammond "was not as
dour as Lind, but quite as dignified . . . and very reserved."

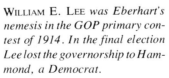

ADOLPH O. EBERHART, *whose re-*
tirement from the governorship
was a major goal of progressive
action, served in that post from
1909 to 1915.

WILLIAM E. LEE *was Eberhart's*
nemesis in the GOP primary con-
test of 1914. In the final election
Lee lost the governorship to Ham-
mond, a Democrat.

OLE O. SAGENG, *an Otter Tail Count[...] farmer-legislator, was an effectiv[...] champion of woman suffrage, county o[...] tion, prohibition, and stringent utili[...] regulation.*

GUNNAR B. BJORNSON, *editor of the Minneota Mascot and a prominent GOP progressive, initiated the successful drive against Governor Eberhart's renomination in 1914.*

EDWARD E. SMITH, *Minneapolis attorney, was a power behind the throne during Eberhart's governorship.*

JOHN F. MCGEE *conducted a furious crusade against Minnesotans suspected of disloyalty during World War I.*

ARTHUR C. TOWNLEY *and the Nonpartisan League ignited a "political prairie fire" that spread from North Dakota to Minnesota and other states.*

CARL A. WOLD, *editor of the* Park Region Echo *of Alexandria, suffered mob violence during World War I for his support of the Nonpartisan League.*

CHARLES A. LINDBERGH, SR., *ran for governor with Nonpartisan League backing in 1918. Mob action barred his meetings in many Minnesota communities.*

JOSEPH A. A. BURNQUIST, *governor during the turbulent years from 1915 to 1921, prevailed over Lindbergh in the GOP primary of 1918. He based his campaign on the "loyalty" issue.*

JAMES A. MANAHAN, *a fiery Bryan Democrat and severe critic of Governor John A. Johnson, served one term as Congressman-at-large (1913–15) and as legal counsel for the Equity movement and Nonpartisan League.*

FRANK B. KELLOGG *represented Minnesota in the U.S. Senate from 1917 to 1923. Following his defeat for re-election, he served the Coolidge administration first as Ambassador to Great Britain and later as Secretary of State.*

HENRIK SHIPSTEAD *helped establish the Farmer-Labor party as a force in Minnesota politics by defeating Kellogg for the U.S. Senate in 1922.*

ANNA DICKEY OLESEN, *Democratic candidate for the U.S. Senate in 1922, waged a brilliant campaign that failed to break a male monopoly on high state-wide elective office in Minnesota.*

J. A. O. PREUS, *(left), governor from 1921 to 1925, unidentified child, and Preus's mentor, Senator Knute Nelson, are shown in this photo taken about 1921.*

successfully proselytized Polk County. In some townships 95 per cent of the farmers became members.[21]

Townley and his associates knew that victory in Minnesota could not be won with the votes of discontented wheat farmers alone. However, the support of other agricultural and small-town groups seemed unlikely. The grievances of the dairy and corn-hog farmers of the south and southeast were less acute than those of the wheat growers. Small-town professional and business men were even less probable allies. The tradition of league hostility to main street, which would be a significant factor in the breakup of the progressive coalition in Minnesota, was already firmly established.[22]

The alienation of the small town left the labor movement as a possible ally of the Nonpartisan League. For several years the Equity movement and the trade unions had nourished the old populist ideal of farmer-labor co-operation by exchanging fraternal delegations at their respective conventions. Experience had demonstrated the difficulty of such co-operation, but the ferment stirring within the Minnesota labor movement offered Townley some hope.[23]

A buoyant optimism was evident within the Minnesota trade union movement in 1915. In his report to the annual convention of the Minnesota Federation of Labor, President E. George Hall announced "a paid up membership larger than the Federation has ever had," and reported what he believed to be "the largest number of new affiliations for any year in its history." The *Union Labor Bulletin*, which spoke for the conservative wing of Minneapolis unionism, sounded a similar optimistic note in its Labor Day editorial, commenting that many "unions have increased wages, and the building trades . . . have been granted the Saturday half-holiday."[24]

A similar self-confidence was apparent nationally. By 1915 organized labor's prospects cheered trade unionists throughout the nation. Ten years earlier the situation had seemed less rosy, as a powerful employer-directed open-shop campaign, public and judicial hostility, and defensiveness on the part of the American Federation of Labor had dogged union advance. To some extent these barriers still hampered the labor movement in 1915, but the apparent friendliness of the Wilson administration, increasing public acceptance of unionism, an upward trend in AFL membership, and a rising level of union activity augured well.[25]

Under such conditions the prospects for industrial peace were not especially good in centers of uncompromising resistance to unionization. Minneapolis was such a center. Since 1903 an employers' fraternity known as the Citizens Alliance had successfully upheld the sanctity of the open shop in the city. According to one of its officials, members of the Citizens Alliance included "many of the leading banks, and other business con[c]erns," and the scope of its activities was broad. A carefully cultivated aura of secrecy obscured the extent and nature of its involvement, but for several years, according to the same official, the alliance had "taken a hand in the adjustment of all important labor disputes" in Minneapolis. "It is our policy to avoid any unnecessary publicity with respect to such matters," he added.[26]

The Citizens Alliance operated on several levels. It conducted an educational campaign, primarily through the publication of a monthly *Bulletin*, which argued the case for the group's basic principle that closed shop unionism was un-American. It kept its members informed of current trade union activities, presumably gathering the information through its mysterious espionage apparatus. Last but not least, it stood ready to assist members who were plagued by strike threats.[27]

Technically, such assistance was not automatically forthcoming. A besieged employer had to appeal to the directors of the alliance, who would then appoint a committee to investigate the dispute. If the committee found the employer's position fair and just, the organization would furnish him with support. This might include legal help in case of court action; the recruitment of workers — or "scabs" as trade unionists impolitely called them — to replace employees on strike; and procurement of guards if violence threatened the destruction of property.[28]

Appropriately, perhaps, a labor movement more radical than the national mean confronted this wall of employer intransigence. For several years socialist trade unionists had controlled the Minneapolis Trades and Labor Assembly, and with it the *Minneapolis Labor Review*, a state of affairs that bred dissension within the Minnesota labor movement. At the 1915 convention of the Minnesota Federation of Labor, for example, conservative delegates pushed a motion to exclude the Minneapolis delegation because the *Labor Review* had caustically attacked the federation's leadership. Although this move failed by a narrow margin, mutual recriminations continued for many months. Moderate Minneapolis unionists also refused to let the Trades and Labor Assembly represent them. In 1914 the Union Card and Label Council of Minneapolis and the Minneapolis Building Trades founded their own paper, the monthly *Union Labor Bulletin*, which undertook to speak for the nonsocialist wing of the city's labor movement.[29]

The very attitude of the Citizens Alliance, however, tended to reduce the divisive effect of ideological conflict within the ranks of Minneapolis labor. The alliance refused to distinguish between moderate and radical unionists and seemed determined to win an unconditional victory in every confrontation. In times of crisis, such as the teamsters and machinists strikes of 1916 and the streetcar strike of 1917-18, the city's trade unionists — whether standing for bread and butter or the overthrow of capitalism — drew together to defend what they regarded as labor's vital interests.[30]

In addition to controlling the Trades and Labor Assembly, Minneapolis socialists had become an important force in city politics by 1915. A network of socialist locals, some based on ward boundaries and others on ethnic identity (Scandinavian, Finnish, German, Jewish, Lettish, and Russian), covered the city. These locals maintained year-round schedules of activities, which included not only standard lectures on the principles of socialism, but also picnics, dances, and organized efforts on behalf of Socialist party candidates for public office.[31]

The leadership roster of this active movement included several men who survived the Socialist party's virtual demise during World War I and later found fulfillment in the Minnesota Farmer-Labor party. Among them were Lynn Thompson, Thomas E. Latimer, George B. Leonard, Andrew O. Devold, and Thomas Van Lear. The latter was a machinist, a trade unionist, and an extraordinarily effective platform orator who combined emotional fervor with a shrewd pragmatism. A remark made during one of his campaigns illustrates Van Lear's style: The opposition, he said, wanted him "to give an academic talk on socialism." He rejected this putative suggestion, saying, "Why, bless you, I'm so busy telling the people how to avoid being robbed by the street railway company that I have no time to give an academic talk on any subject."[32]

To a considerable extent, Van Lear's leadership and popularity account for the success which Socialists were beginning to enjoy in the precincts of Minneapolis. In 1914 four Socialist party members won seats on the twenty-six-man city council. Although this success might have been discounted because technically municipal elections were nonpartisan, Van Lear in 1914 ran an impressive race as the official Socialist candidate for congress from the fifth district. In the final count he polled more than 10,000 votes, only 2,000 less than his successful Republican opponent. Two years later the voters of Minneapolis elected him mayor.[33]

A study made by *Fortune* magazine in the 1930s found a striking contrast between the embattled labor relations of Minneapolis and those of its immediate neighbor. "St. Paul has no labor troubles," the magazine reported. "Its labor was unionized years ago in a nice A.F. of L. way, about the time the city stopped growing." According to *Fortune*, this difference was part of a larger pattern. St. Paul had adjusted quietly to the adverse economic circumstances which arose after the turn of the century, while Minneapolis remained "So preoccupied . . . with its own growth that it failed to notice when it ceased to grow *with* the Northwest and began growing *at the expense* of the Northwest" — including its own working force.[34]

Whatever the merits of this analysis — and it was a highly controversial one at the time — its description of the difference between labor relations within the two cities contained both a grain of truth and an element of exaggeration. St. Paul could not remain completely unaffected by the labor situation in Minneapolis, for firms like the Twin City Rapid Transit Company operated in both cities. Moreover, St. Paul union spokesmen did worry about antiunion activity, including campaigns which received support from the American Anti-Boycott Society, and they were far from uninterested in politics. St. Paul unionism had a well-established tradition of rewarding friends and punishing enemies who ran for public office. For example, Carl C. Van Dyke, who served as fourth district congressman from 1914 until his death in 1919, was a progressive Democrat and staunch noninterventionist who depended primarily on labor support in his successive campaigns. St. Paul employers, however, did not push their antiunion drive to the point of ultimate confrontation, and the comparative absence of extremism within their ranks was matched by moderation in the labor movement. Socialist candidates for public office polled fewer votes than in Minneapolis, and conservative unionists remained at the helm of the St. Paul Trades and Labor Assembly until after the war.[35]

A strike which closed most of the iron mines of northern Minnesota during the summer of 1916 forcefully called attention to the explosive situation in that part of the state. Although management claimed that the strike was inspired by the IWW, the evidence indicates that the initial walkout was spontaneous and unpremeditated. One historian writes that the strike began when an Italian miner after seeing "that his pay check reflected a lower contract rate than he believed he was entitled to . . . threw down his pick" and walked away from the mine. The entire shift "went along with him." News of the walkout spread quickly, and "Within a week most of the mines throughout the entire Range were closed."[36] In the nine years since the first bitter range strike of 1907, company vigilance had kept union organizers out of the mines. Management also took another precaution; it permanently blacklisted the striking miners, replacing them with more docile laborers imported from the Balkan countries. For a time these tactics prevented work stoppages, but they certainly did not promote good feeling.[37]

Some of the blacklisted workers, who were largely of Finnish descent, remained in the area, engaging in occupations other than mining. They also continued to support a radical movement that carried on vigorous agitation against the mining companies. Spokesmen for the companies, in their turn, saw the IWW lurking in every suggestion that the mines be unionized. Meanwhile, controversy concerning the level at which mining properties should be taxed by local authorities aroused middle-class resentment toward the companies. Against this background the deplorable working conditions in the mines bred a sullen anger which boiled to the surface with the June, 1916, walkout.[38]

Like its predecessor in 1907, the 1916 strike collapsed, for the miners still lacked the resources to combat a deadly combination of hunger and coercive pressure. But there were important differences between the two strikes. In 1907 middle-class opinion in the numerous small towns that dotted the range had stood with management. In 1916 for a number of reasons it identified to a considerable extent with the strikers — a change in attitude that produced tangible support. In 1916 range merchants extended credit to the striking miners until Duluth wholesalers, apparently under pressure from the mining companies, cut off credit to the merchants. The mayors of range communities, working through the recently formed Range Municipal League, attempted to bring the contending parties into negotiation; leaders of the strike responded affirmatively, but management refused. Finally, range citizens who were not directly involved in the strike gave information about it to public and private investigators whose published reports communicated the sorry details to an extensive audience beyond northeastern Minnesota.[39]

These reports persuasively challenged the theory that the strike was a fracas stirred up by the IWW for its own subversive ends. They made it clear that substantial grievances — particularly those inherent in the contract system of labor under which the miners worked— had precipitated the walkout. Wobbly organizers had been brought in, but only after the strike had started and because other leadership was unavailable. The reports questioned practices like deputizing private mine guards as police officers and the propriety of trying the strike's IWW leaders for the murder of a mine guard killed by a householder whose home had been invaded, allegedly in a search for illegal liquor. They also pointed out the apparent subservience of some government officials to company control.[40]

The impact of these revelations, which were widely circulated by the liberal and labor press, was far-reaching. The Minnesota Federation of Labor, already under pressure from Mayor Victor L. Power of Hibbing to organize the mines, gave the miners complete moral support but declined on jurisdictional grounds to assume leadership of the strike. The federation also demanded — and got — an impartial investigation of the strike by the state Department of Labor and Industries.[41]

Outside of the labor movement reaction was mixed. "The state cannot afford to permit . . . conditions which make it sure that miners and their families must always be human clods," asserted the *St. Paul Daily News.* Other comment indicated a reluctance to accept as worthy any cause tainted by association with the infamous IWW. The *Minneapolis Journal* proclaimed that "Iron Range miners who have submitted themselves to . . . [IWW] leadership must learn . . . that violence does not win strikes in Minnesota." According to the *Northfield News*, "everyone familiar with the situation knows that had it not been for the I.W.W. agitators . . . there probably would never have been any trouble at all."[42] The *Blue Earth County Enterprise*, also identified with small-town progressivism, took a similar view.

Thus by midsummer of 1916 the major forces that shortly would undermine Minnesota's progressive movement and produce two new alignments — the one a grouping of radical progressives, and the other a combination of conservatives and hitherto moderate progressives — were operative. Townley's organizers had created an embryonic Nonpartisan League within the state, and the discontents that the league hoped to mobilize were highly developed. At the same time middle-class progressivism was showing signs of reacting ambivalently to the new movement. In North Dakota many progressives had been "frightened by the rural radicals into an alliance with right-wing Stalwarts."[43]

Although it was too early to detect a similar tendency in Minnesota with regard to the Nonpartisan League, it was clear that some progressives perceived a parallel threat in the Socialist taint of Minneapolis unionism and in the strike activity of the IWW on the iron range. Lurking in the background, too, were the highly charged tensions aroused by the European war, tensions held in check for the moment by grudging German observance of the *Sussex* pledge.

CHAPTER ELEVEN

The Campaign of 1916

AT FIRST GLANCE the results of the 1916 election in Minnesota seem to elude rational interpretation. In the race for governor, the Republicans won the most impressive victory in state history. The presidential vote, however, was exceedingly close. Charles Evans Hughes, the GOP contender, ran ahead of President Wilson by a plurality of less than 400 votes. Republican Frank B. Kellogg, who campaigned as an advocate of preparedness and firm defense of American rights, triumphed in the contest for United States senator, an outcome that delighted interventionists and near-interventionists. On the other hand, predictions that voter resentment over the Gore-McLemore resolutions would retire most of the House delegation proved mistaken. Only one of Minnesota's ten congressmen lost his bid for re-election.[1]

If this outcome taken as a whole is confusing, separate analysis of the four contests yields a number of interesting conclusions. Republican victory in the governorship contest is attributable primarily to a virtual disintegration of the Minnesota Democratic party following the death of Hammond in December, 1915. The size and distribution of Wilson's large vote suggested the possibility of an effective farmer-labor coalition; the wheat-farmer and trade-union vote went overwhelmingly for the president. Kellogg's victory disclosed that a pro-Ally candidate could win in Minnesota if his personal prestige topped that of his rivals and he ran against a divided opposition. The congressional returns indicated that firm, uncompromising defense of American maritime rights was not the first concern of Minnesota voters.

Before Hammond's death a number of prominent Republicans, including Congressman Charles A. Lindbergh, had indicated an interest in their party's nomination for governor.[2] The succession of Lieutenant Governor Joseph A. A. Burnquist, a Republican, created a new set of circumstances. As an incumbent with only one year of service, Burnquist enjoyed a kind of presumptive right to the nomination, other things being equal. Moreover, memory of the 1914 defeat encouraged cultivation of party unity, an end that a hard-fought battle for the nomination would scarcely serve.

Burnquist's background further reinforced his claim to run for re-election. Despite his youth — he was thirty-seven in 1916 — he had nearly a decade of experience in public life. A native of Dayton, Iowa, he graduated from Carleton College at Northfield in 1902, took graduate work at Columbia University, and in 1905 completed the course offered by the University of Minnesota college of law. After practicing law in St. Paul for three years, he won election in 1908 to the Minnesota House of Representatives where he served for two terms. As we have seen, he became lieutenant governor in 1912, a post to which he was re-elected in 1914.[3]

As a state legislator, Burnquist gained the reputation of being an uncompromising progressive. His consistent support of measures like county option, the direct primary, and stringent utility legislation led Lynn Haines, the reform publicist, to give him an exceptionally high rating as a creative insurgent. Backed by a small coterie of supporters, Burnquist ran for House speaker in 1911 as a reform candidate. Defeat did him no harm; he emerged from the contest as a courageous young crusader who had dared challenge the Smith machine. After becoming lieutenant governor he had less opportunity to push progressivism, but county option supporters were grateful for the help he rendered their cause as presiding officer of the Senate in 1915.[4]

Burnquist's reputation of being a staunch progressive followed him into the governorship. Shortly after Hammond's passing, the *Park Region Echo* of Alexandria, whose editor, Carl Wold, would shortly become a Nonpartisan League spokesman, remarked that the new governor was "fair to all in his political views and transactions." The *Minneota Mascot* called him an adherent of "the progressive school of political thought" and an official whose record demonstrated that "No special interests dictated to him." After conferring with Burnquist in early 1916, Lindbergh reversed his intention to seek the Republican nomination for governor. "The principles for which he stands and the objects which he wishes to attain, are in accord with my own," said Lindbergh.[5]

Fortified by these testimonials from progressive Republicans, and facing no opposition from the party's discredited machine wing, Burnquist easily captured the nomination. In the primary election of June 19 he prevailed over his only opponent, the former state auditor, Samuel G. Iverson, by a margin of more than three to one.[6]

Shortly after Burnquist's impressive primary victory, his standing with those progressives who sympathized with the striking miners on the iron range sharply deteriorated. Nearly every aspect of the governor's strike policy displeased labor spokesmen and their liberal allies. They charged that he assented to and even encouraged the infamous practice of deputizing mine guards as police officers. His secretary, Gustaf Lindquist, whom Burnquist sent to the range on an inspection tour, refused to meet strike leaders and accepted lavish hospitality from the representatives of management. Worse still, the governor counseled St. Louis County authorities to try arrested persons at Duluth rather than in the range towns, presumably because "steel trust justice" was more certain at Duluth.[7] A number of delegates to the 1916 Minnesota Federation of Labor convention, which met in July while the range strike was still in progress, demanded impeachment of the governor. The convention declined to endorse this proposal, but a strong anti-Burnquist feeling was clearly evident within the federation.[8]

Although Burnquist's response to the range difficulty unquestionably favored management, it would be unjust to say that he thereby repudiated his commitment to progressivism. Like many middle-class progressives of his generation, Burnquist feared the "excesses" of radical labor even more than the alleged machinations of wealth. At a time when developments such as the range conflict and the rise of the Nonpartisan League indicated mounting militance within the reform movement's left wing, moderate progressives often became zealous defenders of the status quo. They still accepted the premise that an evil conspiracy endangered the American way of life, but the seat of conspiracy, in their view, had shifted from Wall Street to IWW headquarters.[9]

Criticism of Burnquist's strike policy continued throughout the campaign. In September former Congressman Frank M. Eddy, a Republican, predicted that "the Union Labor vote will be cast almost solidly against [Burnquist]." Eddy also noted that Nonpartisan League adherents who had "made some headway" in organizing "the Red River Valley and . . . the sixth district" were "talking against him." Other reports confirmed Eddy's observations and attributed Nonpartisan League hostility toward Burnquist to a desire to cultivate labor support on the range.[10]

Burnquist's opposition faced an insurmountable handicap in the lack of an acceptable alternative candidate. The organizational effort of the Nonpartisan League in Minnesota had just begun, and it was not yet in a position to be effective. Nor did the Democrats offer an appealing choice. Internal dissension, a chronic disease of the old Minnesota Democratic party, was unusually virulent in 1916. An open brawl developed on the train carrying the Minnesota delegation to the Democratic national convention at St. Louis between supporters and opponents of National Committeeman Fred B.

Lynch. When the delegates reached St. Louis, the Lynch and anti-Lynch men booked rooms in separate hotels to avoid further hostilities.[11]

Although these two factions battled lustily for the gubernatorial nomination, neither won. "While they were fighting over the bone the unknown dropped in and run off with it." The unknown was Thomas P. Dwyer, a Minneapolis boilermaker who had filed for the nomination before Hammond's death in order to show Hammond that he had friends in Hennepin County. Political writers found it impossible to explain his nomination. Some speculated that many voters may have confused Thomas Dwyer with James Dwyer, who was a prominent legislator from Hennepin County.[12]

Dwyer was an impossible candidate, scarcely known outside Hennepin County. Shortly before the election a poll of eighty-one Northfield business-men disclosed that sixty-eight could not identify him. Nor did his quoted statements inspire confidence. On one occasion he affirmed opposition to county option, prohibition, woman suffrage, and all such "fads." On another he proclaimed, "Let every man eat and drink what and when he pleases." He also advocated the enactment of a statute prohibiting the use of profane language in public.[13]

Obviously such a candidate could not hold the normal Democratic vote, let alone capitalize on the developing disaffection with Burnquist. Realizing this, Democratic leaders cut Dwyer adrift, leaving him "paddling his own canoe." Occasionally rumors of his withdrawal circulated. One report told of plans to substitute Mayor Victor Power of Hibbing in the hope that Power could hold the Democratic vote and draw additional support from organized labor and farmers already committed to the Nonpartisan League. But Dwyer doggedly refused to quit, and since he was the legally nominated candidate, Minnesota Democrats were stuck with him. Of course, they did not have to vote for him. Eddy found Democrats among his circle of acquaintances "not interested, in the slightest degree in their candidate for Governor." He noted that "the majority of them . . . would very much prefer to see him defeated." The election returns fulfilled this wish. Burnquist polled nearly 246,000 votes to slightly over 93,000 for Dwyer.[14]

While Burnquist backers had a right to rejoice at the magnitude of their victory, they must have realized that it was won largely by default. The deep split within progressive ranks over range strike issues which had developed during the campaign was a more reliable harbinger of the future than the size of Burnquist's majority.

The supporters of Charles Evans Hughes were optimistic about Minnesota at the outset of the 1916 campaign. Never in its history had the state gone Democratic in a presidential election, although the Bull Moose movement had carried it in 1912. The feuding factions within the Minnesota Democratic party could give little help to the national ticket, while German-American hostility to Wilson created an opening for Republican capture of many normally Democratic votes.[15]

As the campaign proceeded, however, Republican managers noted with alarm a rising tide of Wilson support. Many farmers, it seemed, were grateful for improved commodity prices and the recently created Federal Land Bank system. The president's espousal of the eight-hour railroad labor law and the Keating-Owen child labor bill had convinced many trade unionists that Wilson was their friend. One Republican county chairman wanted "a copy of the Rural Credits bill, the Child Labor bill and the Adamson bill" because he found it impossible to convince "A great many people . . . of the fallacies of those measures untill [sic] they see the bill or have the objectionable features actually read to them."[16]

The personalities of the competing candidates also had an anti-Hughes impact. Frank Day characterized Hughes as "a lobster — apparently without tact or human sympathy." Day was a Democrat and a strong Wilson supporter, but the same complaint came from Republican sources. One GOP leader in southwestern Minnesota deplored Hughes' inability "to reach the every day fellow." A Minneapolis attorney who on "the day Hughes was nominated . . . didn't care whether he or Wilson was elected" later became persuaded that "Hughes has the viewpoint of New York City, and Wilson that of its victims."[17]

Since New York was the center of interventionist agitation as well as high finance, the image of Wilson as spokesman for "victims" of the metropolis heightened the credibility of the Democratic slogan, "He kept us out of war." One labor paper charged that "Ermine" Hughes had the support of "the jingo press" and Roosevelt, "the Republican-Bull Moose-Progressive military political boss." An apprehensive Republican found the conviction that Wilson had kept America out of war "deep seated" indeed. "A lot of the people have been led to believe that the election of Hughes may mean war and the election of Wilson peace," wrote a prominent Duluth Republican.[18]

Scandinavian Americans in particular responded favorably to Democratic peace claims. According to one Republican party official: "the trouble lies largely with the Scandinavian people of the State. There are two things which seem to have laid hold of them . . . the mistaken notion that Wilson has kept us out of the war; [and] . . . that they are now receiving high prices for their products." Other Hughes partisans pushed the same panic button.[19]

Late in the campaign a few Republicans began to fear that even German-Americans, whose dislike of Wilson supposedly anchored them securely to Hughes, were shifting their allegiance to the national Democratic ticket. This view proved to be unduly pessimistic. However, many German-Americans who could never accept Wilson became increasingly disturbed by eastern interventionist support of Hughes. According to Charles J. Moos, a prominent Republican who served as a liaison man between his party and the German-American community, German-American voters on the eve of the election still preferred Hughes personally to Wilson, but they feared he would "be so dominated by Roosevelt, Root, Lowden etc. that he will be even more pro-Allied than is Wilson."[20]

Spurred by an apparently spontaneous swing toward Wilson, the president's friends put together a loose, improvised campaign organization. Since no effective help could be expected from the dissension-torn state Democratic party, they negotiated unofficial and in some cases unannounced alliances with a number of reform groups. Labor spokesmen, including the trade-union press, campaigned vigorously for Wilson. In Minneapolis, political writers detected signs of an informal Democratic-Socialist coalition. And in northwestern Minnesota, Nonpartisan League organizers reportedly were working quietly for the president.[21]

The election returns vindicated Republican pessimism. Hughes won by less than 400 votes. Wilson decisively carried the areas most susceptible to the combined "progressivism and peace" appeal: the wheat-growing Red River Valley; the Twin Cities, particularly the labor wards; and the iron range. On the other hand, he failed to win the entire noninterventionist vote. As expected, many German-American Democrats bolted their party. Despite an almost unbroken record of Democratic fidelity, Stearns County cast 4,312 votes for Hughes and only 3,350 for Wilson. Brown County, which usually went Democratic in close elections, voted nearly two to one for Hughes.[22]

The failure of a solid noninterventionist front to develop is attributable to several factors: the pro-Hughes orientation of the German-language press; deep German-American hostility to Wilson; and the absence of a direct Hughes-Wilson confrontation on the issue of foreign policy. The Democrats entered the campaign under attack from two sides. Both the pronounced interventionists and the convinced neutralists were critical of administration policy. The Wilson men responded to this double attack by claiming that American rights had been upheld by a president who had also "kept us out of war." The Republicans faced the problem of winning and holding the allegiance of two incompatible groups — those who felt Wilson's policies were not sufficiently pro-Ally, and those who believed them to be excessively so.

In states like Minnesota, where most interventionists were Hughes supporters to begin with, the Republicans had to secure and retain the backing of Wilson's neutralist critics. The interventionist exuberance of prominent Hughes campaigners like Theodore Roosevelt made this a difficult challenge. Minnesota Republicans met it by peevishly denying the president's right to claim that he had kept the country out of war.[23]

The election returns indicate that the claim was not completely persuasive. With German-American help, the Hughes camp carried Minnesota by a paper-thin margin that could scarcely be called a victory considering the impressive advantages the Republicans had enjoyed at the beginning of the campaign. Especially in northwestern Minnesota many noninterventionist Republicans voted for Wilson. Many of them may have done so because they approved the progressive turn which Wilson's domestic policy took with such measures as the Federal Land Bank system, federal aid to vocational education, and federal regulation of grain exchanges. However, as Professor Arthur S. Link insists, "peace and progressivism" were inseparable parts of a single appeal in 1916.[24]

Despite the dire warnings of interventionists after the Gore-McLemore vote, Minnesotans returned eight of their ten congressmen to Washington. Lindbergh, who represented the sixth district, did not run for re-election; Harold Knutson replaced him. George R. Smith, the fifth district incumbent, lost in the Republican primary to Ernest Lundeen, who won in November. Unable to derive much comfort from these results, pro-Ally spokesmen insisted lamely that had Smith not voted against tabling the McLemore resolution, Minneapolis Republicans would have worked for him instead of remaining inactive and letting the nomination go to Lundeen.[25]

Pro-Ally commentators also interpreted the election of Frank B. Kellogg to the United States Senate as a great victory for their cause. The strength shown by the future secretary of state in areas having a heavy foreign-born population seemed especially encouraging. According to the *Minneapolis*

Journal, "Voters of Scandinavian and German birth showed themselves real American citizens, prompt to rise above nationality considerations and to rebuke those who wave the Hyphen."[26]

Such claims had an element of plausibility. Both in the primary and in the fall election campaigns, Kellogg unequivocally endorsed preparedness and the vigorous defense of American rights under international law. As he informed Hughes after the primary results were known, he had "talked preparedness in nearly every speech." This delighted Theodore Roosevelt, who wired Kellogg, "It is good omen you should have won on preparedness."[27]

Whether Kellogg's success in the campaign represented a popular mandate for intervention is another question. He captured the Republican senatorial nomination in a four-man race that pitted him against two outspoken noninterventionists — incumbent Senator Clapp and Congressman Lindbergh — and ex-Governor Eberhart, whose foreign-policy commitments were hazy but whose following certainly included noninterventionists. Significantly, the combined primary vote cast for Clapp, Lindbergh, and Eberhart exceeded that for Kellogg by nearly 35,000 votes. In the fall campaign Kellogg faced two opponents — Daniel W. Lawler, the Democratic candidate, who campaigned as a noninterventionist, and Prohibitionist Willis G. Calderwood, who coupled his antiliquor stand with demands for the eight-hour day, attacks on the grain trade, and strictures against militarism. Again Kellogg won by less than a majority; the combined vote of his two rivals exceeded his by approximately 10,000.[28]

Other factors as well as a divided opposition on the issue of foreign policy had worked for Kellogg. His personal prestige, fortified by a national reputation, overshadowed that of his opponents. Lawler was by this time a perennial candidate with an unbroken record of defeat in state-wide contests; and Calderwood, who ran a good race considering his handicaps, was a minor-party candidate. Moreover, Kellogg's managers had conducted an astute campaign contrived to win support within every group in the state. Active Kellogg supporters included not only established leaders of the Republican party who closed ranks to elect him, but also such political insurgents as James Manahan and Mayor Power of Hibbing, as well as a few important labor spokesmen and prominent Democrats. Some of these reform-minded supporters had misgivings which may not have been altogether groundless. Early in the campaign the general solicitor of the United States Steel Corporation assured Kellogg that "everything we can do to further your success will be done with the greatest pleasure."[29]

In addition, German-Americans voted for Kellogg in large numbers.

This fact led some pro-Ally observers to hope that Minnesota German-Americans were shifting their views on foreign policy. Other explanations appear more credible. Moos had secured for Kellogg, as he had for Hughes, the support of the German-language press. Presenting the Kellogg case to German-American voters was obviously a delicate operation, given the candidate's commitment to preparedness and other pro-Ally policies. One circumstance helped: for the duration of the *Sussex* pledge the United States experienced more unpleasantness with Great Britain than it did with Germany, a fact that made it plausible to give Kellogg's vigorous defense of American rights an anti-British slant. "Frank B. Kellogg is certainly not in favor of permitting Great Britain to rifle our mail and not be held accountable for that gross action," commented the *Brown County Journal*.[30]

A brief period of restless uncertainty followed the election. Spokesmen for Minneapolis business worried about a rising tide of radicalism both in the factories and on the prairies. Congressional passage of the eight-hour railroad labor law in September had convinced several of them that the militance of labor threatened to wreck American institutions. After November they also faced the distasteful necessity of putting up with a city administration headed by a Socialist, a prospect that made John McGee "sick."[31]

However, Van Lear's election scarcely meant that the Socialists had become the majority party in Minneapolis politics. Van Lear had campaigned primarily on the issues of street railway regulation, scandals in the police department, and failure of the incumbent administration to eradicate vice. His ability to make these issues work for him was matched by a capacity to assure non-Socialists that his commitment to the class struggle did not inhibit him from serving the entire community. After the election he attributed his victory to the support of "the union workingmen, the socialist workingmen and the level-headed business men."[32]

It is doubtful that the elements represented by the Citizens Alliance were reassured. Van Lear, after all, was a Socialist whose program called for municipal ownership of public utilities and a ban on the use of policemen as strikebreakers. His power as mayor was limited, and non-Socialists overwhelmingly dominated the city council, but control of the police department was vested in his office. This could mean a great deal if labor troubles like the machinist and teamster strikes of 1916 should recur.

Reports from Bismarck, North Dakota, also were disturbing. After the turn of the year, the deliberations of North Dakota's legislature indicated that the Minneapolis business community indeed faced the prospect of stiff competition from state-owned enterprises. Before the session convened, legitimate hopes that Townley lacked the ability or inclination to enact the radical league platform into law could be entertained. But as the farmer-dominated legislature transformed one plank after another into laws which the league-elected governor approved as a matter of course, it became clear that a political prairie fire was in fact sweeping North Dakota.[33]

Country editors in Minnesota would shortly make up their minds on the Nonpartisan League, but for a time they reserved ultimate judgment. Spokesmen for Minneapolis business immediately concluded that grave danger was approaching. In February a *Commercial West* editorial quoted "a prominent citizen of North Dakota" as saying that capital found itself "under the gun" in his state to the extent that "bankers and prosperous citizens, other than farmers" found it expedient to avoid "unnecessary attention." League progress in northern Minnesota, the editorial continued, had brought the peril within range of the Twin Cities: "Isn't it high time that something be done? Those who have invested capital in Minnesota and who believe that the Nonpartisan League can accomplish little in this state reckon without their hosts."[34]

By this time a sudden and ominous turn in relations between Berlin and Washington was pushing foreign affairs into the forefront of public concern. To some extent the campaign of 1916 had reduced neutralist-interventionist tension within Minnesota. A quest for Republican unity and German-American votes had led the pro-Ally backers of Hughes and Kellogg to mute attacks on the patriotism of noninterventionists. Moreover, reasonable German observance of the *Sussex* pledge had kept American-German relations free from crisis. High officials knew the pledge was wearing thin, but talk of a negotiated peace obscured this unpleasant reality from public view.

Shortly after the election Wilson made his last effort to mediate the war. The first step was a request that the belligerents define their war aims. On December 12, 1916, six days before Wilson delivered the war aims request, Theobald von Bethmann-Hollweg, the German chancellor, announced to the imperial Reichstag and to the world that his government was willing to talk peace. The appearance of collusion between Bethmann and Wilson chagrined both Allied leaders and American pro-Ally advocates, but neutralist optimism rose. Perhaps the war could be ended short of total victory by either side.[35]

Behind the scenes, prospects were less favorable. Germany's military and naval leaders, who were now more dominant in the councils of the imperial government than they had been at the beginning of the war, argued that the submarine fleet had developed sufficient capability to assure German victory if it were employed in unrestricted fashion. An imperial conference on January 9, 1917, broke down civilian resistance to this line of reasoning and produced a decision to repudiate the *Sussex* pledge by resuming unrestricted submarine warfare.[36]

During the three-week interval that separated the making of this decision and its announcement to the world, Wilson went ahead with his peace offensive. He continued to press the belligerents for statements of war aims, and on January 22, 1917, he delivered the "peace without victory" speech, which defined his views on the proper basis for negotiating a settlement. Neither side, said the president, should demand unwarranted territorial cessions or financial indemnities of the other, and both should respect the claims of national self-determination, a formula that delighted American neutralists and liberal opinion in the Allied countries.[37]

The rapid pace of events soon negated Wilson's initiative. On January 31 the German government delivered two communications to Washington. The first responded to Wilson's request for a statement of war aims. The second, which diverted all attention from the first, announced an immediate resumption of unrestricted submarine warfare. Since Wilson had made continuance of diplomatic relations with Berlin contingent on abandonment of such warfare, he now was obliged to sever regular relations, a step he took immediately. This put Germany and the United States on a collision course, culminating in the American declaration of war on April 6, 1917.

⊠ CHAPTER TWELVE

Storm and Stress

A CRISIS such as the one produced by American severance of relations with Germany ordinarily inflames patriotic feeling, spurs jingoistic utterance, and breeds unreasoning, belligerent hysteria. In February, 1917, two additional factors reinforced emotion throughout Minnesota. First, the reluctance of many Minnesotans, whether for ethnic or other reasons, to make war on Kaiser Wilhelm II outraged people who had persuaded themselves that Germany was the devil nation. In the second place, the high-pitched fear of radicalism which recently had developed became entangled with the diplomatic crisis. Socialists and IWW spokesmen stood in the forefront of the antiwar movement, and nonsocialist radicals like Congressman Lindbergh and Senator La Follette refused "to stand by the president" under any and all circumstances. To those who insisted on viewing the world in simple, uncomplicated terms, patriotism presently became synonymous with conservatism, and sedition with radicalism.

Events in Minneapolis soon heightened suspicions that an unholy alliance linked radicalism and treason. A few days after the diplomatic break with Germany, Mayor Van Lear issued a statement taking sharp issue with the patriotic cry that now was the time to "follow the flag" and "back the president." The flag, said Van Lear, sometimes had been used to sanctify unworthy causes. He could not, for example, have followed it "up the hill" at Ludlow, Colorado, where the mission of its bearers was "to shoot the helpless women and babies of the striking miners." As for supporting the president, Van Lear professed a lack of faith in Wilson's social and foreign policies, so how could he support him?[1]

The statement infuriated local war enthusiasts. The *Minneapolis Tribune* questioned Van Lear's authority to speak for Minneapolis, and other papers took a similar line. In response, Van Lear called a mass meeting in the Minneapolis Auditorium on Saturday evening, February 10, to protest Wilson's action. How many people attended cannot be ascertained. Prowar observers placed the crowd at "probably five or six thousand "; the Socialist

New Times reported an "immense throng of nearly 25,000"; and the *Union Labor Bulletin*, no friend of Van Lear, called it "an overflow meeting."[2]

Whatever the size, Van Lear's rally provoked an immediate reaction. The next day his adversaries sponsored gatherings both in the auditorium and in neighboring churches to place "Minneapolis in good standing with the rest of the country as regards her duty in a national crisis." These meetings formally endorsed the creation of a Minneapolis Loyalty League under the presidency of Cyrus Northrop. A printed statement affirming support of the president was signed by 36,000 "loyal" citizens and subsequently forwarded to Wilson through Senator Nelson.[3]

A sense of crisis also came to dominate proceedings of the Minnesota legislature, which met in regular session from early January to mid-April. Not all domestic concerns were sidetracked: the session submitted a state prohibition amendment to the voters in the 1918 election and enacted a comprehensive "Children's Code" that was a model of progressive legislation in the field.[4] However, the most celebrated enactment of the session was the one creating a Minnesota Commission of Public Safety.

> This body was to consist of seven members, including the governor and attorney general on an ex-officio basis. It was sweepingly empowered to do all acts and things non-inconsistent with the constitution or laws of the state of Minnesota or of the United States, which are necessary or proper for the public safety and for the protection of life and public property or private property of a character as in the judgment of the commission requires protection, and shall do and perform all acts and things necessary or proper so that the military, civil and industrial resources of the state may be most efficiently applied toward maintenance of the defense of the state and nation and toward the successful prosecution of . . . war, and to that end it shall have all necessary power not herein specifically enumerated and in addition . . . specific powers.[5]

Several aspects of the Safety Commission bill and its history invite comment. The fact that its preamble assigns first priority to protection of property and mentions assisting the war effort almost as an afterthought strongly suggests that the bill's sponsors anticipated a radical labor uprising within the near future. The near record speed with which the measure passed through the legislative process further hints at a sense of desperate urgency. It was introduced in the Senate on March 31 and passed that body on April 10 after a suspension of the rules permitted earlier consideration than would have been possible under regular procedures. The House approved it on April 12, also under a suspension of the rules. Since the two versions did not agree, a conference committee had to reconcile the differences. It did so in only two days. Both houses approved the compromise bill, the Senate unanimously and the House with one dissenting vote. Three days later Governor Burnquist signed the measure and simultaneously announced his appointments to the commission.[6]

Significantly, the bill encountered very little opposition. Only two House members, Andrew O. Devold of Minneapolis and Ernest G. Strand of Two Harbors, both Socialists, voted against it at any stage. Several future critics of the commission, including Henrik Shipstead and Magnus Johnson, either voted for the measure or were absent when the crucial votes were taken. No organized presentation of a case against it was ever made.[7]

Although John McGee was not a member of the legislature, his influence apparently shaped the Safety Commission bill and contributed to its passage. McGee's candidacy for membership on the commission also seems to have developed early. On April 11 he confessed to Senator Nelson that "Many people here, in banking, grain and milling circles, want me to go on the commission," a suggestion which McGee found flattering. Senate passage of the act elated him. He informed Nelson that the commission's teeth, which he noted were "eighteen inches long," and the appropriation of two million dollars to finance commission activities augured well for social stability and for a fruitful Minnesota contribution to the war effort. He added: "if the Governor appoints men who have backbone, treason will not be talked on the streets of this city and the street corner orators, who denounce the government, advocate revolution, denounce the army and advise against enlistments, will be looking through the barbed fences of an interment [sic] camp out on the prairie somewhere."[8]

On the whole Burnquist's appointments to the commission met these specifications. McGee was one, and he soon emerged as the body's symbol. In addition to Burnquist and Attorney General Lyndon A. Smith, the other members were John Lind, who resigned from the commission in early 1918 because he could not get along with McGee; Charles H. March of Litchfield; Anton C. Weiss, a conservative Democrat and the publisher of the *Duluth Herald*; and Charles W. Ames of St. Paul. With the possible exception of Lind, these men were more acceptable to business than to organized labor. From the outset trade union spokesmen complained that the commission included no labor representation and that some of its members were bitter enemies of unionism. These complaints increased in volume as time went by.[9]

While action on the Safety Commission bill was pending, the House considered a proposal requiring the registration of all aliens residing in the state. Unlike the other measure, the alien registration bill generated an acrimonious debate. Proponents argued that it "gives us a chance to show whether we stand by the president in this crisis," claimed that it was "aimed at the Kaiser's spies in this country," and insisted that no one opposed it "except aliens, and why should we care for their feelings at a time like this?" Such reasoning offended some foreign-born legislators, and a few mustered sufficient courage to speak out. John B. Hompe of Otter Tail County, who had been born in the Netherlands, had fought in the Civil War, and had been active in Minnesota politics since the Populist era, saw "no reason to hale inoffensive people before a court and make of them spy suspects." Swedish-born Magnus Johnson affirmed his willingness "to shoulder a gun to defend the United States," announced his intention to vote against the bill, and asserted defiantly, "I am not a copperhead." The bill did not become law, but later the Safety Commission, acting on its own authority, put the registration provisions into effect.[10]

The pressure mounted by militants like McGee no doubt frightened a number of antiwar advocates into silence. An assertion in *Commercial West* that "The truckling groveling Bryan . . . should be interned" indicates how poisoned the climate became following the diplomatic break with Germany. Nevertheless, neutralist activity continued at a brisk level until the declaration of war on April 6. Several country editors stuck to the view that the prerogatives of organized wealth rather than the rights of humanity were responsible for the crisis. Frank Day commented in his *Sentinel* on March 2: "Begins to look as though there would be no peace negotiations between the warring powers so long as loan negotiations are possible." His attitude was shared by others like Gunnar Bjornson of the *Minneota Mascot*, Carl A. Wold of the *Park Region Echo*, and Nels T. Moen of the Fergus Falls *Ugeblad*.[11]

Although college and university students were not in the forefront of the peace crusade in 1917, Minnesota recorded one notable instance of campus involvement. Late in March the Macalester College Neutrality and Peace Association, a student organization, sent a circular letter to Minnesota's congressional delegation condemning militarism, attributing the drift toward war to munitions manufacturers, and praising the congressional minority that had "the bravery to stand up for what it believed to be the best interests of the American people."[12]

In a well-publicized reply to the circular letter, Congressman Clarence

B. Miller of Duluth accused the students of being "pro-enemy and anti-American." The charge against munitions makers, Miller continued, was "the cry of the yellow streaked and coward soul when confronted by duty, seeking to justify its welching by ascribing improper conduct to others." Stung by Miller's rebuttal, "the rest of the student body and most of the faculty exerted themselves to prove that the majority opinion had not been represented in the unfortunate communication," according to Franklin Holbrook and Livia Appel in their book, *Minnesota in the War with Germany*. Fifteen of the school's eighteen faculty members signed a message to President Wilson asserting that "The United States owes it to the cause of democracy, the rights of humanity and its own good name to engage actively in the war and help overthrow those tyrannous and lawless survivals of a barbaric age." Campus "loyalists" circulated petitions pledging support of the government and organized patriotic rallies. Several Macalester men enlisted in the naval reserve to "vindicate the honor of the school." However, the offending students were not left entirely bereft of support. An angry editorial in Bjornson's *Minneota Mascot* of March 30 not only defended their action but also pointedly implied that Miller was beholden to the United States Steel Corporation, the wealthiest property holder within his district and a firm not adversely affected by the war.

With more zeal than prudence, many German-Americans also continued to crusade for peace. Although statements by some German-American spokesmen suggested resignation to the inevitability of war, elements within the community seemed to believe that peace might still be preserved. On February 10 the *Brown County Journal* counseled its readers not "to rock the boat." It admitted that the situation was grim, but the administration's record in Mexico allowed the journal to hope that Wilson might backtrack at the last minute. By March 30 such a hope seemed forlorn indeed. Nonetheless, on that date a mass meeting of about a thousand persons at New Ulm endorsed resolutions affirming the loyalty of all present to the United States, protesting the drift toward American involvement in the European conflict, and demanding a popular referendum on the fateful question of peace or war. On March 31 an antiwar coalition sponsored a similar rally in St. Paul. An informal vote taken in New Ulm a few days later showed that of 485 ballots cast, 466 favored peace and 19 war. Early in April a delegation of New Ulm citizens went to Washington for the purpose of registering a last-minute protest against the pending war resolution— an action that editor Day of the *Sentinel* saw as "Perfectly natural but probably impolitic."[13]

Evidently the vigor of Minnesota's peace crusade impressed the con-

gressional delegation. Senators Nelson and Kellogg supported the war declaration, but four of the ten congressmen voted against it. Three of these —
Charles R. Davis of St. Peter, Van Dyke of St. Paul, and Harold Knutson
of St. Cloud — represented districts with large German-American populations; they would win comparatively easy re-election victories in 1918.
The fourth, Ernest Lundeen of Minneapolis, committed political suicide.
His standing within Minneapolis Republican circles never had been high,
and his antiwar vote made him a pariah. Nevertheless, he would poll a
respectable vote in his bid for renomination in 1918.[14]

Following American entry into the war, most of the progressives whose
opposition to it had rested on other grounds than ethnic loyalties adapted
to the new situation with apparent ease. The example of Gunnar Bjornson
is instructive. On March 16, 1917, his paper had asserted that the war
had "no issue, no principle. Except . . . Which set of commercial pirates
shall rule the world." By August 10 he had discovered that:

> Our Allies have no imperialistic ambitions. The imperialistic
> ambitions of Germany moved her to aggression. France, Great
> Britain, Italy, and now free Russia, as well as ourselves, are
> in the war to resist imperialistic ambition and not to achieve
> such ambitions of their own. It is not the desire to break Ger-
> many, but to establish there a democracy.[15]

Two weeks later Bjornson suggested a relationship between the struggle
against autocracy abroad and privilege at home. "The trusts . . ." he
asserted, "are having their inning just now. . . . Victory in this war will
make victory in the struggle, between 'swollen fortunes' and toiling men
. . . more easily won by the toilers." On February 1, 1918, the *Mascot*
proclaimed: "When the cannons of war shall have ceased to boom their
messages of death and destruction, the cannons of public opinion will begin
to thunder their no less effective bombardment of the systems that have
taken their unjust toll from the toiling masses for all these centuries."[16]

Bjornson's comments reflected the thinking of many progressives. Whatever the war had been before American entry, it was now a crusade against
tyranny. As Wilson's war aims became explicit, the notion that progressivism
was being projected beyond American boundaries gained wide acceptance.
Moreover, the needs of war could be used to justify adopting the progressive
program at home. "Why should not the war serve . . . as a pretext to

foist innovations upon the country?'' asked the *New Republic*. Also, war-inspired idealism would spur impatience with domestic inequities. A public address delivered by Walter Lippmann during the first month of the war confidently predicted:

> We who have gone to war to insure democracy in the world will have raised an aspiration here that will not end with the overthrow of Prussian autocracy. We shall turn with fresh interests to our own tyrannies — to our Colorado mines, our autocratic steel industries, our sweatshops, and our slums.[17]

Despite the official antiwar stand taken by the majority wing of their party, many American Socialists shared the hope that World War I was releasing creative forces which would produce a new and more humane society. In a series of articles published in the *Gaa Paa*, a Minneapolis Norwegian-language weekly, Andrew Devold, a local Socialist who hovered uncertainly between the prowar and antiwar factions of his party, forecast a bright postwar future. Munitions profits, wrote Devold, were enriching America's economic barons, who also hoped to capture the markets made available by the wreckage of European economies. In other words, capitalism seemed to be entrenching itself. However, argued Devold, opposing forces "predicting the coming of a new age are stirring within the depths of society." Revolutionary restlessness was plaguing the established European order, and in the United States organized labor was becoming increasingly militant. Devold also saw "the farmers' revolt in the Northwest" as an encouraging portent. He hoped that a farmer-labor coalition would dominate postwar midwestern politics. Meanwhile, Devold pointed out, wartime economic mobilization had brought European socialism fifty years nearer realization.[18]

Although most progressives and some Socialists concluded that a war which promised to advance their aims deserved support, not all adherents of either persuasion did so. Socialist spokesmen in particular continued to insist that wicked capitalistic intrigue had brought the United States into the conflict. Front-page headlines carried by the Minneapolis Socialist weekly, *New Times*, on April 7 invited patriotic retribution. In bold type they proclaimed: INFAMOUS COMMERCIAL WAR ENTERED UPON WITH HYPOCRITICAL PLEAS OF LOFTY MOTIVES. . . . WAR DECLARED TO SAFEGUARD INVESTMENTS OF WALL STREET IN BONDS OF ALLIES. Commenting on recruiting difficulties a few weeks later, *Gaa Paa* observed: "If the present regime could smoke out all its secret and hidden enemies within the country and if then it

resolved to arrest all of them, it would have no army left to send overseas."
Several Socialist leaders were arrested and convicted either for resisting
the draft or discouraging enlistments, offenses punishable under both state
and federal law.[19]

Progressives who still entertained doubts about America's great crusade
generally were more circumspect than the Socialists, but a few exceptions
seemed to justify the conservative thesis that the loyalty of any reformer
should be suspect until proven. Through 1917 editorials in Carl Wold's
Park Region Echo maintained a critical attitude toward the war, infuriating
Alexandria's business and professional people. James A. Peterson, the Minneapolis attorney who had opposed Senator Nelson for renomination in
1912 and would do so again in 1918, published an article disputing the
accepted view that the United States had gone to war to uphold international
law. Although the article stopped short of advocating resistance to conscription, its appearance resulted in Peterson's indictment— though not
in his ultimate conviction— on a charge of sedition.[20]

Guilt by association was only one difficulty inhibiting complete rapport
between the progressive movement and the war. The problem of how it
should be waged created a number of troublesome issues for the progressive
conscience. To what extent did the need for national unity justify the suppression of basic freedoms? Mayor Van Lear, who grudgingly accepted the
war after April 6, articulated the doubts of many when he facetiously remarked that perhaps the country was exporting so much democracy overseas
that none remained for people at home. And what about conscription?
Many reformers professed a willingness to accept the drafting of men for
the armed forces only on the condition that wealth and property were subject
to the same call. Closely related was the question of what steps the government should take to eliminate profiteering in the necessities of life.[21]

The possibility of negotiating peace before a total Allied victory was
won also aroused controversy. In 1917 peace proposals began to come
from a number of sources. Soon after the overthrow of Czar Nicholas
II of Russia, a group of left-wing Russian revolutionaries, Bolshevik and
non-Bolshevik, called for an end to hostilities on the basis of "no annexations,
no indemnities," a proposal strikingly similar to the formula laid down by
Wilson in his "peace without victory" speech. The German Reichstag
passed a peace resolution along the same line in July, 1917; and the Pope
held his good offices in readiness. Most Americans emphatically rejected
these possibilities. "To suggest talking peace to such a monster [*imperial
Germany*] is as foolish as to try to pet a mad dog or to reason with a
raving maniac," commented *Commercial West.*[22]

A few American reformers, including both progressives and Socialists, believed that negotiation on the basis of "no annexations, no punitive indemnities" deserved exploration. To facilitate this end, they established in the summer of 1917 an organization called the People's Council of America for Democracy and Peace, more commonly known as the People's Council for Peace, or the People's Council. Its announced objectives called for "an early democratic and universal peace based on no annexation, no punitive indemnities and the right of all nations to determine their own destiny." It also endorsed the creation of an "international organization for the maintenance of world peace." Its home-front program included repeal of conscription and resolute maintenance of democratic liberties in wartime.[23]

At its inception the People's Council claimed the affiliation and support of several distinguished citizens, including David Starr Jordan, naturalist and president of Leland Stanford University; ex-Senator John D. Works of California; Florence Kelley, a prominent social worker; and Senator La Follette. In Minnesota it won the backing of local Socialists, a few German-American spokesmen, and a number of prominent progressive politicians such as James Peterson and Sylvanus A. Stockwell, a long-time state legislator from Minneapolis.[24]

Substantial local support, coupled with the sympathetic attitude of Mayor Van Lear, led the council to schedule its first national convention in Minneapolis for the first week of September, 1917. As the date approached, the sponsors encountered more and more difficulty. An adequate meeting place could not be secured; those who owned or controlled halls and auditoriums refused to make them available for a cause so suspect. This problem was solved by a plan to hold the convention and the accompanying mass meetings in two large tents which were to be erected on property owned by Stockwell near Minnehaha Park. But demands to suppress the projected assembly became insistent, and Governor Burnquist bowed to them. A few days before the convention was to open he prohibited the People's Council from meeting anywhere in the state on the grounds that public order would be prejudiced.[25]

The conservative prowar press applauded the action, while the *New Times* proclaimed on September 1: KAISER BURNQUIST SUSPENDS U.S. AND MINNESOTA CONSTITUTIONS. Samuel Gompers, president of the AFL, disapproved the ban, although he was working hard to counter People's Council influence within organized labor. Other prowar labor leaders were "equally disappointed." They wanted to "argue it out" with the People's Council "on a basis of reason and not of bayonets."[26]

During the summer of 1917 Minnesota's German-American community passed through a painful crisis which not only reinforced Burnquist's impulse to ban any and all suspicious meetings, but also influenced the community's postwar political behavior. The outbreak of war found many German-Americans psychologically unprepared. The sympathetic ties binding them to the European homeland could not be severed by a simple act of will. Moreover, for nearly three years the German-language press, the only news source available to many, had pleaded the justice of Germany's cause, bitterly condemned Britain, and interpreted interventionist agitation in America as propaganda inspired by Wall Street to lure unsuspecting people into an unjust war.[27]

Following the diplomatic break with Germany, responsible German-American leaders had belatedly sought to prepare their following for the inevitable hostilities. Early in February Julius Moersch, president of the Minnesota Union of the National German-American Alliance, had indicated to the local branches under his jurisdiction that he held little hope for peace. "Our hearts may bleed and break," wrote Moersch, "but that does not relieve us from the necessity of fulfilling our duty to the land of our adoption." But Moersch was not ready to accept American participation in the war as a great moral venture. "About the justice or the injustice of the declaration of war, a higher power and the later history of the world will give judgment," he asserted, adding that "Germany never sought war with America."[28]

Moersch correctly anticipated his people's adjustment to the fact of war. German-Americans generally accepted the April 6 decision because their sense of obligation as American citizens dictated that they do so, and in the end their record of support proved impeccable. But they refused to regard the war as a holy crusade against the forces of evil. To them it was an unpleasant enterprise of dubious origin that had to be concluded in the shortest possible time. While such an attitude held no threat of outright sabotage, it fell short of what "patriots" like McGee demanded. According to a Minnesota Safety Commission statement, "The test of loyalty in war times is whether a man is wholeheartedly for the war and subordinates everything else to its successful prosecution."[29]

Contemporary observers disagreed on how well Minnesota German-Americans met their difficult situation. Two weeks after the United States declared war the *Martin County Sentinel* reported: "We haven't heard an unpatriotic expression from a single German." Writing from St. Paul in mid-April, ex-Congressman Frederick C. Stevens informed Senator Nelson, "our German people are acting very well, but not many volunteer enlistments can be expected from them." Stevens predicted, however, that German-Americans would "not object to compulsory service" and would "do their share with the others." Edward J. Lynch, Collector of Internal Revenue in St. Paul, saw matters in a different light. That German-Americans should suffer distress and grief was only natural, observed Lynch, but "some cases" had been brought to his attention which indicated that a number were "ugly and apparently not at all loyal to the country of their adoption." More than a month later, on May 22, the excitable McGee reported: "in centers of population strongly German . . . drilling is going on preparatory to resisting the draft."[30]

McGee exaggerated, but developments in New Ulm soon demonstrated that Stevens was overly optimistic. At first, all went well in the German-American city. "Registration day, Tuesday, June 5, passed quietly in Brown county," reported the *Brown County Journal*. Two weeks later, however, Albert Steinhauser's *New Ulm Review*, a liberal Democratic weekly which already had become critical of wartime suppressions of freedom and the campaign against German culture, supported a proposal that German-American draftees be exempted from service on the battlefields of France. Embodied in a resolution prepared by Congressman Frederick A. Britten of Illinois, the proposal was being pushed by *Viereck's Weekly*, an important national spokesman for German-Americanism. The *Review* argued that its adoption would relieve young German-Americans of the agonizing responsibility of striking "at the breast that nourished them or their fathers." Steinhauser's paper emphasized that the Britten resolution did not exempt German-Americans from military responsibility or confine them to noncombatant service. The battle areas outside of Europe also required manpower.[31]

Discussion of the Britten proposition undoubtedly helped prepare the way for the famous New Ulm antidraft rally of July 25, 1917, although the genesis of the rally is not completely clear. The Safety Commission implicitly accepted the theory that local leaders and officials planned and organized it, but the *Brown County Journal*, which after the declaration of war resolutely opposed all so-called pro-German activity, reported that the rally was "part of a nationwide propaganda which has for its object . . . that the draft law will be changed and those who have been drafted will not be forced to go to Europe unless they volunteer to do so." On the day of the rally, the *New Ulm Review* carried a front-page story announcing it and identifying the People's Council of America as its sponsor.[32]

This statement concerning sponsorship raises questions, for a New Ulm branch of the People's Council was not organized until a month later. Nevertheless, the claim of council involvement is significant. Before the war Albert Pfaender, New Ulm's city attorney and the rally's leading personality, had not traveled with the reform elements that dominated the council. By Lynn Haines' standards, Pfaender's record as a state legislator in 1911 had been consistently conservative. His apparent shift of affiliation illustrates that if enthusiasm for the war tended to draw some progressives into alliance with conservatism, the reverse could also happen, and conservatives who entertained doubts about the war could find common ground with reformers who were cool to it. The subsequent history of the Nonpartisan League in Minnesota would underscore this fact.[33]

Whoever initiated the July 25 New Ulm gathering — which attracted an enthusiastic crowd of 10,000 — the purpose was scarcely seditious. Mayor Louis A. Fritsche, the presiding officer, opened the formal program with a denial of intent "to cause any disaffection of the draft law." The chief aim of the rally, said Fritsche, was to request "congress and the government . . . not [to] force those drafted to fight in Europe against their will." Petitions to this effect were circulated and signed by many of those present.[34]

Pfaender delivered the main address. He began by proclaiming the loyalty of German-Americans to the United States, pointing to their records in the Civil War and the Spanish-American conflict as proof. He also recognized that the United States was at war, a reality which imposed inescapable obligations on all American citizens, but he questioned whether the congressional decision for war conformed to the desires of a majority of Americans. A constitutional amendment requiring a popular referendum before war could be declared seemed to him a wise step for the future.

Pfaender then turned his attention to congressional powers in wartime, particularly to the recruiting of military forces. There was no question, he said, that congress had power to draft men to repel invasion, but he doubted the constitutionality of a draft for overseas duty, an issue which he said deserved judicial examination. For the time being, Pfaender felt, two courses of action should be followed: young men who were called up should faithfully comply with the draft law, and petitions should be addressed to congress requesting a revision of the law to permit only volunteers to serve in Europe.

From the standpoint of constitutional law and the American civil liberties tradition, defenders of the New Ulm meeting had a persuasive case. Even hostile observers conceded that while Pfaender and the other speakers questioned the draft, they did not advocate forcible resistance to it or to any other law. Unfortunately, however, the war to guarantee democracy throughout the world had created an atmosphere that discouraged democratic liberties at home.

As news of the July 25 event spread— some of it in distorted form— New Ulm rapidly became an outcast city. Daniel Lawler called the rally a "traitors' meeting . . . addressed by a lot of . . . traitors." "It will," added Lawler, "take New Ulm a quarter of a century to live down the infamy with which it has been stamped by these traitors." "Is it any wonder," queried editor Dunn of the *Princeton Union*, "that there are those who regret the Sioux did not do a better job at New Ulm fifty-five years ago?" The tendency of other German-American communities to follow New Ulm's example also infuriated Dunn. "Seditious meetings are being held with impunity all over Minnesota," he asserted on August 9, adding: "The Copperheads are rampant." In Fergus Falls the *Ugeblad*, which had opposed war up to the last minute, reacted more moderately, but it, too, questioned the propriety of discussing the measures taken to wage the war. The antiwar Socialist press supported the New Ulm rally, but this hardly countered the volley of criticism.[35]

A few days later the Safety Commission swung into action. It accused the "ringleaders" of "a cunning, but futile effort to observe the letter of the law, while outraging its spirit." According to the commission, the New Ulm speakers had "excited responsive enthusiasm in their audience" when describing drafted men as "martyrs, dragged to an unjust fate by a tyrannical and cruel government." Burnquist, who was a commission member, indicated his agreement with these conclusions. The meeting, he charged, was "unpatriotic and un-American." It tended "to create among the drafted men who attended . . . a feeling that the draft . . . was unjust and illegal"; and the "intended effect . . . was to interfere with the plan of the United States government in the raising of its army and in the prosecution of the war."[36]

Before the commission had completed its investigation, Burnquist suspended three public officials who had participated in the rally: Mayor Fritsche, City Attorney Pfaender, and Brown County Auditor Louis G. Vogel. Fritsche and Pfaender thereupon submitted their resignations to the New Ulm city council which, on the instruction of the Safety Commission, refused to accept them. The Safety Commission wanted the case under its own jurisdiction. Under the Minnesota constitution the three officials had to be given hearings. These resulted in the exoneration of Vogel and the removal from office of Fritsche and Pfaender.[37]

After employing the mailed fist on New Ulm's leaders, the Safety Commission subjected the city's residents to a patriotic brain washing. On September 4 New Ulm held a "Dedication Day" rally in honor of departing draftees. Resolutions pledging unconditional submission to the draft law and rejecting any criticism of it were enthusiastically acclaimed. Governor Burnquist delivered the main address, describing German autocracy as the blackest force in the universe and extolling the American war effort as a crusade to democratize the world. The remarks of Julius A. Coller, a Shakopee businessman and Democratic politician, gave the rally a proper German-American tone. Coller proclaimed:

> "I am of German blood. . . . prior to 1917 I yielded to no man in the earnestness of my hope that the German eagles should emerge supreme in the conflict across the sea. But the call of blood, strong though it may be, sinks into insignificance when there comes the call of my own, my native land.[38]

Many responsible Minnesotans hoped the September rally would help redeem New Ulm's reputation, but much of the damage inflicted by the July affair and its aftermath was irreparable. The strong public reaction to such gatherings — or to reports of them in the press — reinforced a disposition to make war not only on the German government but on Germans and German-American culture as well. The rally on July 25 widened the alienation of German-Americans from other segments of the Minnesota community and impeded the mental and emotional adjustment of many to the reality of war between the United States and Germany.

In theory the Safety Commission's stern action against New Ulm officials was supposed to separate the leaders of the rally from their followers, who would then happily accept new leadership. This, of course, did not happen. Ex-Mayor Fritsche remained popular, and many New Ulm citizens urged him to seek vindication by again running for office in 1918. Pressure from Minnesota German-American leaders, who feared a Fritsche candidacy would revive the entire controversy, dissuaded him; but a "sticker candidate" who functioned as a Fritsche surrogate polled 506 votes out of a total of 1,208 cast.[39]

Serious questions also can be raised concerning the effectiveness of Safety Commission propaganda both with respect to the New Ulm rally and German-Americans generally. *Minnesota in the War*, the commission's official bulletin, showed little compassion for the plight of German-Americans; neither did it insist, as President Wilson's war message had, that the war was against the imperial government, not the German people and their culture. Although the commission stopped short of outlawing the German language — a proposal that it considered — it encouraged hostility to German ways and counseled German-Americans to remove suspicions from themselves by buying more liberty bonds and making larger Red Cross contributions than their neighbors. The German-American, declared one writer employed by the commission, "has got to declare himself through open and spontaneous acts of loyalty if he is to escape the suspicion of being disloyal."[40]

The Safety Commission thus did little to heal the tragic breach between Minnesota German-Americans and other citizens. At the same time it unwittingly encouraged the alienation of German-Americans from the conservative wing of the Minnesota Republican party. Technically the commission was bipartisan, but its policies came to be inseparably identified with McGee, a practicing Republican, and with the Burnquist administration. In the postwar years, the quest for retribution against "McGeeism" would ally a large and normally conservative German-American bloc with union labor and Nonpartisan League farmers. This coalition provided the Minnesota Farmer-Labor party with the bulk of its voting strength throughout the early 1920s.

The apparent success of the September 4 New Ulm rally encouraged prowar conservatives to feel that they were winning the mind of Minnesota. Other developments reinforced confidence. Monster loyalty gatherings throughout the state were mobilizing support for the war. Federal seizure of IWW headquarters and imprisonment of the organization's leaders had removed one fearsome threat. Comparative calm prevailed on the iron range where serious labor strife had been expected. The German-American press was under "loyal" control, and the People's Council seemed on the point of expiring. A prowar labor organization, the American Alliance for Labor and Democracy, which held its first national convention in Minneapolis early in September, was countering "sedition" within the trade unions. A *Commercial West* editorial of September 15, entitled "Disloyal Elements Subsiding," defined an emerging conservative view of the situation.[41]

This optimistic mood would be short-lived. On September 20 a spontaneous exchange between Senator La Follette and members of his audience at a Nonpartisan League gathering in St. Paul would reactivate concern about the loyalty question, bring the league directly into the line of "loyalist" fire, and set in motion a chain of events that profoundly affected the electoral campaign of 1918.

CHAPTER THIRTEEN

The Rise of the Loyalty Issue

"THAT LITTLE NON-PARTISAN LEAGUE CLOUD, now no larger than a man's hand, is quite likely to envelop the heavens," commented Frank Day in the *Sentinel* on February 2, 1917. "If we were in the republican household," he continued, "we would send in an S.O.S. order for lightning rods." Two weeks later the *Sentinel* chided the Twin Cities press for abusing the league in such an "ugly manner." This treatment, the editor thought, boded "well for the movement."[1]

Day spoke prophetically. When the diplomatic crisis with Germany erupted, Townley and his associates were in the process of moving their national headquarters from Fargo to St. Paul. Several structural changes accompanied the move. A Minnesota Farmers' Nonpartisan League, distinct from the National Nonpartisan League and nominally directed by a separate slate of officials, came into being. Townley also employed Joseph Gilbert, an idealistic reformer with considerable experience in the labor movement, to serve as liaison man with the Minnesota trade unions. In theory this reorganization was more significant than in fact, for Townley, who held the position of National Nonpartisan League president, maintained tight control over the entire enterprise.[2]

Nevertheless, the move to St. Paul was important. It indicated a serious intent on Townley's part to shift the movement's base to a more populous and diversified area than North Dakota. It also heralded an intensified organizational drive in Minnesota. By September, 1917, the Minnesota Farmers' Nonpartisan League claimed a membership exceeding thirty thousand and the spiritual affiliation of many more. League activities in centers where the movement was strong generated an enthusiasm not seen in Minnesota since Populist days. A 1917 Labor Day rally at Alexandria, for example, attracted a huge crowd that reveled in the evangelical atmosphere created by emotional league oratory.[3]

The nervousness of Minneapolis business and industrial leaders kept pace with growing league membership. In the spring of 1917 a small group of grain trade men founded the so-called Minnesota Nonpartisan League which they equipped with a routine and program superficially similar to that of Townley's organization. The bogus league caused some brief confusion, but within a few months the transparency of the scheme discredited its sponsors more than it hurt the Townley movement.[4]

Main street reacted more slowly than the Minneapolis business community, but as the league campaign proceeded, it, too, grew increasingly hostile. Initial exposure to the league message undoubtedly impressed some small-town progressives. Townley's rhetoric was more strident than the progressive variety, but there were striking similarities. Both excoriated the financial interests and professed deep concern for the common man, and both proclaimed the right of the people to rule.[5]

However, it quickly became clear that Townley wanted no small-town influences within his organization. The Nonpartisan League was a movement for, by, and of the "producers," a category including actual farmers and wage earners, but not merchants or bankers. After hearing a Townley speech which in some respects pleased him, Gunnar Bjornson observed: "Personally we should have liked to have heard him come out stronger than he did for co-operation and unity between and among the farmers and the people of the small towns." Perhaps verbal inclusion of small-town business and professional men within the fold of God's children would have helped, but it is doubtful that such a strategy would have been enough. Those for whom free enterprise was an article of faith were appalled by the socialism of the Nonpartisan League platform. Rumors of close ties between the IWW and the league also alarmed moderate progressives.[6]

More important, the league program threatened the small towns with murderous competition. It promoted a network of co-operative enterprises which could succeed only at the expense of existing small-town trading firms. Unless they submitted unconditionally to Townley's direction, country editors also faced tough rivalry from league-owned newspapers. In other words, the Nonpartisan League imperiled the status of small merchants, lawyers, bankers, and editors more directly and more immediately than had eastern corporations, whose menace earlier had led these groups to affiliate with progressivism. Thus the new threat exerted pressure away from reform and toward defense of the existing order.[7]

First reports of league progress in Minnesota had produced anxiety within political circles. In commenting on internal GOP difficulties immediately following the election of 1916, a Republican official observed to Senator-elect Kellogg that the Nonpartisan League "must be considered in the plans made for future work, or there will be additional trouble." Significantly, he failed to recommend any particular course of action. Practitioners of a craft, the chief function of which is the reconciliation of divergent interests, scarcely knew how to respond to a movement that spurned compromise and demanded unconditional acceptance of its program as the price of support. By the summer of 1917 other reactions had given way to deep apprehension. Writing to Senator Nelson in mid-August, Fred B. Snyder, university regent and prominent Minneapolis civic leader, noted that the league was making "threatening progress" throughout the state. "Unless something is done to counteract this movement," added Snyder, "I fear that our State offices and the control of the Legislature will pass into the hands of that organization."[8]

Contrary to a widely held view, Townley and his advisers did not stumble heedlessly into what many people interpreted as downright opposition to the war. To judge by their actions and statements, the league leaders were keenly aware of both the perils and opportunities of the situation, and they tried to avert the perils and capitalize on the opportunities.

Before the diplomatic break with Germany, nearly all league supporters, whether ex-Socialists or not, had been zealous neutralists. During the period between the severance of relations with Germany and the American declaration of war, the organization stuck to this position. However, with American entry into the conflict, the league announced unqualified support of the war effort. Its newspapers not only explicitly accepted the decision for war but urged support of the first liberty bond drive. In justifying this to a Socialist friend, Henry G. Teigan, who was then secretary of the National Nonpartisan League, remarked that "it is not wise to . . . separate ourselves from the rest of society" as the majority wing of the American Socialist party had done when it adopted a pacifist position.[9]

Issues relating to the war soon became central in the league's propaganda effort. Several simple propositions were reiterated time and again by Townley and other speakers: the war should be accepted as a crusade against German militarism and on behalf of democracy; the manpower draft could also be accepted, provided wealth was conscripted as well as lives; and the war must not be used to justify suppression of democratic liberties. Among these points, the conscription of wealth was stressed most frequently. Townley interpreted this to mean the establishment of national food control along lines advocated by his organization— that is, nationalization or government control of processing and distribution. It also meant financing the

war out of the immense profits being garnered by munitions and other
manufacturers. To tax these profits, said Townley, was a simple act of
justice when the sons of humble folk had to die in Europe. Such a policy,
he argued, would protect the integrity of the war as a "people's" enterprise
by limiting its money-making potentialities.[10]

A special election in North Dakota on July 10, 1917, necessitated by
the death of Congressman Henry T. Helgesen, afforded the Nonpartisan
League an additional opportunity to elaborate its position on the war. John
M. Baer, the league-endorsed candidate, campaigned on a platform of conscripting wealth. He also discussed suitable terms for peace. Germany,
Baer pointed out, held "conquered territory . . . equal in area to her own
European territory, prior to the war." Britain held "conquered German
territory . . . five times the area of the German Empire in Europe." Neither
conquest could be countenanced. "To allow . . . profit from the war,
either in the Imperialistic acquisition . . . or . . . punitive indemnities,
will but incite to future wars. *Imperialism whether made in Berlin or made
in London, is the same. — the curse of the world*," proclaimed Baer.[11]

Although Baer won the North Dakota congressional seat, his campaign
aroused ugly suspicions concerning the basic loyalty of the Nonpartisan
League. In the supercharged atmosphere of the time the candidate's comparison of Germany and Britain, even if complimentary to neither, carried
a hint of pro-Germanism. The argument for conscripting wealth also was
open to distortion. At the commencement of hostilities, Townley often
contended that the war should be financed out of heavy taxes on swollen
profits rather than by liberty bonds purchased out of the limited savings
of working people. His enemies interpreted this line of reasoning as an
attack on the first liberty bond drive. Moreover, Townley's acceptance
of the draft seemed grudging and reluctant. His lurid descriptions of bat-
tlefield horrors correctly depicted the realities of war, but they hardly encouraged a rush of young men to the recruiting stations.[12]

The composition of the Nonpartisan League's following heightened suspicion of its commitment to the war. "Whether Townley intended it or not,"
wrote one of his associates years later, ". . . every anti-war element rallied
to his support in all of the various states where the organization existed."
Only in German-American towns did the league manage to breach a solid
wall of main street hostility. Shortly after the war, Teigan noted that
"businessmen in general are on absolute 'outs' with the farmers," except
"in German communities." While this phenomenon could be attributed
to the league's championship of democratic freedoms in wartime, most

people in 1917 were easily persuaded that it cast doubt on the loyalty of the organization.[13]

After the Baer campaign the league leadership dealt more cautiously with explosive war issues. Townley did not mute his attacks on the "money autocracy" nor retreat from the demand that profits finance the war, but he earnestly exhorted his audiences to buy liberty bonds and donate to the Red Cross. The league also held the People's Council at arm's length. Along the same line, Townley made a show of strictly enforcing a ban on discussion of the war by his speakers. In August he canceled a meeting at Lester Prairie where Mayor Van Lear was scheduled to discuss foreign policy.[14]

During the summer of 1917 Townley and his associates devoted considerable thought to the problem of building understanding between the farmers' movement and organized labor. They soon found the issue of food policy to be a major impediment. Farmers wanted the highest price the market would allow for commodities such as wheat, while wage earners keenly resented every increase in the cost of living. The league leaders soon formulated a compromise which they hoped would surmount the difficulty: acceptance by the farmers of the National Food Administration's ceiling price of $2.20 a bushel for wheat, provided the government nationalized food processing and distribution, instituted rigid control of consumer prices, and subjected war profits to confiscatory taxation.[15]

To publicize this program and to provide opportunity for discussion of related issues, Townley organized a three-day Producers' and Consumers' Conference which opened in the St. Paul Auditorium on September 18. In planning the agenda, league leaders had rigidly excluded discussion of foreign policy, and the roster of speakers included men who had supported as well as opposed the declaration of war on Germany. Senator William E. Borah of Idaho, who had voted for the war resolution, addressed the gathering on the opening day. Senator La Follette, who had vigorously opposed war up to the last minute, was scheduled to speak two days later.[16]

La Follette arrived in St. Paul on September 19, one day before his appearance, without a prepared speech. He repaired this deficiency by closeting himself in a hotel room for thirty-four hours of intense labor, producing a finished address which defended the maintenance of free speech in wartime. Upon seeing the text shortly before the senator was to speak, league officials James Manahan and William Lemke questioned the propriety of delivering such an address, given the inflamed state of public opinion. La Follette offered to withdraw, a solution Manahan and Lemke refused to accept.

In response to pleas from the two men, the senator consented to speak extemporaneously.[17]

When the three arrived at the auditorium, they found a packed house. The streets were also crowded with people drawn there by a desire to see and hear the famous senator. The enthusiasm sparked by La Follette's arrival inside the auditorium led Manahan to change his mind concerning the suitability of the senator's prepared address; but since La Follette had left the text at the hotel, he had no choice but to speak extemporaneously, and he was thus deprived of the opportunity to weigh carefully what he said. La Follette's speech on this occasion "became one of the least read and most criticized speeches ever delivered by a United States Senator," although the presence of three stenographers who recorded his remarks in full made it possible to ascertain exactly what he said. Distorted press dispatches conveyed the impression that La Follette had given a seditious tirade. Actually his references to the war were incidental to the main drift of the speech and were made in response to interpolations from his audience.

In accordance with his hastily improvised plan, La Follette began with a discussion of representative government. As he approached the subject of financing the war, the central concern of the address, he interjected a comment that he had not favored going to war. He then added: "I don't mean to say that we hadn't suffered grievances; we had— at the hands of Germany. Serious grievances!" By this time the audience was reacting strongly, and for the most part approvingly, whereupon La Follette specified the basic grievance: "We had cause for complaint. They had interfered with the right of American citizens to travel upon the high seas — on ships loaded with munitions for Great Britain." Applause and laughter followed. The senator called for silence, and added: "I would not be understood as saying that we didn't have grievances . . . We had a right, a technical right, to ride on those vessels. I was not in favor of the riding on them, because it seemed to me that the consequences resulting from any destruction of life that might occur would be so awful."

At this point interruptions from his listeners broke the continutity of La Follette's discourse. Following an exchange with questioners, some friendly and some unfriendly, he completed his thought: "I say this, that the comparatively small privilege . . . of an American citizen to ride on a munition-loaded ship, flying a foreign flag, is too small to involve this Government in the loss of millions and millions of lives." Further heckling followed. One hostile voice persisted in asking about the *Lusitania*. In reply La Follette asserted that Bryan had warned Wilson four days before the great liner sailed that it was carrying six million rounds of ammunition.

The senator further remarked that "the passengers who proposed to sail
. . . were sailing in violation of a statute of this country: that no passenger
shall sail or travel upon a railroad train or upon a vessel which carries
dangerous explosives. And Secretary Bryan appealed to President Wilson
to stop passengers from sailing on the *Lusitania*." After recapitulating
his remarks relative to the war, the senator proceeded to discuss financing,
agreeing with Townley's view that heavy taxes on war profiteers should
be the government's main source of revenue. At the conclusion of the
speech the audience gave the senator an enthusiastic ovation.

Even accurate reporting of La Follette's speech would have produced
angry public reaction, but actual accounts aroused a furious storm. The
Associated Press dispatch, which was telegraphed from St. Paul to more
than a thousand papers, quoted the senator as saying, "We had no grievance
against Germany" when as a matter of fact he had said the opposite. The
dispatch contained other inaccuracies, for it stated that La Follette had
said the sinking of the *Lusitania* was justifiable, and that loans and munitions
profits were the only American stake in the war. But any comparison of
the dispatch with the stenographic record was academic, for it was the
widely circulated Associated Press version, not the stenographic record,
that determined public reaction.[18]

Immediately following La Follette's departure from St. Paul, hell broke
loose in Minnesota. Politicians and business leaders bent on destroying
the Nonpartisan League now had a weapon which few human beings in
their position could have resisted using. The thesis linking defense of the
status quo with patriotism, and militant reform with sedition, had received
powerful support. An organization committed to radical political and
economic change had sponsored a "traitorous" speech by a sharp critic
of the established order. From the conservative point of view, it followed
that the fight against the Nonpartisan League was part of the struggle to
save America. A *Commercial West* editorial published nine days after La
Follette's appearance stated the conservative position with characteristic
bluntness: "The chronic business baiters who have kept up a clamor for
radical legislation for the past decade or more, are the same people who
are now unable to see their duty of loyalty to their own government."[19]

Many former admirers of the Wisconsin senator and many sincere friends
of the Nonpartisan League were unable to forgive his bringing the state
into disrepute at a time when memories of the February meeting in
Minneapolis, the July rally in New Ulm, and the fracas over the People's
Council remained fresh. Community leaders who had worked to overcome
the reluctance of their people to support the war felt defeated and frustrated.

La Follette, some of them reported, had fortified German-American inclinations to oppose the war. And many Minnesotans were persuaded that La Follette actually had embraced treason. The *Fairmont Daily Sentinel*, which had strongly supported the senator in the past, commented: "A great career . . . has been turned to ashes because Senator La Follette lost his head and betrayed his country in its hour of need. Too bad! Too bad!"[20]

As might be expected, the Safety Commission launched an immediate investigation of the incident. In announcing the probe, Burnquist said that La Follette's arrest and return to the state for trial under the espionage law were being considered. Although this threat was not carried out, the Safety Commission did pronounce the speech to be disloyal and seditious and petitioned the Senate to expel its errant member. The same demand came from other parts of the country, and a resolution to that effect (introduced by Senator Kellogg) remained pending in the Senate until after the war, when it was dropped.[21]

The complicity of the Nonpartisan League in the affair also drew the Safety Commission's attention. On September 25 the commissioners summoned Townley to appear and subjected him to a grueling examination. Two principal points emerged from his testimony: a denial of Nonpartisan League responsibility for the speech, and what the commission interpreted as an admission that La Follette's views were "seditious and disloyal." According to the league president, La Follette had violated an understanding not to discuss the war, and Townley had not approved the senator's remarks for delivery.[22]

With slight modifications in emphasis — chiefly a more charitable treatment of La Follette — the league press echoed the main points in Townley's testimony. The Fargo *Courier-News* called the senator's view of the war "mistaken" and commented: "Notwithstanding the evils which have accompanied the war, we believe still that it is justified and inevitable upon the high ground which President Wilson has placed it." The *Courier-News*, however, refused to call the senator a seditionist, remarking, "we can understand Mr. La Follette's attitude. It is the result of the life long fight that he has waged against the forces of exploitation in this republic." Carl A. Wold, editor of the *Park Region Echo* of Alexandria, whose loyalty also was under attack, disclaimed any wish to discuss the disloyalty of the La Follette speech "except to point out that it was very clearly not the intention of the management to display any favoritism in either direction."[23]

Opponents of the league resolutely refused to permit such disclaimers to quiet suspicions. In fact, it soon became evident that conservatives intended to make the September 20 incident the basis for an attack which they hoped would rout Townley's organization in the election of 1918, if not before. A group of businessmen, politicians, editors, educators, and some labor leaders met in St. Paul on October 7 "for the opening of a campaign to combat the traitorous and seditious influences . . . which have centered very largely in the Nonpartisan league."[24] A comparison of "notes" by those present developed an interesting consensus with respect to the Townley movement.

The conferees agreed that the league was opposing the war effort both covertly and overtly. Its leaders, they felt, were seeking to make the second liberty bond drive a failure. They believed that throughout the state "hundreds" of leaguers were openly insulting the flag and that in some communities league influence had so poisoned the atmosphere that those who supported the war found themselves in a position similar to Unionists residing in the Confederate states during the Civil War. In short, the group said, "the league . . . is actually a pro-German organization and is doing more than any influence to make it appear that Minnesota is not loyal to the government." They also saw the league as threatening the existing economic order. Boycotts sponsored by it were endangering the business life of some towns, and "the commercial life of Minnesota" would "be attacked by legislation if the league" obtained "a large voice in the next senate and house." The group thought that such a possibility menaced some sectors of business more than others, and that "the mining interests of northern Minnesota" would "have a special drive made against them."

After reassuring itself of the enmity of Townleyism both to patriotism and the status quo — which by implication were inseparable allies — the group discussed ways and means of countering the rampant disloyalty which supposedly had been unleashed by the Nonpartisan League and Senator La Follette. One delegate favored "shooting such men as La Follett[e] and Townl[e]y." Possibly this suggestion appealed to many, but they chose instead to authorize a gigantic loyalty demonstration in the Twin Cities. Before adjourning, the conference appointed a committee of fifteen to organize the demonstration and to secure, if possible, a representative of the national administration as the main speaker.

Critics of the Burnquist administration who also were unaffiliated with the Nonpartisan League saw the October 7 meeting and the planned loyalty spectacular as the first move in the governor's re-election campaign. According to these critics, the governor would run nominally as a Republican, but in fact he would be backed by a "loyal" coalition held together by a desire to save Minnesota and the nation from sedition and pro-Germanism. It was hoped that as a return favor for support of the national administration by Burnquist and Senator Nelson the Democratic party would not contest the re-election of either man. Unless the Nonpartisan League expired within the year — an unlikely prospect, although determined efforts to smash it were in the offing — there still would be an election, but a "yellow" Townley ticket, supported only by immovable pro-Germans and intransigent radicals unresponsive to the call of patriotism, would suffer ignominious defeat.[25]

When this strategy was applied to the political realities, however, it soon became clear that Burnquist would have to settle for a narrower base of support than originally envisioned. Although the Minnesota Democratic party entered no candidate in opposition to Nelson in 1918, it did feebly contest the governorship. More important, the national administration refused to participate in the crusade against the Nonpartisan League.

When the arrangements committee for the Twin Cities loyalty demonstration, which was held in mid-November, requested Washington to send either a cabinet member or the president as a speaker, the administration's high command replied it would do so if Townley were also permitted to "have a place on the platform and be allowed to speak." Since the goal of the demonstration was "to offset the injurious effect of the activities of the Nonpartisan league," the committee rejected this stipulation, whereupon the administration sent a lesser official, Assistant Secretary of Agriculture Carl S. Vrooman, a liberal Democrat from Missouri. Vrooman's address scarcely furthered the antileague campaign. After making an unfavorable comparison between the loyalty of the farmers and the weak patriotism of profiteers, he called upon liberals of all political parties to make common cause against vested privilege, reaction, and antisocial standpatism.[26]

Early in December Townley journeyed to Washington for a series of conferences with federal officials. Among others, he met with President Wilson, Herbert Hoover, the national food administrator, and George Creel, director of the Committee on Public Information, who arranged the league president's itinerary. From Townley's point of view, these conferences were highly satisfactory. They did not forge an actual political alliance between the administration and the Nonpartisan League, but both sides understood the other better than they had before. The influence of Congressman Baer worked toward the same end. Shortly after taking office he established an intimate relationship with high officials in the liberal wing of the administration.[27]

Minnesota conservatives soon blamed Creel for the refusal of the administration to join their "loyalist" crusade. On April 8, 1918, Senator Nelson called Creel's attention to intimations of "an alliance . . . of some kind between" the Committee of Public Information "and the Leaders of the Non-Partisan League." Creel's reply not only throws light on Townley's conferences with Wilson and Hoover, but also illuminates the administration's relationship with the Nonpartisan League:[28]

> As you must understand, the business of this Committee is to try to put the people . . . thoroughly and enthusiastically behind this war. Last summer it came to my attention that the Nonpartisan league was not in harmony with the national purpose, and when Mr. Townley came to Washington, I insisted that he call upon me. I sent him also to Mr. Hoover, and . . . the President. The whole point of these interviews was to bring home to him that this was not a "rich man's war," that it was a war of self-defense, that no classes were being favored at the expense of any other class, and that the very life of the country depended upon understanding and support. I can say truthfully that, since that time, the Nonpartisan league has done nothing, so far as my knowledge goes, that could not be approved by every patriotic citizen.

Creel also stated that he had never "given official or unofficial approval of the Nonpartisan league" and had no "connection direct or indirect" with it. He had not sent government speakers to league meetings, although he had complied with a request to supply "the names of individuals who might be able to address its loyalty meetings." Creel defended this action by saying, "If, as claimed in Minnesota, the Nonpartisan league is disloyal, I feel it the more reason that speakers of ability and highest loyalty should be permitted to address its meetings."

Immediately following the La Follette speech, the prospect of bringing the moderate wing of the Minnesota labor movement into the projected "loyal" coalition seemed promising. Though objecting to the composition of the Safety Commission, conservative unionists nevertheless professed a desire to be "fair with the commission and assist it in every legitimate undertaking."[29] Burnquist's antilabor policy in the range strike still rankled, but he had partially redeemed himself by bowing to the Minnesota Federation's request for an investigation of the range situation which yielded, from labor's point of view, a balanced and objective report by the state Department of Labor and Industries. Other issues had dimmed memories of the strike. Moreover, the outbreak of war had exacerbated the tension between radical and moderate trade unionists. The latter had pointedly abstained from participating in such aggressive peace campaigns as that led by Mayor Van Lear in the two months before the commencement of hostilities.

The declaration of war by the United States in April, 1917, further complicated labor's internal situation. The moderates wholeheartedly identified with the AFL in completely supporting the war. The Socialists, both of the trade-union and white-collar varieties, split at least three ways: some accepted the St. Louis platform of the American Socialist party which declared continuing opposition to the war, some adhered to the prowar faction, a position that aligned them with the labor moderates; and a third group followed the lead of Mayor Van Lear, who reluctantly fell in line while reserving the right to criticize wartime policy and to co-operate with movements like the American Council for Peace and Democracy.[30]

Representatives of the three groups exchanged nasty recriminations during the early months of the war. At the convention of the Minnesota Federation of Labor which met at Faribault in July, 1917, a contingent of nearly a hundred delegates, most of them Socialists, voted against resolutions placing the Minnesota labor movement squarely behind the war. Following the adoption of these resolutions by a vote of approximately two to one, a group of about forty Socialists angrily left the convention. Later in the summer the moderates sought to counter the influence of movements such as the People's Council by co-operating with the American Alliance for Labor and Democracy. They also affiliated with Labor's Loyal Legion, a local organization founded by William C. Robertson, managing editor of the liberal *Minneapolis Daily News*, for the purpose of rallying the labor movement to the war.[31]

As the weeks passed moderate unionists became firmer in their support of the war. The *Union Labor Bulletin* was prepared even to risk a split in the labor movement, saying:

> It now behooves the . . . labor movement to guard against
> . . . the now harnessed and broke pacifists of the country (and
> this vicinity in particular) using the name and prestige of
> organized labor to carry on the work of German intrigue so
> decisively checked by the government's secret service. . . .
> it will be better to divorce these radical elements within our
> ranks than to suffer with them when the final reckoning comes.[32]

Such a state of mind predisposed many labor leaders to reject co-operation
with the Nonpartisan League, particularly after the La Follette episode.
Immediately following the senator's St. Paul appearance, President Hall
of the Minnesota Federation of Labor was quoted as saying that the Nonpartisan League was "a seditious outfit" which made promises to working
people that could not be fulfilled. A little later the executive council of
the state federation passed a resolution unalterably opposing the endorsement
of any candidate known to be hostile to the AFL declaration of March
12, 1917, which pledged unqualified support of the president.[33]

The Nonpartisan League claimed to be in accord with the March declaration, but its reputation created presumptions to the contrary. Fortunately
for the Townley movement, however, the Burnquist administration soon
took a stand that virtually threw the Minnesota trade unions into the arms
of the Nonpartisan League.

Beginning in the late summer of 1917, a campaign to organize a Twin
City Rapid Transit Company union sponsored by the AFL aroused tension
between the company's open-shop management and those carmen who co-
operated with the unionization effort. The intervention of the Safety Commission terminated a strike which interrupted service for several days in
October. The settlement ending this strike yielded the employees a number
of benefits, including more desirable split-shift arrangements, an increase
in pay, and reinstatement of a number of carmen who had been discharged
for union activity.[34]

The vital issue of union recognition remained unresolved, however, and
new tensions soon developed. Labor spokesmen accused the company of
failing to carry out its promises to reinstate the discharged men. A so-called
button war (competitive display of insignia) developed between members
of a company-sponsored union and the carmen affiliated with the AFL
local. Again the Safety Commission intervened. On November 19 its committee recommended "The total disuse and abandonment of buttons or
other insignia symbolizing the Union or Non-Union organizations" and
the cessation of "all solicitation for. . . the Union . . . on the company's
property," and instructed the company to discipline violators of "the forego-
ing recommendations."[35]

Defenders of this so-called button order claimed that it treated all parties
equally because it placed the same burden on adherents of both the company
union and the AFL local. Labor spokesmen, however, pointed out that

company unionists wanted to get rid of their buttons, since displaying them on duty subjected the wearers to contemptuous treatment by streetcar passengers who were partial to the AFL. More important, the order appeared to deny constitutional rights explicitly recognized by the national administration. While federal labor policy by no means countenanced strikes inimical to the war effort, it did not agree with the contention of the Minneapolis Citizens Alliance that for the duration of the conflict no unions should be permitted to organize where they did not exist before the outbreak of hostilities, a contention that the Burnquist administration fully accepted.[36]

After the commission issued its button order, trade unions throughout the state rallied solidly behind the aggrieved carmen. "Before making this ruling," commented the *Union Labor Bulletin*, "the safety commission was dealing with about one thousand street car employes, but after making the ruling it was dealing with about 50,000 workers." Protests and mass meetings dominated newspaper headlines. On Sunday, December 2, in St. Paul's Rice Park, James Manahan, then serving as attorney for the Nonpartisan League, State Representative Tom J. McGrath, and Oscar E. Keller, who was later elected to congress, were arrested and immediately indicted "for inciting riot and sedition, in large part because they denounced the Safety Commission, the Governor and their orders." When the accused came up for trial, all charges were dropped for lack of evidence.[37]

The apparent threat to law and order as well as the possibility that essential production might be interrupted aroused the apprehension of federal authorities. On December 4 Secretary of War Newton D. Baker wired the Safety Commission, requesting a suspension of the button order and offering to mediate the dispute. At a mass meeting held the following day in St. Paul the labor movement accepted Baker's offer while the streetcar company and Safety Commission, acting in concert, pursued an opposite course. In a telegram to the secretary of war, Burnquist stated that "a re-opening of the decision" on the button order "as matters . . . now stand would be a surrender of government by reason of riots and agitation and would be an incentive to further riots and agitation." Consistent with this rhetoric, Burnquist had already removed the sheriff of Ramsey County for failing to maintain order in St. Paul and had mobilized the local home guard. Following the exchange with Baker he ordered home guard units from eight other Minnesota cities into Minneapolis and St. Paul.[38]

Contrary to later claims of the Safety Commission, this show of strength did not contain the crisis, and only a presidential request coupled with a renewed offer of federal mediation averted a general sympathy strike

scheduled for December 13. The unions unconditionally accepted the mediation tender. Burnquist's response was less cordial. In a telegram to the
secretary of war he argued that if the federal government had affirmed
the obligation of both parties "to abide by the orders of the State tribunal
practically all attempts to defy the state government would now be at an
end." A public statement issued to the press interpreted the federal government's role as one of "investigation" rather than mediation. "There
can be," the governor said, "no mediation without consent of both parties."
In other words, the button order remained in force.[39]

During the prolonged negotiations which followed, the Safety Commission
and the Minneapolis Citizens Alliance, which represented the streetcar company, insisted that no concessions to unionism should be made for the duration
of the war. The federal mediators, who in the final analysis lacked authority
to force a settlement, eventually abandoned the struggle. "I regret very
much to advise you," wrote one of them on March 13, "that the President's
Mediation Commission has been unable to bring about a settlement. . . .
The company has positively refused to agree to the findings of the Commission. . . . *They have thus put themselves on record in opposition to
the war policies of our government at this time.*"[40]

Organized labor quickly took advantage of the mediator's implication
that the Twin City Rapid Transit Company was engaged in an unpatriotic
obstruction of the war effort. The firm recruited workers from rural Minnesota
to replace the locked out strikers, and this policy in a time of labor scarcity
on farms gave the union an additional opportunity to impugn the loyalty of
management. Failing to see the humor of this reverse twist to the loyalty
issue, friends of the company developed their own version of the strike's
relationship to patriotic obligation. A Norwegian-language editor, employed
by the Safety Commission to oversee the Scandinavian-American press,
attributed the strike to "Leaguers, socialists, pacifists and other servants
of Germany, including, no doubt, some hired German agitators and spies."[41]

Even the loyalty of officials serving the national administration came
into question. Otis P. Briggs, chairman of the executive committee of
the Citizens Alliance and the chief negotiator for the transit company,
saw only two choices open to "an able bodied person" while the war
lasted:

> . . . either go to the firing line in France and fight as no
> man ever fought before or stay at home and work as no man
> ever worked before. It is no time for strikes and lockouts and
> discussions of academic questions. . . . if the United States

Government, under direction of the President, would come out at this time in a general declaration that so far as unionism and non-unionism are concerned, a condition of status-quo must remain until this war is over, it would remove endless difficulties . . . all over the United States.

The refusal of the federal mediators to adopt this view led Briggs to conclude that one of them was "just as much a Socialist as Mr. Van Lear."[42]

Briggs also noted that the "street railway matter is now being taken up by the Non-Partisan League," as indeed it had been for some time. From the beginning of the strike, league officials like Manahan conspicuously backed the carmen. In its issue of December 8 *Commercial West* noted that Manahan and a colleague

. . . went out of their way during the recent disturbance in St. Paul, to defend the position taken by the labor agitators in this street railway affair. While Mr. Townley . . . was assuring President Wilson of his patriotism and the loyalty of the league, his manager and attorney were lending aid and encouragement to trouble-makers endeavoring to muss up the industrial situation in the Northwest. One of these men emphasized his Bolsheviki tendency by an entirely uncalled for attack upon Otto H. Kahn, the eminent New York banker, who recently made such stirring loyalty addresses in the Twin Cities.[43]

The league's co-operation with organized labor on behalf of the carmen brightened the prospects for a farmer-labor combination and further dimmed any hope that Burnquist's "loyalist" coalition could win moderate trade union support. A delegation of league farmers, meeting in St. Paul in mid-February to protest the banning of their organization in many parts of the state, also conferred with a group of trade unionists for the purpose of working out a common approach to the streetcar company dispute. One labor paper paper hailed this joint effort as "The first step to merge organized labor of Minnesota with the Nonpartisan league in an effort to 'clean house at the state capitol.' " A few weeks later Minneapolis unionists founded a Municipal Nonpartisan League which stood ready to negotiate coalition arrangements with Townley's movement. On the state level, however, the Nonpartisan League and the Minnesota Federation of Labor would not achieve a co-operative relationship until after the all-important 1918 primary campaign.[44]

While a process of interaction between the loyalty issue and other concerns was forming the battle lines for the campaign of 1918, a broad but unco-ordinated drive to destroy the Nonpartisan League as an organization got under way. At one level this drive proceeded through the courts. During the autumn and winter of 1917 several county attorneys instituted suits against league officials, usually on charges of discouraging enlistment in the armed forces, and thereby initiated the prolonged litigation that came to be known as the Townley trials. These terminated in convictions and prison sentences for a number of league leaders, including Townley and Gilbert.[45]

At another level the anti-Nonpartisan League drive wore only the thinnest veneer of legality. In a score or so of counties, mostly in southern Minnesota, local bodies undertook to outlaw the league within their jurisdictions. The Faribault County Commission of Public Safety, for example, passed a resolution noting that the league had sponsored La Follette's St. Paul address, "the most seditious and unpatriotic speech recorded within this State"; deploring the league's "objects and purposes as being unpatriotic and in-opportune in these war times"; and recommending its exclusion "from our homes, our halls, our churches, our schools and all other places of public gathering."[46]

Backed by small-town opinion, local officials made a determined and generally successful effort to enforce these questionable enactments. After hearing of plans to hold a league meeting within their jurisdiction, officials of the National Defense League of Jackson County served notice that they would "use every measure at our disposal to prevent" Townley speakers from appearing. A number of league adherents scheduled a meeting at a schoolhouse near Alden in Freeborn County. Upon learning of the meeting, the Alden postmaster contacted a member of the county safety commission who in turn informed the county attorney and the captain of Alden's home guard. These two gentlemen acted promptly; the county attorney ordered the meeting stopped, and the captain mobilized three auto loads of guardsmen, who went to the scene and converted the proceedings into a Red Cross and thrift stamp rally.[47]

Occasionally violence broke through the façade of legality. Carl Wold of Alexandria, one of the few Minnesota editors to place his paper at the disposal of the Nonpartisan League, suffered both physical assault and the wrecking of his presses. A communication to Senator Nelson from one of Wold's townsmen reveals the depth of feeling against the editor. "We still believe we can get him legally," the writer confided, "and get him we must for he is a menace to any respectable community. . . . The rough element are in for beating them [*Wold and his associates*] up, decorating them with tar and feathers and chasing them out." As it turned out, the vendetta against Wold had a backlash effect. In the summer of 1918 it became known that he was afflicted with incurable cancer, and his death before the end of the year elevated him to the status of a martyr.[48]

The state Public Safety Commission responded to the drive against the league on the local level with a *laissez faire* policy. It took no steps itself to outlaw the organization, but it ignored league appeals for protection against the zeal of local officials. On February 26, 1918, Townley bluntly asked the governor, "Is the National Nonpartisan League to be regarded by the executive and peace officers of the State as an outlaw?" Burnquist replied equivocally that "Insofar as your league complies with the laws of the State and Nation, it is not an outlaw."[49]

The official attitude of the Safety Commission was scarcely more helpful. A statement appearing in the March 30, 1918, issue of the commission's bulletin seemed to place the onus for mob action on the victims rather than the perpetrators:

> It is hard to conceive of a more contemptible coward than the near traitor and seditionist who makes every effort . . . to discourage patriotism of the militant sort. When the patience of the loyalists is thus tried to the breaking point, and drastic action is taken by the citizens themselves, he is the first to emit a squeal of mortal terror, and rush to the protection of the very law that he has openly scorned and defied. . . . the ever increasing number of cases daily noted where it [*mob law*] is used on pro-Germans . . . should at least indicate to the near-traitor that he is surely and certainly bringing the day of reckoning nearer every hour that he persists upon his despicable course. The time to "get right" is NOW, and in a manner that will leave no doubt of sincerity. Noses are sure to be counted in every community.[50]

Although Safety Commission releases such as this one encouraged rather than restrained a rising vigilante spirit, McGee and his colleagues did not personally conduct hostilities against the Townley movement. The league challenge to main street, punctuated by frequent agrarian threats to boycott small-town business enterprise, was sufficiently ominous to spur a determined war against Townleyism. The La Follette episode, which raised suspicions that the organization was pro-German to the level of firm conviction, provided an extraordinarily effective base for attack. In the aftermath of the Wisconsin senator's "seditious" remarks, everything seemed to fit a neat pattern: The unwillingness of many Minnesotans to accept the war with appropriate enthusiasm was attributable to German-inspired league influence. The league's ties with Socialism and the IWW, its strident radicalism, and its obvious intent to array class against class all worked for Germany by weakening American capacity to wage a successful war.

This premise sustained the extra-legal drive against the Nonpartisan League until after the armistice of November 11, 1918. It also provided the anti-Townley forces with a platform in the Minnesota campaign of that year.

CHAPTER FOURTEEN

The Campaign of 1918

IN PLANNING the first Minnesota state convention of the Nonpartisan League, which opened in St. Paul on March 17, 1918, the leaders of the organization committed a serious blunder. For some unaccountable reason they invited Governor Burnquist to address the gathering. As must have been expected, the governor declined. It also should have been anticipated that Burnquist would take full advantage of any opportunity to put the case against Townleyism on record. This is precisely what he did in replying to Arthur Le Sueur, manager of the Minnesota branch of the National Nonpartisan League, in whose name the invitation had been sent. The governor's statement captured newspaper headlines shortly before the league convention met, and its substance provided a rich mine of material for the editorial columns of antileague journals while Townley's convention was in session.[1]

Burnquist's letter of refusal recapitulated most of the current charges against the farmers' movement. League leaders, wrote the governor, had "been closely connected with the lawless I.W.W. and with Red Socialists." They had "catered to that faction of labor which has violated the law and been opposed to compliance with just orders of duly constituted authority" — an obvious reference to the streetcar strike. Moreover, "The cheering and applauding of the unpatriotic utterance of Senator La Follette at your last convention put a stamp of disloyalty on it [*the league*] that can never be erased." Burnquist also noted that Le Sueur was "the attorney who defended the murderers in the I.W.W. trouble on the Range two years ago," but he failed to mention that the case against Le Sueur's clients had been dismissed for lack of evidence before coming to trial. Following another reference to the IWW— "this law-breaking Bolshevik element in our society" — the governor defined the basic premise of those who doubted Nonpartisan League loyalty:

> He who in normal times needlessly arrays class against class
> is most often the ambitious demagogue, but any individual who

will do so when our nation is in a life-and-death struggle is
knowingly or unknowingly a traitor to his state and to his country.
. . . for me there are during this war but two parties, one
composed of the loyalists and the other of the disloyalists.[2]

This unwitting surrender of campaign initiative to the opposition apparently did not dent the morale of league followers as their convention got
under way. In several respects this meeting bore a striking resemblance
to its North Dakota counterpart in 1916. Townley's leadership dominated
both gatherings, and the same enthusiasm gave life to the ,proceedings.
Both conventions worked to gain control of state government by naming
a ticket which would file in the Republican primary; and both platforms
incorporated the basic Nonpartisan League demands for state ownership
of terminal elevators, mills, warehouses, insurance systems, and credit
facilities.[3]

But there was one significant difference. In 1918 the Nonpartisan League
had to come to terms with the war. The campaign of its opponents to
label the organization disloyal was already well advanced. Success or failure
in the forthcoming election depended on meeting the challenge effectively.
A full recognition of this reality is reflected in convention proceedings
and speeches and in the line taken by Nonpartisan League papers. It is
also to be seen in the pronouncements of Charles A. Lindbergh, the convention's choice to run against Burnquist in the Republican primary.
Throughout its sessions, the convention paid proper deference to the flag,
the Red Cross, and the sacred obligation of all Americans to purchase
liberty bonds. The platform proclaimed all-out support of the crusade against
German autocracy, wholeheartedly endorsed President Wilson's war aims,
and pledged continued support of all war activities.[4]

The organization's strategists proposed to go beyond merely defending
it against accusations of being pro-German. They aggressively affirmed
that the war effort needed the league program. The "main problem" facing
the nation, said Lindbergh in accepting the endorsement for governor, "is
to manage a war so as to lose the least number of lives . . . and at the
same time to win." Accomplishing this, he continued, "is no less an
economic problem than a military one." The platform's prescription for
the economic problem was massive extension of governmental regulation.
One plank demanded a strengthening of presidential price-fixing authority.
Another called for increased tax levies on large incomes. Still another recommended that the government operate strike-bound industries as well
as munitions plants in order to eliminate all direct profit from war.[5]

In the course of an active campaign, Lindbergh returned again and again to the theme that victory in the war depended on enactment of the league program. A statement issued when he filed for the Republican nomination asserted that reform "is our patriotic duty as well as our right," and asserted that the war disclosed "the absolute necessity" of reconstructing the economic order. "Until we do this," he maintained, "we cannot develop our full national strength which we will need to win the war."[6]

A month later in a speech at Rochester Lindbergh elaborated the point. Modern war, he said, depended as much on production as on military tactics. Britain, France, and Italy had recognized this by placing essential industry under efficient government control. The failure of Russia to do so had led to that nation's collapse. "There is," said Lindbergh, "only one remedy, and that is to have the government conscript industry." The Nonpartisan League, he claimed, was the only organization in the country "backing up President Wilson in his fight with the politicians and profiteers to carry out the program." The "profiteers" were "the real disloyalists." In an obvious reference to a suggestion made a few weeks before by McGee that firing squads be set up to dispatch disloyal Swedish- and German-Americans, Lindbergh added, "if there should be any firing squads here . . . they should first seek out these traitors" — that is, the profiteers.[7]

Perhaps another candidate could have handled this message more persuasively than did Lindbergh. Many farmers responded to his leadership with reverent awe, but he failed to win the confidence of other influential groups. His opposition publicized evidence that he was anti-Catholic. Most trade unionists reacted to him with coolness and reserve. The *St. Paul Daily News*, unable to "make a recommendation as between" Lindbergh and Burnquist, called the league candidate "visionary" and "obsessed with a hallucination about an arch-enemy . . . the 'money trust.' " The *Mesaba Ore* of Hibbing, which spoke for range liberals, believed that "the non-partisan league made the mistake of its life . . . when it picked up Lindbergh as its candidate for governor."[8]

Lindbergh's most serious handicap grew out of his authorship of a book published in 1917 under the intriguing title *Why your Country is at War and What Happens to You after the War, and Related Subjects*. Lindbergh's opus proclaimed the solemn obligation of every American to support the war effort. In a perverse way it even articulated the hopes of prowar liberals by saying: "The war has boosted the Money Trust to its highest power, and it is due to have its farthest fall. This has now become a war for freedom." But, like La Follette, Lindbergh found it impossible to repress memories of his own last-ditch battle against American entry. "Trespass upon our rights on the high seas makes our cause just," he wrote, "still

I do not claim that it was wise to enter the war. . . . Our purpose is humane, nevertheless I believe . . . that a certain 'inner circle' . . . adroitly maneuvered things to . . . make it practically certain that some of the belligerents would violate our international rights and bring us to war with them."[9]

There were also passages that were open to damaging distortion. The one most often quoted out of context read: "We should spurn as contemptible to the idea of democracy the oft-heralded statement of 'Stand by the President.' " Since standing by the president had come to rank with God and country, the league opposition got considerable mileage out of this apparent rejection of the highest duty of citizenship. The complete passage conveyed a quite different meaning: "We should spurn as contemptible to the idea of democracy the oft-heralded statement of 'Stand by the President,' in the sense of its present frequent use because it is too often used as a guise to deceive."[10]

The incriminating passages from Lindbergh's book attracted nationwide attention. Testifying before the military affairs committee of the United States Senate in May, Townley found himself confronted with a number of embarrassing Lindbergh quotations, some of which called the war a struggle for commercial supremacy. The league leader sought escape from his predicament by lamely suggesting that Lindbergh may have meant German commercial supremacy, an explanation that failed to satisfy his interrogators.[11]

Certain Nonpartisan League pronouncements on the Russian situation also alarmed the military affairs committee. The recently adopted platform had pledged help and support to all people fighting for democracy, "especially to the people of Russia." In addition, league publicists were fond of using a term which had a prominent place in the Bolshevik lexicon: industrial democracy. Under sharp questioning Townley disavowed any intention to support what the Russian Bolsheviks were doing but hoped that Russia would eventually adopt industrial democracy in the form advocated by the Nonpartisan League.[12]

This rejoinder did little to lift the Bolshevik burden which by now lay heavily on the Nonpartisan League. It had come to rest there partly because league spokesmen persisted in disbelieving the accounts carried by the "monopoly" press and in hoping the Bolsheviks would establish a genuine democracy in the land of the Czars, and partly because the anti-Townley people were alert to every opportunity to attack the movement. Shortly after Lenin and his followers overthrew the Russian provisional government on November 7, 1917, the league's opponents discovered an affinity between the Russian Bolsheviks and Townley's organization. *Commercial West* described "The Bolsheviki" as "the party of extreme radicals, the word signifying those who demand the greatest." After this dubious piece of linguistic analysis, the paper commented:

> We have a similar party in this country headed by the outlaw I.W.W.'s, with the Nonpartisan League as a close second, and with such political leaders as La Follette and his followers giving aid and encouragement to the destructionists and socialists generally. . . . This universal disaster in Russia, following attempts to put in force the crazy notions of radicals, is exactly what would follow in this country if we should adopt the extravagant ideas of La Follette, Townley and Haywood, as a working basis for government and industry.[13]

In March, 1918, Lenin's regime and imperial Germany ratified the treaty of Brest-Litovsk which removed Russia from the war. Although the Russian war effort had collapsed some time earlier, the treaty was a psychological blow to the Allied cause. Crusaders against American radicalism in general and the Nonpartisan League in particular found the Bolshevik action useful indeed. Soon after the pact was ratified, *Commercial West* pontificated on the lessons to be learned:

> The expected has happened in Russia, and the recent betrayal of that country to Germany by the ultra-radical Bolsheviki leaders has surprised no one. . . . The destructionists in America, parading under the various labels of I.W.W.'s, Socialists and Nonpartisan leaguers, are today the greatest hindrances to the vigorous prosecution of the war. Always a great menace to society, even in times of peace, their propaganda in a critical hour like the present, is equivalent to an invasion of America by a foreign foe. Will we heed the lesson of prostrate Russia and take vigorous action to protect this country in time, or will we, through misguided leniency and toadying to the votes of the rabble, permit these obstructionists to keep up their work until America stands helpless in this great struggle?[14]

Later the same periodical perceived a nefarious conspiratorial bond between the German bid for world domination and socialist revolution, stating: "It is only during the last 50 years . . . that the world has been pestered with radical Socialists and lawless anarchists. It is no mere coincidence that the socialistic propaganda throughout the world coincides with the time when Prussia has been plotting for world dominion.''[15] Such a bizarre thesis probably did not command widespread acceptance even in 1918, but the identification of the Nonpartisan League with Bolshevism at a time when many people believed Russia's revolutionary government to be in virtual alliance with imperial Germany strengthened the plausibility of pro-German charges against the organization.

While such assorted handicaps prevented the Nonpartisan League from seizing the initiative in the 1918 primary campaign, the Burnquist forces also experienced serious difficulties. The Republican organization had not recovered from the disarray into which it had been thrown by the demolition of the Smith machine in 1914. The Nonpartisan League threat encouraged the restoration of some unity, and the party tapped the talents of Smith, though the governor did not appoint him to a top party post. Republican officials, however, remained dissatisfied with what they considered to be grave deficiencies in organization.[16]

In planning his campaign, Burnquist adopted the nonpolitical approach appropriate for a candidate whose bid for office rested on claims that he was more patriotic than his opponent. "Personally, therefore," the governor announced, "I intend to make no political speeches during the primary and shall accept, as far as possible, those invitations to deliver patriotic addresses which I have . . . received." He kept this promise. His speeches did not refer either to Lindbergh or to the issues raised by the Nonpartisan League. Near the close of the campaign, he capsuled his appeal by saying: "It is a source of much satisfaction to feel that our people are becoming aroused . . . to the necessity of preventing a disintegration of our forces through ill-advised contests at home or through advocating the formation of such factions as to prejudice the different elements of our state against each other by reason of occupation or location."[17]

Throughout the campaign McGee, who was known to be close to Burnquist, threatened the credibility of this pose. Testifying before the United States Senate military affairs committee on April 19 in support of a proposal to place the nation under the jurisdiction of military tribunals, the safety commissioner committed a major indiscretion. He said:

> A Non-Partisan League lecturer is a traitor every time. In other words, no matter what he says or does, a League worker is a traitor. Where we made a mistake was in not establishing a firing squad in the first days of the war. We should now get busy and have that firing squad working overtime. . . . The disloyal element in Minnesota is largely among the German-

Swedish people. The nation blundered at the start of the war
in not dealing severely with these vipers.[18]

To condemn German-Americans as a group was one thing, but to take
on the state's Swedish-American community as well bordered on political
madness. Under party pressure to which he submitted with evident displeasure, McGee issued a lengthy explanation denying any intention to
brand Swedish-Americans as disloyal. In the course of his statement, however, he reiterated his belief that military courts were needed to eradicate
sedition, saying that his experiences in Chisago County, which had a large
Swedish-American population, and in Brown County, a major German-
American center, had demonstrated to his satisfaction the impossibility of
securing convictions from local juries. A military court, he said, would
be different because "The certainty of conviction of the guilty before such
a court with a prompt appearance of the guilty before the firing squad
would have had and would still have a most restraining influence on the
disloyal, seditious and traitorous."[19]

Burnquist's managers may have deplored McGee's exuberance, but they
could not abandon the loyalty issue as the main reason for their man's
renomination. Too much had been invested in the effort to impeach the
patriotism of the Nonpartisan League's leadership, and the crusade against
the Townley movement had unquestionably impressed many voters. Pending
cases and indictments against Townley and his associates in several district
courts on charges of having discouraged enlistment in the armed forces
raised doubts which prudent citizens, who may have been skeptical of the
accusations of campaigning politicians, could scarcely dismiss.[20]

Moreover, some of Burnquist's most astute backers believed the governor
had no other strong factors working for him. A prominent Duluth Republican
remarked: "The Loyalty issue is the only thing which will save Burnquist."
About two weeks before the primary, Senator Nelson touched on this point
in a statement supporting the governor. He said:

. . . the exigency of the war makes me especially interested
in the nomination and re-election of Governor Burnquist. He
has proved himself a veritable Rock of Gibralter in maintaining
law and order, in sustaining the spirit of loyalty and patriotism,
and in faithfully supporting our federal government in the war.
. . . to defeat Governor Burnquist under these circumstances
. . . would be taking a backward step in the path of patriotism
and loyalty.[21]

On the closing day of the primary campaign, spokesmen for the contending camps issued the customary statements reiterating what they wanted the electorate to believe. Gustaf Lindquist, ignoring McGee's contribution, claimed that the governor's campaign had "been notably clean and free from any discourtesy" and pointed out that his chief had "not mentioned his opponent in any public address." Townley assailed Burnquist for "subserviency to 'big business' and a wilful refusal to co-operate with the federal government." The league leader anticipated a Lindbergh victory by "at least 30,000" votes.[22]

The final count failed to vindicate Townley. Burnquist won renomination with a total of 199,325 votes to 150,626 for Lindbergh; in other words, Lindbergh polled three votes to every four cast for Burnquist. The conservative press hailed this result as a great victory for loyalty and patriotism. The *St. Paul Daily News* interpreted the returns in a different light. "Something like 60 per cent loyalty for Minnesota isn't anything to wave flags about," commented this paper, and added: "But such a standard . . . is utterly false . . . the great mass of the Lindbergh vote was as loyal as the Burnquist vote, but . . . it voiced an emphatic PROTEST against real wrongs as well as fancied grievances."[23]

Three choices, all to some extent unsatisfactory, lay open to the Nonpartisan League following the primary election. The organization could sit out the final election contest, endorse the Democratic candidate for governor, or file an independent ticket. If it elected the first course, could the enthusiasm which had garnered 150,000 votes be held in suspended animation until the next election in 1920? Most league strategists thought not. The outcome of the Democratic primary — which drew less than 10 per cent of the total votes cast on June 17 — prejudiced the second possibility. Fred E. Wheaton, the Democratic nominee, was regarded as more conservative than his opponent, District Judge Willard L. Comstock, who had been backed by Lind and his liberal Democratic circle. Although a few trade unionists ultimately supported Wheaton, most anti-Burnquist spokesmen regarded him as unacceptable. Leaders of the Minnesota Federation of Labor called him "a political weakling" with "few qualifications that would commend him to the mass of the voters."[24]

Wheaton's refusal to withdraw in favor of a candidate capable of leading a broad anti-Burnquist coalition left the Nonpartisan League and its potential allies with the third choice: the filing of an independent ticket. Such a course ran counter to Townley's basic strategy of capturing the Republican party, and a third-party effort launched so late in a campaign offered small hope of success. But this appeared preferable to the other possible courses.

The attitude of organized labor reinforced the case for an independent ticket. Thanks largely to the labor policies of the Burnquist administration, the annual convention of the Minnesota Federation of Labor, which met at Virginia in mid-July, strongly favored the immediate intervention of trade unions in state politics. A motion instructing federation officials to call a political conference to meet not later than August 24 passed by an overwhelming margin. This gathering was held simultaneously with the reconvened convention of the Nonpartisan League. A joint committee representing the two groups agreed on the endorsement of a partial ticket for the fall election, which was ratified by the parent bodies. The endorsed candidates, David H. Evans for governor and Tom Davis for attorney general, later filed by petition and appeared on the ballot under a "Farmer-Labor" designation because the secretary of state ruled that Minnesota election laws precluded their filing as independents.[25] The Minnesota Farmer-Labor party as such did not come into being until after 1920.

Compared to Lindbergh, Evans was obscure but not completely unknown. He was a resident of Tracy, a hardware merchant and a farmer, who had been active in state politics for many years as a progressive Democrat. He had supported Woodrow Wilson both in 1912 and 1916 and had also campaigned for the antiliquor cause. Since American entry into the war, he had worked zealously on behalf of liberty bond drives and patriotic activities in general. Formally he was not affiliated with the Nonpartisan League; he had worked for Judge Comstock in the 1918 primary. He had, however, won the organization's favor by making his farm available for a meeting which Tracy authorities would not permit within their city.[26]

In the main, the Evans campaign followed the course charted by Lindbergh. Evans placed more emphasis on labor issues, but only as a variation in the contention that the war effort needed the league program. Addressing a Labor Day rally in St. Paul, Evans unreservedly endorsed Wilson's war policies. He also assailed the Burnquist administration for failing to curb mob rule, charging that this failure discouraged commitment to the war effort.[27]

The Republicans responded to Evans by continuing to agitate the loyalty issue in somewhat different form than they had during the primary contest and conceivably with diminished effectiveness. Evans was less vulnerable to pro-German accusations than Lindbergh had been; it was difficult to impeach the loyalty of a Wilson Democrat who had taken the lead in organiz-

The mob actions against Nonpartisan League speakers in
various parts of Minnesota were characterized by the league
paper, the Minnesota Leader, as "Good News for the Kaiser"
in a cartoon of May 18, 1918, which hurled the accusation
of league disloyalty back at its opponents.

ing war activities. The league was hurt, however, by disclosures from
seized IWW records revealing that Arthur Le Sueur had served as counsel
for William D. Haywood, the notorious Wobbly leader. The most damaging
document was a widely circulated letter from Le Sueur to Haywood written
on the eve of American entry into the war which, among other things,
asserted: "This damned war business is going to make it mighty hard
to do good . . . radical work of any kind, but I think the fight should
be now centered against spy bills and conscription."[28]

Although there is no doubt that the Le Sueur letter damaged the league's
cause, the loyalty crusade lost some of its steam as election day approached.
For one thing, the mounting tide of Allied victory in Europe diminished
the fear of Germany. For another, nonpolitical catastrophes diverted attention

from the campaign— the influenza epidemic limited public meetings, and the Moose Lake forest fire, which struck in October, destroyed some twenty villages and took about six hundred human lives.[29]

Signs of a reaction against the loyalty campaign also began to multiply. Two well-publicized incidents fed this tendency. The first involved the Luverne Loyalty Club, which in June had undertaken to destroy Townleyism in Rock County by forcing Nonpartisan League members to register and take an oath pledging loyalty to the United States and renouncing their organization. The technique worked brilliantly, and league membership in the county quickly declined from 382 to twelve. The hold-outs soon felt the force of the loyalty club's enforcement machinery. A number of them suffered "deportation" into Iowa.[30]

One of the deportees, an elderly German-American farmer, made the mistake of returning to the Luverne area in August to help his sons with threshing. When local loyalists learned of his return, a mob came to the farm on August 19, seized him, tarred and feathered him, and forcibly deported him to South Dakota.[31]

A few weeks later the action of a mob in St. Louis County brought tragic consequences. A campaign by a Duluth organization known as the Knights of Liberty against foreign nationals pleading alien status to avoid the draft reached the point of violence in September. A Finnish immigrant who had suffered rough treatment at the hands of a mob was later found hanging from a tree. Whether suicide or lynching had taken his life could not be definitely ascertained, but it was obvious that his death was a direct result of mob lawlessness.[32]

The governor, who had taken no action in the Rock County case, felt that the man's death could not be ignored. He issued a proclamation offering a reward for "information leading to the arrest and conviction" of the perpetrators and asserting: "The public welfare demands that persons suspected of disloyalty be given a fair trial and, if guilty, be punished by the lawfully constituted authorities, and that mob violence shall not be tolerated."[33]

The Duluth incident and the governor's response— its tardiness and perhaps its spirit— strained the patience of a sensitive southwestern Minnesota journalist to the breaking point. Gunnar Bjornson, who had supported Burnquist in the primary campaign, penned an editorial expressing the outrage that many people were beginning to feel:

The governor of the state of Minnesota has come out against mob rule.

After due deliberation he has decided that he does not want any more men tarred and feathered or horsewhipped or deported, beaten up, disgraced or shamefully treated, without due process of law. . . .

The governor has made the discovery that there is a law against dragging a man out of his home and beating him up and subjecting him to all kinds of indignities. . . .

Mobs have been doing, — free and unmolested, — so many Hun stunts in this state that we had almost come to believe that the mob was a new form of law and order enforcement.

The governor and the Safety Commission have been silent on the mob atrocities so long that we really did not know what to think about it. . . .

But the governor has saved the day — also he has saved the constitution. . . .

We hope now that he will keep this up and will make his proclamation extend to every corner of the state. We hope that hereafter there will be no more stealing of banners, no more tearing off of the United States flag from cars that carry a Nonpartisan League banner, no more of the dirty, sneaking yellow paint brigades, no more of this tarring and feathering, no more of the disgraces that have taken place in Rock County, no more deporting of citizens, nor more of the hundred and one different kinds of outrages that have gone unmolested and unnoticed, if not encouraged, by state and county officials.[34]

Unexpected developments in the contest for United States senator and the race for congress in the eighth district — the range area — enlivened the closing days of a flagging campaign. Senator Nelson had filed for re-election anticipating only minor opposition. The Democratic state convention, meeting in March, had declined to back him officially, but the Democratic State Central Committee formally endorsed him, and prominent Democrats, including Lawler, Lynch, and Richard T. O'Connor, participated in his campaign. James A. Peterson, Nelson's opponent in the 1912 primary election, had again challenged the senator's renomination, but suffered overwhelming defeat. From Nelson's point of view, only one flaw marred the primary outcome: Peterson had carried Douglas County, the veteran senator's home base, where the Wold controversy was creating an anti-Nelson backlash.[35]

In the final election campaign, Nelson faced only one opponent, Willis G. Calderwood, candidate of the National party which was a temporary amalgam of prowar Socialists, a Bull Moose Progressive remnant, and the left wing of a fragmented Prohibition party to which Calderwood had belonged. The Nelson people regarded Calderwood as more of an annoyance than a threat. They expected the old Republican senator, whom they pictured as the symbol of a sturdy Americanism that transcended partisanship but abhorred the Nonpartisan League, to win an unprecedentedly one-sided victory that would cap his career and help seal the doom of Townleyism. They also cultivated the impression that President Wilson heartily desired Nelson's return to the Senate— an impression which was rudely upset a few days before the election.[36]

On October 23 John Lind received a telegram from the Democratic National Committee which he immediately released to the press. The communication "strongly" endorsed Calderwood, calling "his election as of the utmost importance not only in the matter of supporting President Wilson's conduct of the war but also for the purpose of cooperating in the reconstruction policies and progressive measures . . . which will follow cessation of hostilities."[37]

Nelson and his managers felt betrayed. Searching for explanations of the Calderwood endorsement, Nelson himself concluded that the responsibility rested on Lind who, he wrote a friend, had always "been hostile to me" because "he has always felt that I have had the place that he ought to have." Information from Nelson backers within the Minnesota Democratic camp confirmed the suspicion that Lind had indeed worked for Calderwood's endorsement.[38]

Apparently it did not occur to Nelson that other considerations might also have influenced Wilson and the Democratic National Committee. The central premise of the senator's campaign was that he deserved the support of all "loyal" voters, a category which seems to have included everybody except intractable pro-Germans, Nonpartisan League members, Socialists, Wobblies, and other "Bolshevik" varieties, none of whom deserved representation in any case. Such a premise left no room for discussion of the urgent issues on which men of comparable virtue and patriotism disagreed. Although Nelson would in the future support the League of Nations, he pointedly ignored Calderwood's efforts to draw him out on Wilson's Fourteen Points, disarmament, and postwar domestic policy, all of which were becoming highly controversial throughout the country.[39]

The Democratic National Committee's pronouncement stimulated the final phase of the Calderwood campaign. Nelson's friends noted a proliferation of Calderwood signs along Twin Cities streets and an increased circulation of his literature. Late in October the unofficial links already connecting the Evans and Calderwood campaigns also became firmer when the *Minnesota Leader*, the official organ of the state Nonpartisan League, flatly endorsed Calderwood. An editorial in the *Minneapolis Tribune* interpreted the meaning of these developments from a "loyalist" point of view:

> Nonpartisanship, Socialism, political Prohibition and John Lind Democracy have struck hands . . . in support of W. G. Calderwood. What a composite of class politics, sedition and intrigue! . . . This combination will also gather to itself all the pro-German, Bolsheviki, I.W.W. and uncatalogued flotsam and jetsam of the state.[40]

Vituperation, however, did not cover the embarrassment created by the national administration's embrace of Calderwood. Throughout the campaign, political writers hostile to Townleyism had called the Nelson-Burnquist team the "loyal" ticket and the Evans-Calderwood slate "yellow." The battle cry of the "loyalists" was "stand by the president." Now it developed that the president desired the election of one of the "yellow" candidates.

As expected, Nelson won his bid for another term, polling more than 206,000 votes to Calderwood's 137,000, a majority of approximately 69,000. Under the circumstances his margin, though substantial, could hardly be called a landslide. Calderwood approached the finish line burdened with the handicaps of a late start, minor-party status, conspicuous identification with the dry cause, which prejudiced his appeal to trade unionists and German-Americans, and the invidious implication of being a "yellow" candidate. Nelson had the benefit of immense prestige, a buildup as the epitome of loyal Americanism, overwhelming newspaper support, Scandinavian identity, and the open backing of prominent Minnesota Democrats, several of whom rejected the stand of their national committee.[41]

In 1918 range politics followed a logic that eluded the interpretive skill even of experienced eighth congressional district observers. The most obvious reality was that the Nonpartisan League had failed to establish rapport with range reformers. The central labor body in Duluth had refused to send representatives to the Producers and Consumers Conference in 1917; Victor Power, the mayor of Hibbing, had declined endorsement as the league's candidate for attorney general in March, 1918; Duluth representatives left the Minnesota Federation of Labor's political conference of August, 1918, before its proceedings concluded; and the Duluth *Labor World* supported Democratic candidate Fred Wheaton for governor. Most important, Burnquist trounced Lindbergh by two to one in St. Louis County, which embraces Duluth and most of the range. Few significant pockets of league strength were discernible.[42]

A number of irritations seem to have contributed to this lack of amity between the Nonpartisan League and the range protest movement. Townley may have found personal relations with Mayor Power difficult; neither man took kindly to rivals. The issue of iron-ore taxation created additional unpleasantness. Range liberals had no desire to leave the mining companies untaxed, but they objected to proposals that higher levies on mining go to the state rather than into local revenue funds.[43]

Since the European homelands of most ethnic groups in the northeastern area stood to gain by Allied victory, the Nonpartisan League's pro-German reputation also blunted its appeal in many range communities. In analyzing the outcome of the 1918 primary, Sigvart Rødvik, a competent political writer employed by the Nonpartisan League to maintain liaison with the Norwegian-language press, attributed Lindbergh's poor showing in St. Louis County partly to Slavic-American distrust of any man or movement accused of being pro-German. A belief that imperial Germany stood back of the conservative "white" faction in the tangled Finnish civil war that broke out in 1917 predisposed radical Finnish-Americans to hold the same point of view.[44]

The absence of an effective Townley organization coupled with the failure of eighth district Democrats to run a candidate, encouraged Republican Congressman Clarence B. Miller to be complacent about his own re-election. However, late in the campaign a combination of reform groups sponsored the candidacy of William L. Carss on an independent "Union Labor" ticket which in the closing weeks of the contest gained momentum and in the final count defeated Miller by more than 4,000 votes.[45]

Carss's victory is attributable partly to the success of his supporters in outmaneuvering Miller on the loyalty issue, and partly to voter displeasure with the congressman's alleged friendliness to the so-called steel trust. After the severance of diplomatic relations with Germany in February, 1917, Miller had been a militant supporter of all-out war against Germany. Before that he had voted for the McLemore resolution and had written sympathetic letters to local pacifists which, Carss spokesmen argued, indicated "doubtful loyalty." Carss, according to his backers, had forthrightly favored the Allied cause from the very start of the war. While Miller had consorted with neutralists, the union labor candidate had advocated American entry into the war rather than "waiting until insult after insult had been heaped upon us."[46]

The *Minnesota Leader* hailed Carss's election — the major political upset of the year — as a Nonpartisan League victory. Since Carss had received moral and possibly financial support from the Townley movement, the claim was in a sense justified. However, his campaign had remained formally separate from the league, and he could scarcely be accused of "pandering to a treasonable sentiment," a charge that was made by the Safety Commission against the Townley movement. Precisely how McGee reacted to this successful appropriation of the loyalty issue by the opposition is not a matter of record.[47]

Burnquist won re-election by considerably less than a majority of the votes cast for governor. He polled 166,515 to 111,948 for Evans and 76,793 for Wheaton. Two minor-party candidates, a Socialist and a National, received a combined total of 14,422. Minnesota had been saved for "loyalty," but if a charismatic leader could have commanded the entire non-Burnquist vote, the governor would have lost by a substantial margin.[48]

The meaning of the primary and final elections in 1918 is disclosed by the distribution of the returns rather than by the total vote for the contenders — a truism that applies to most elections. As measured by the Lindbergh and Evans vote, and to a lesser extent by the vote for Calderwood, the Nonpartisan League appealed most strongly to three segments of the electorate: the farmers of the Red River Valley and adjacent areas; German-Americans throughout the state; and the working people of the Twin Cities. Although the organization failed to win impressive support on the iron range, the Carss victory forecast the future Farmer-Labor orientation of that region also.

The strong preference for the league registered by Red River Valley voters surprised no one. The grievances of wheat farmers had spawned the Townley movement, and northwestern Minnesota had been a center of Populist strength in the 1890s. Conceivably the loyalty issue reduced the league vote, particularly in the small towns, but the neutralist tradition of the region (which was heavily Scandinavian-American) acted as a brake on excessive hysteria.

If anything, the size of the league vote in German-American precincts exceeded expectations. Lindbergh carried Brown County by more than two to one, and Evans polled a majority of the votes cast in the five-man contest for governor. Notwithstanding its two-to-one majority against the state prohibition amendment, Brown County also gave Calderwood, the lifelong antiliquor crusader, a three-to-two majority over Nelson. Stearns County, too, returned a substantial majority for Lindbergh, and a plurality for Evans, although Nelson prevailed over Calderwood. Closer to the Twin Cities, and farther from Minnesota's wheat belt, Carver County, like Brown, voted for Lindbergh by more than two to one, cast 1,521 ballots for Evans to 984 for Burnquist, and gave Nelson a slim margin of 60 votes over Calderwood.

The strong league tide in the German-American counties carried even some villages and small cities, in spite of the pronounced bias of small towns against the organization. New Ulm voted for Lindbergh by more than three to one and for Evans and Calderwood by substantial majorities. Chaska, Waconia, Norwood, Young America, and Jordan returned league majorities or pluralities in the primary or in the final election or both. Springfield, Sleepy Eye, and Shakopee voted the other way.

The claim of some league spokesmen that German-Americans voted for Townley candidates on domestic policy grounds is extremely dubious. Senator Nelson, whose experience in Minnesota politics went back to the 1870s, noted that German-American farmers "as a rule" had "not been in the habit of going into any agrarian movement." He added, "They were not numerous in the Farmers' Alliance, among the Grangers, or among the Populists." A Townley organizer recalled that initial league recruiting "proceeded rapidly" in northwestern Minnesota, "but in southern Minnesota, which was largely populated by conservative and wealthy farmers of German descent, the organizers ran into a stone wall and were unable to get any appreciable number of members until war was declared in 1917." In short, the issues related to the war account in large part for the heavy German-American support of the Nonpartisan League.[49]

This is not to say that the league won German-American backing by "pandering to a treasonable sentiment." The Safety Commission's simultaneous crusades against German-Americanism and the Nonpartisan League, together with constant reiteration of the pro-German charge against the Townley movement, cast the state administration in the role of persecutor both of the league and the German-American community. Few political bonds are more powerful than a common enemy. The league, moreover, had the temerity to protest the suppression of democratic freedoms in wartime, and German-Americans understandably interpreted this protest to embrace their own grievances.

Although Hennepin County voted for Burnquist over Lindbergh by approximately two to one, the labor precincts of Minneapolis gave substantial support to the Nonpartisan League. In the primary Lindbergh carried the sixth, ninth, eleventh, and twelfth wards. Evans carried the same wards in the final election, although his total vote in the county was smaller than that of Lindbergh. Conceivably the pro-German issue lost the league some Minneapolis labor support. The first ward, which had a large Polish-American population and which became a Farmer-Labor stronghold in later elections, went for Burnquist in the primary and for Wheaton in the final election.

In Ramsey County, where numerous German-American votes and a respectable trade union movement created a substantial base for the Nonpartisan League, Lindbergh and Evans polled a larger share of the vote than they did in Hennepin. Evans carried St. Paul by a tiny plurality, though Burnquist won Ramsey County by an equally thin margin. Contrary to the trend in Minneapolis and in the state as a whole, Evans also outpolled Lindbergh in St. Paul. The zealous effort on the eve of the primary to place material relating to Lindbergh's alleged bias against the Roman Catholic church in the hands of every St. Paul voter may well account for this break in the general pattern.[50]

The 1918 election signaled the end of the Progressive era in Minnesota. The old bipartisan coalition of moral reformers, small-town business and professional men, and farmers that had sustained the progressive movement was shattered beyond repair. Out of the wreckage, the Nonpartisan League appropriated progressivism's rhetoric, much of its crusading spirit, and the support of its left wing. In addition the league gained the allegiance of organized labor and a substantial segment of the German-American community, two elements whose affiliation with progressivism had been limited. This coalition of radical progressives, trade unionists, and German-Americans constituted the voting base which the Nonpartisan League would pass on to its successor, the Minnesota Farmer-Labor party.

If the emergence of the Nonpartisan League provided left-wing progressivism with organizational sponsorship, conservatism also gained reinforcement. Without abandoning their basic suspicion of Wall Street and big business, moderate progressives, caught up in a fear of Nonpartisan League radicalism, moved into a closer relationship with their old adversaries, the so-called standpatters, a development symbolized by Edward E. Smith's restoration to a position of influence within the Republican party. For the next decade this alliance would largely determine the course of Minnesota Republican politics.

CHAPTER FIFTEEN

The Aftermath of Minnesota Progressivism

PARADOXICALLY, the Nonpartisan League helped restore partisanship to Minnesota. From the turn of the century until 1918 a consensus based on progressivism had dominated state politics, at least on the rhetorical level. On most policy questions there was little to distinguish the three Democratic governors, Lind, Johnson, and Hammond, from their Republican adversaries, Van Sant, Jacobson, and Lee. Even Eberhart attempted to identify with progressivism, and Burnquist began his career as a proponent of reform. The propriety of voting for men rather than parties also gained wide acceptance, a logical point of view given the similarity of official Republican and Democratic pronouncements on the issues of the day.

Townley's invasion of Minnesota, which was both a symptom of and a contributing factor to a breakdown of the progressive consensus, drastically altered this pattern. Beginning in 1918 the most important factor shaping state politics was a spirited contest for power between two coalitions separated from one another by highly visible differences on questions of public policy. The Townley movement attracted groups whose complaints against the status quo were acute — notably grain farmers, trade unionists, left-wing progressives, and pragmatic Socialists — as well as those who harbored resentful memories of the wartime "loyalty" crusade. The Republican party commanded the support of defenders of the established order along with that of former progressives who feared Nonpartisan League radicalism more than they welcomed change.

While the 1918 election returns clearly underscored the existence of these two coalitions, the institutional framework within which they would confront one another was not yet developed. Defeat in the Republican primary of that year had obliged the Townley people to enter a third-party ticket in the final election without discrediting in their thinking the technique of

182

attempting a capture of the GOP. The Farmers' Nonpartisan League continued to operate on the assumption that seizure of the Republican party was a viable goal. At its 1919 convention the Minnesota Federation of Labor authorized creation of a Working People's Nonpartisan Political League, an organization designed to engage in joint political activity with the Farmers' League.[1]

On March 24, 1920, the two groups held endorsing conventions which by prearrangement met in the same hotel. By this time disagreement on strategy had developed, not between the two leagues as such, but within each organization. One faction advocated independent political action through a permanent farmer-labor party. The other favored adherence to Townley's original strategy. A compromise temporarily resolved the dispute. Candidates for three state offices were filed under Farmer-Labor designation, while the main effort was directed toward gaining the Republican gubernatorial nomination for Henrik Shipstead. Like Lindbergh in 1918, Shipstead failed to win the primary, whereupon he filed as an independent candidate for the fall election, which he lost by a considerably wider margin than the primary. The other candidates suffered a similar fate.[2]

This record of failure weighted the balance in favor of permanent third-party action. In 1922 the endorsees of the two leagues filed as Farmer-Labor candidates, with Shipstead running against Kellogg for the United States Senate and Magnus Johnson contesting the re-election of Governor Jacob A. O. Preus. Shipstead defeated the prestigious Kellogg, and Johnson lost by a sufficiently narrow margin to encourage hopes for the future. The victories of the Reverend Ole J. Kvale in the seventh congressional district and of Knud Wefald in the ninth augmented the elation generated by Shipstead's triumph. As historian Arthur Naftalin has noted, "The 1922 election established the Farmer-Labor party as the second party in the state."[3]

This impressive achievement did not signal a wholesale conversion of Minnesota voters to Farmer-Labor radicalism. Rather, it reflected the need for an opposition party capable of representing aggrieved grain farmers, trade unionists, and ethnic groups victimized by wartime and postwar nativism. For a number of reasons the Minnesota Democratic party was neither willing nor able to assume this role. Writing in 1924, John Lind asserted that "what is left of the Democratic organization in this state (with few exceptions) consists largely of the old ward-heeler element[s]," which, according to Lind, had substantially controlled party affairs for several years. "Their ambition," he added, "seems to have been, in most instances, to act as handmaidens for . . . the Republican party."[4] Another

Democratic handicap was identification of the national party with World War I — ''Wilson's war'' — a factor that alienated many German-Americans from their traditional political allegiance. Finally, several interpreters of Minnesota political history have surmised that Scandinavian-American voters of anti-Republican orientation were loath to affiliate with the Democratic party because they resented the dominance of Irish Catholics within its leadership.[5]

Although the role of surrogate for the Democratic party broadened Farmer-Labor opportunities, it also created serious problems. A party whose name, antecedents, and rhetoric carried intimations of a class movement committed to radical goals found the compromises required to hold a disparate coalition together distasteful. Perpetual tension existed between those Farmer-Laborites who regarded principled advocacy of the movement's semisocialist program as more important than the next election and those who, hungering for immediate political success, sought to mute Farmer-Labor radicalism. The question of whether limited working arrangements with Communists were tolerable or desirable was another divisive issue. Moreover, basic conflicts of interest between agriculture and labor were an ever-present difficulty, and the passing of time dimmed the wartime memories that for a few years operated so powerfully on behalf of Farmer-Labor unity. There was also the constant possibility that a Democratic renaissance might undercut the Farmer-Labor electoral base, a possibility pointed up in 1928, when the Democratic vote for governor quadrupled over its level of two years earlier.[6]

Ultimately these and other factors undermined the Farmer-Labor movement. Until 1938, however, several countervailing forces worked for its preservation. Notwithstanding Franklin D. Roosevelt's leadership on the national level, dissension within party ranks continued to blight hopes for a Democratic revival in Minnesota. The Republicans also faced a unity problem, attributable in part to the clashing ambitions of individual politicians and in part to the old difference in viewpoint between insurgent and standpatter. In addition, the GOP's conservative orientation nationally handicapped the Minnesota organization, whose leadership in the period between the administrations of Theodore Christianson (1925–31) and Harold E. Stassen (1939–43) was not impressive. During Floyd B. Olson's governorship (1931–36) the Farmer-Labor party suffered no such leadership gap. Most important, perhaps, economic hardship in rural Minnesota throughout the 1920s followed by the Great Depression of the next decade tended to broaden public tolerance for Farmer-Labor radicalism.

The bad feelings engendered by the campaign of 1918 continued through 1919, merging with the hysteria of the so-called red scare. According to the *Minneota Mascot*, a compulsion "to beat" the Nonpartisan League dominated the legislature of that year — Townley's movement having succeeded in electing 24 members to the lower house and eight senators. Early in its proceedings the session managed to ratify the eighteenth amendment to the federal constitution (prohibition), but congressional failure to submit the nineteenth (woman suffrage) until June necessitated a special session which met in September. The regular session also failed to deal with iron ore taxation, but the special session passed a tonnage tax measure which Burnquist vetoed.[7]

House File Number 1 fared better than the tonnage tax; it became law. Popularly known as "the flag bill," this measure outlawed "display within the state of Minnesota [*of*] any red flag, or black flag, . . . any flag or banner, ensign or sign having upon it any inscription antagonistic to the existing government of the United States, or the state of Minnesota." The act further specified that "possession . . . of any such flag . . . or facsimile thereof . . . shall be deemed evidence of an intent . . . to display the same." Two exceptions were allowed: "the use of a red flag by any employee of a railroad company as a signal, or the display of a red flag on a public highway as a warning of obstruction."[8]

The hysteria that produced legislation such as the flag bill receded perceptibly in 1920. In accepting the call of the state GOP convention to run for governor, Jacob A. O. Preus proclaimed the chief issue of the forthcoming campaign to be "Townleyism," which he described as "a political cult that would take away from us our property and our homes." Association of the Nonpartisan League with "free love" was another early theme of the Republican campaign. Nevertheless, 1920 was not a repetition of 1918. Realizing that the McGee-Burnquist image was creating a backlash, Republican leaders readily accepted the governor's decision not to seek re-election and permitted the safety commissioner to fade from public view. The state convention pledged enactment of a "fair and equitable tax on iron ore," and endorsed farm co-operative marketing agencies as a more viable approach to agriculture's problems than state ownership, the solution advocated by the Nonpartisan League.[9]

On the campaign trail, Preus reiterated these positions again and again. His performance at Marshall early in October impressed Gunnar Bjornson. As quoted by the *Mascot*, Preus acknowledged that the Nonpartisan League owed its existence to "various problems that confront the farmers and it

After the allegation that the Nonpartisan League was pro-German began to lose credibility, adversaries of the league charged that it promoted sexual freedom. This cartoon from the January, 1920, issue of the Red Flame, *an opposition anti-Bolshevik journal published by the Citizens' Economy League of North Dakota, appeared over the caption, "Fathers, Mothers, What Do You Think of It?".*

proposes a constructive platform which must be answered by fair and reasonable discussion." He then contrasted the Nonpartisan "government ownership way" with the Republican "co-operative way," claiming that experience and rationality vindicated the latter. He also stressed the Republican commitment to enact a tonnage tax.[10]

Upon taking office in January, 1921, Preus mounted an ambitious effort to win legislative approval of the program embodied in the 1920 Republican platform. According to GOP partisans, he succeeded brilliantly, and the *Minneapolis Tribune* claimed that the 1921 legislature redeemed "every promise, made by the Republican party in its campaign, against the forces of Townleyism last year." The assessment of Carl J. Buell, a reform publicist who continued Lynn Haines's tradition of publishing a critique of each legislative session, was more restrained. He called the session "a disappointment to both extremes, — the extreme radical and the extreme reactionary, — and a satisfaction to reasonable people who do not expect to reform all evils at one session."[11]

There can be little doubt that most old progressives who still retained a trace of their prewar militancy basically agreed with Buell. Few legislative sessions in the history of the state have enacted more laws designed to assist agriculture. One statute dealt with a fundamental Equity and Nonpartisan League complaint against the grain trade by declaring commodity exchanges to be open markets obliged to admit co-operative selling agencies as members; another applied the same rule to livestock exchanges; still another expanded the range of activities open to co-operative enterprise; and a constitutional amendment permitting the state to operate a rural credits agency was submitted to the voters. In the realm of taxation, "an occupation tax equal to 6 per cent of the valuation of all ores mined or produced . . . in addition to all other taxes provided for by law" was imposed on iron mining companies operating within the state. To guard against a judicial overturn of this levy, the legislature submitted an amendment to the state constitution authorizing it.[12]

If these measures tended to blunt the Nonpartisan League appeal, other enactments created issues for the 1922 campaign. The Brooks-Coleman act, which divided regulatory authority over street railways between the Railroad and Warehouse Commission and the municipalities served, was regarded by many old progressives as an unwarranted departure from the tradition that local units of government should control their own utilities. Failure of the legislature to supplement the occupation tax on iron ore with a levy on royalties also rankled. In addition, the legislature vitiated the effect of the occupation tax by limiting the power of range communities to tax the mining companies. Finally, the session passed an amendment to the primary law authorizing endorsement conventions in advance of the primary election, specifying that candidates endorsed by such conventions should be so designated on the primary ballot, and prohibiting defeated primary candidates from making a second try in the fall election. Principled progressives who feared a restoration of machine politics as well as those members of the Nonpartisan League who still nourished hopes of capturing the Republican party denounced this law as an abomination.[13]

Negative public reaction to the Brooks-Coleman law, to the new primary law, and to the legislature's failure to act more decisively on iron ore taxation, coupled with discontent arising from the 1921 depression, which struck rural Minnesota with particular force, sustained the powerful Farmer-Labor bid for power in 1922. Preus won over Magnus Johnson, but by a plurality of only 14,277 votes. In addition to electing a senator and two congressmen, the Farmer-Labor party augmented its strength in the state legislature, increasing its representation in the lower house by ten members. A substantial number of conservatives who had opposed iron ore taxation also were defeated by professed adversaries of the so-called steel trust.[14]

Preus responded to the situation by moving to the left. His recommendations to the 1923 legislature included a rural credits program (the amendment authorizing such a program having been approved by the voters in the 1922 election), a royalty tax on iron ore, and submission of an amendment authorizing a state income tax. The legislature honored the first two recommendations but declined to submit an income tax amendment. It also modified the primary law, striking out the specification requiring convention endorsed candidates to be designated as such on the ballot.[15]

Shortly after the 1923 legislature adjourned, the death of Senator Knute Nelson raised a serious personal complication for Preus. The governor had been regarded as Nelson's heir apparent, and if the senator had survived until expiration of his term in 1924, undoubtedly Preus would have been the favored contender for the post. The question now was how Preus could achieve promotion from governor to senator. A suggestion that he resign the governorship with the understanding that Lieutenant Governor Louis L. Collins appoint him to the Senate evoked adverse public reaction. Thereupon Preus called a special election. As expected, the governor won the Republican nomination in the primary, but in the final election conducted a month later he lost decisively to the colorful Magnus Johnson who ran on the Farmer-Labor ticket. Apparently Preus's obvious eagerness to secure higher office produced a negative response among voters.[16]

Although the special election of 1923 abruptly terminated Preus's political career, it did not diminish the significance of his administration. Under his leadership the Minnesota Republican party had quietly repudiated McGeeism, returned to a course reasonably acceptable to the party's old progressive wing, and in the process realized a number of deferred progressive goals. Iron ore taxation was the most striking case in point. In both style and substance, the Preus administration anticipated the "modern Republicanism" of Governors Stassen, Edward J. Thye, Luther W. Youngdahl, and Elmer L. Andersen.

Theodore Christianson, Preus's immediate successor, eludes classification. His record was discernibly more insurgent than that of Preus. While the latter was winning advancement within the Minnesota Republican hierarchy as a protégé of Knute Nelson and a loyal organization man, Christianson entered politics as a La Follette backer. In 1912 the *Dawson*

Sentinel, which he edited in conjunction with his law practice, had strongly supported Peterson against Nelson for the Senate and Manahan for congressman-at-large. By 1924 the insurgent tint was less visible than ten years earlier, but apparently a trace remained. Officials of the United States Steel Corporation distrusted Christianson sufficiently to explore the possibility of an understanding with Floyd B. Olson, his Farmer-Labor opponent in the race for governor, before reluctantly deciding to back Christianson.[17]

Nevertheless, the causes with which Christianson most clearly identified as state legislator and as governor were tax reduction and low government spending. Up to a point both were compatible with progressivism, but Christianson's dogmatic advocacy of them created the impression of insensitivity to human needs. He also abhorred public ownership, a program which he associated with profligate government spending. Burnquist and Preus, he wrote, had sought "to check the Townley movement by offering . . . an alternative program," but he chose to meet "the issue of public ownership with a frontal attack." Economy, he added, was an essential component of this attack. As he expressed it, "confiscatory taxation, if continued long enough, would ultimately draw the country into socialism."[18]

In terms of the creed that Christianson professed, his administration was a success. It resisted increases in state expenditure, including school aids, limited the operations of the Rural Credit Bureau, and initiated an extensive reorganization of state government. Minnesota voters responded positively to this program. After winning over Olson by a comparatively narrow margin in 1924, Christianson was triumphantly re-elected two years later and again in 1928. Obviously the voters responded more positively to Christianson than Preus.[19]

During Christianson's third term, however, a number of adverse circumstances undermined Republican vitality. The first shock of the Great Depression discredited the Hoover administration, intimations of irregularity in the management of several executive departments diminished confidence in Republican incorruptibility, and internal dissension disrupted party unity. In 1930 Christianson failed to wrest the senatorial nomination from the incumbent, Thomas D. Schall, whose narrow victory in the fall election appalled rather than elated many Republicans. The *Minneapolis Journal*, for example, backed Einar Hoidale, Schall's Democratic opponent. The race for governor intensified GOP gloom. The Republican candidate, Ray P. Chase, whose conspicuous participation in the loyalty crusade ten years earlier was vividly remembered by German-Americans as well as by old Nonpartisan Leaguers, lost overwhelmingly to Olson. Republican fortunes remained at a low ebb for the next eight years.[20]

In one important respect, Republican and Farmer-Labor history ran parallel through the 1920s and 1930s. Both coalitions had an image problem: essentially, "Townleyism" and "McGeeism." Their efforts to deal with the problem reinforce the parallel. Basically, both sought to counter accusations that they were extremist by moving toward a center based on the style and values of prewar progressivism.

This strategy helped the Preus administration rehabilitate Republican fortunes in the early 1920s. A similar if less successful effort was evident within the Farmer-Labor movement. The selection of David Evans as candidate for governor in 1918 was clearly a concession to moderation, as was the endorsement of Henrik Shipstead for the same office two years later.

A practicing dentist, Shipstead was neither an Equity member, a trade unionist, nor a Socialist, the usual access routes into the Nonpartisan League movement. His moderately reformist political outlook had been shaped in part by the Scandinavian Populist milieu of Kandiyohi County, where he was born in 1881, and in part by a deep admiration for Governor John Peter Altgeld of Illinois, developed while he was a student in the dental school of Northwestern University. After establishing a practice in Glenwood, the young dentist became active in civic affairs and politics. He served for a time as mayor of Glenwood, participated in the 1914 insurgent Republican crusade against the Smith machine, and two years later won election to the Minnesota House of Representatives.[21]

According to Martin Ross, Shipstead's admiring biographer, the relationship of the future senator to the Nonpartisan League was that of a sympathetic "bystander" until November, 1917, when an episode connected with the loyalty crusade edged him toward involvement. A group of Pope County farmers had engaged a hall in Glenwood for the use of a Nonpartisan League organizer. Under pressure from local business leaders and the county Public Safety Commission, the owner of the hall canceled his agreement with the farmers. The latter then consulted Shipstead who rented the hall in his own name, made it available to the organizer, and personally intervened when a mob forced the visitor to leave town. Ross adds that Shipstead's initiative on this occasion aroused sufficient hostility against him to undermine his dental practice. It also pushed him into the mainstream of Nonpartisan League politics. With league backing, he contested the renomination of Congressman Volstead in 1918. Although unsuccessful by a narrow margin, this venture pointed up Shipstead's qualities as a campaigner, thereby laying the basis for his subsequent political career.[22]

In campaigning for the governorship Shipstead subordinated the Nonpartisan League's public ownership program to such themes as iron ore taxation, the Public Safety Commission's assault on civil liberties, the need to limit use of injunctions in labor disputes, the malpractices of Wall Street, and the unhappy consequences of American participation in the war. When he ran against Kellogg in 1922, Shipstead found this line of attack even more rewarding. The depression of 1921 had intensified agricultural discontent, disillusionment with the war was deeper than ever, and Kellogg symbolized the influence of big business in politics along with zealous support of the war. Both in 1920 and two years later, Shipstead's rhetoric was sharp and militant, but it belonged in the Populist-progressive rather than the Socialist tradition. Unmistakably it called for a redress of grievances within the existing system, not a radical restructuring of society.[23]

The same pattern marked the adaptation of Shipstead, Kvale, Wefald, and Magnus Johnson to their responsibilities in Washington. Arrival of the four Farmer-Laborite men in the capital aroused curious interest, but it was clear immediately that they did not propose to function as an isolated group of carping radicals. Instead they became respected members of the powerful farm bloc within congress that sponsored such legislation as the McNary-Haugen bill which introduced the concept of price parity for agriculture, opposed Coolidge's fiscal policies, and in general helped to maintain progressivism as a vital force in national politics.[24] Shipstead in particular achieved high prestige; for nearly two decades Minnesota office seekers grasped his coattails at election time.

Magnus Johnson, whose rustic style and earthy speech contrasted sharply with Shipstead's unruffled poise and dignity, also surpassed original expectations. During the campaign of 1923, Senator George H. Moses of New Hampshire had quipped: "If Magnus Johnson goes to the Senate, there'll be another vacancy in it. When [Senator Henry Cabot] Lodge hears him speak, he'll drop dead." Johnson soon confounded such prophets. Shortly after the new senator took office, a prominent journalist wrote: "A wide gulf separates the real Magnus Johnson from the Magnus Johnson of popular opinion. . . . He *can* carry on a conversation in an undertone. . . . He knows a lot about what's wrong with the farmers."[25]

Unhappily for continued Farmer-Labor success, a crisis within the movement that tended to undermine the reassuring impression created by Shipstead and his colleagues developed in 1923.[26] The precipitating factor was a conviction held by many Farmer-Laborites that their organizational structures should recognize the permanance of third-party activity. By 1923 three entities shared status within the movement: the Farmers' Nonpartisan League, the Working Peoples' Nonpartisan Political League, and the so-called legal Farmer-Labor party, which in accordance with state law was headed by a committee selected by victorious Farmer-Labor candidates in the 1922 primary. It was suggested that the two leagues merge into a Farmer-Labor Federation, whose function would be to support and direct the legal party. Townley, who retired from leadership of the farmers' league early in 1922, stoutly opposed such a merger. So did Thomas Van Lear and the *Minneapolis Star*, the movement's principal journalistic organ. William Mahoney, president of the working people's league, and Henry Teigan, executive secretary of the farmers' league, led the drive for federation.

The 1924 joint convention of the two leagues, held in St. Cloud in March, favored federation. Granting a few concessions to the minority faction failed to promote universal happiness. A remnant of the farmers' league vainly attempted until 1926 to maintain a separate existence, while a larger number accepted the new federation with serious reservations. Socialists and the radical wing of labor, it was feared, would henceforth dominate the movement. The rise to prominence of the Communist issue in 1924 nourished and reinforced such fears.

While working for establishment of the Minnesota Farmer-Labor Federation, Mahoney and Teigan also had been involved in the affairs of the national Federated Farmer-Labor party, whose leaders aspired to sponsor La Follette for the presidency in 1924. However, many La Follette supporters remained aloof from this group, basically because Communist participation in its management was clearly apparent. Mahoney and Teigan were less circumspect. At their urging the St. Cloud convention approved plans for a joint Minnesota Farmer-Labor and Federated Farmer-Labor convention to be held in St. Paul on June 17 for the ostensible purpose of nominating La Follette and possibly also to lay the basis for a permanent national third party.

A chain of disastrous repercussions followed. Shortly before the convention met, La Follette issued an open letter dissociating his candidacy from it and calling attention to its Communist tint. Convention deliberations produced further distress for Mahoney and Teigan: attendance was far below estimates; the Communist-dominated majority humiliated Mahoney by defeating him for permanent chairman; La Follette was repudiated, not as a response to his open letter, but because the Communist party had just abandoned the tactic of seeking coalitions with non-Communist left-wingers; and a pair of obscure radicals who later withdrew in favor of the Communist ticket were nominated for president and vice president. Subsequently, the convention sponsored by the Conference for Progressive Political Action which met in Cleveland, Ohio, on July 4 to tender La Follette an acceptable nomination, not only refused to seat Mahoney but also reprimanded him for his "depraved" associations. At the same time, La Follette declined to run in Minnesota under the Farmer-Labor label, although a loose co-ordination between his campaign and that of the Minnesota Farmer-Labor ticket was achieved.

Conceivably political observers both in 1924 and later have overestimated the impact of the June 17 episode. Improvement of economic conditions during the summer worked powerfully for the GOP, and Christianson was a formidable candidate. Moreover, the Farmer-Labor showing was reasonably creditable. Olson, the candidate for governor, ran ahead of La Follette by 26,000 votes and lost to Christianson by less than 40,000. Johnson lost to Schall by the narrow margin of 10,000 votes. A Republican victory of such modest proportions could well have been won without intrusion of the Communist issue into the campaign.[27]

Nevertheless, Minnesota third-party leaders attributed prime importance to the fiasco. The 1925 state convention formally abolished the Farmer-Labor Federation, replacing it with a structure called the Farmer-Labor Association. In most respects the new organization was modeled on its predecessor, but there was one important difference: the association excluded Communists from membership. Farmer-Labor spokesmen also cultivated a moderate approach to public policy issues without formally repudiating the public ownership program written into the association's constitution. The movement, it appeared, "was seeking to consolidate its political position within the framework of a capitalistic system which it tacitly accepted."[28]

The voters of Minnesota did not immediately reward this strategy of moderation. Not only did Christianson triumph decisively in both 1926 and 1928, but Wefald lost his congressional seat in the former year, and the Farmer-Labor bloc in the state legislature dwindled. However, when both the national and Minnesota GOP began to slip in popular esteem during Christianson's last term, the Farmer-Labor party could plausibly claim an identification with old-fashioned progressivism that rendered it an acceptable alternative to the party in power.

Olson's campaign for the governorship in 1930 jealously guarded this claim. The platform drafted at the state convention under the candidate's careful supervision combined a number of mildly reformist planks, the most drastic being one calling for public works to ameliorate unemployment, with vigorous advocacy of regional interests like the St. Lawrence Seaway and the McNary-Haugen bill, plus a strong rhetorical commitment to such hallowed causes as tax reduction. In defending his innocuous document before the convention, Olson remarked: "As I regard the political situation in Minnesota it is not up to the Farmer Labor party to introduce new and unique ideas of government. It is up to this party, as I see it, to restore the fundamentals of good government."[29]

The platform set the tone for the entire campaign. Confident that the radical wing of his party would not defect, Olson zealously courted the support of groups traditionally susceptible to the old progressive appeal. To small businessmen he promised legislative action against chain stores and chain banking. He assured good government advocates that his appointments would be based on merit, not partisan affiliation. He sought rapport with farm audiences by reiterating his commitment to the principle of farm parity. Coupled with Olson's personal magnetism, the virtual noncandidacy of Edward Indrehus, the Democratic nominee, and the handicaps burdening Ray Chase, the Republican contender, this strategy produced an impressive victory in November. Olson won by a plurality of nearly 185,000 votes and in the process carried all but five of the state's 87 counties.[30]

The caution and moderation practiced in the 1930 campaign also marked the early stages of Olson's governorship. At the outset, if not later, administration patronage policy commanded more approval among old civil service reformers than among Farmer-Labor partisans. The first inaugural message called for several important reforms, including tighter regulation of security sales, a state-wide old-age pension law, and the banning of injunctions in labor disputes, but it studiously avoided "references to the infirmities of the capitalist system." Since conservative majorities controlled both houses, the failure of the legislature to honor most of these recommendations was attributable more to partisanship than to their inherent unacceptability.[31]

In terms of tangible legislative achievement, the second Olson term was more productive than either the first or third. The legislature of 1933, whose lower house was controlled by a coalition of Farmer-Laborites and liberals from the other two parties, performed creditably notwithstanding an ongoing battle between the governor and leaders of the conservative Senate. Among other things, it established Minnesota's income tax, enacted the famous mortgage moratorium law; passed a number of important labor bills (including bans on yellow dog contracts and on the use of court injunctions and a statute limiting employment of women in industrial jobs to a fifty-four-hour week); outlawed further power development and logging operations on state lands in the border lakes area; created thirteen state forests on tax-delinquent lands in northern Minnesota; and appropriated relatively generous sums for unemployment relief.[32] Although impressive, this program could scarcely be called radical. To discover within it any hint of the co-operative commonwealth blueprinted in the constitution of the Farmer-Labor Association would require an extraordinarily fertile imagination.

Other facets of administration policy deviated more sharply from tradition. In responding to the Minneapolis truck drivers' strike of 1934, the governor pursued an unprecedented course disturbing to many middle-class progressives. As his biographer, George H. Mayer, writes, "Olson forthrightly endorsed labor organization and sought to implement the collective bargaining provisions of the N.I.R.A. [National Industrial Recovery Act] long before responsible national leaders took a definite stand . . . [and] helped orient people to the revolutionary concept that labor as well as management deserved legal protection of its rights." The long-range consequences, Mayer believes, were important. In his opinion Olson "paved the way for more cautious leaders to pass the Wagner Act."[33]

If Olson's labor policies aligned him with the second wave of New Deal reform rather than with conventional Minnesota progressivism, his rhetoric from 1934 until his death two years later tended to place him to the left of both. This tendency corresponded to a radicalization of the Farmer-Labor movement that expressed itself fully in the party platform of 1934, a document proclaiming the failure of capitalism and the advent of a co-operative commonwealth.[34] That such a trend developed is not surprising. The innovative spirit and permissive political milieu of the early New Deal years encouraged dedicated leftists to believe that deliverance was at hand, not necessarily from Roosevelt, but conceivably under the auspices of a new national third party.

The extent to which Olson's apparent swing to the left reflected inner personal conviction is uncertain. Mayer insists that the famous governor was "more a rebel than a radical," a pragmatist who rejected the ideological approach to politics. Upon discovering the heavy political liabilities created by the 1934 platform — the content of which had been strongly influenced by a militant Olson speech to the convention that adopted it — the governor attempted the extraordinary feat of interpreting it as a reformist rather than a radical manifesto. At the same time he continued to resist efforts by radicals to use the Minnesota Farmer-Labor organization as a base for national third-party action. He often verbally endorsed the third-party concept, but he maintained a reasonably warm rapport with the New Deal

and consistently refused to break with the president, a stance that helped
frustrate an attempt by co-operative commonwealth advocates to launch
a third party in 1936.[35]

Whatever the depth of Olson's commitment to radicalism, the 1934 election carried intimations of an adverse voter reaction to the leftward swing.
Massive defections in rural and small town Minnesota, including German-
American areas, reduced the Olson plurality by more than 100,000 votes
compared with 1932. In 1936, however, several circumstances combined
to reverse temporarily the decline and produce the largest Farmer-Labor
vote in history. United with the overwhelming psychological effect of Olson's death from cancer on August 22 were a less provocative platform,
withdrawal of the Democratic candidates for governor and United States
senator, and Roosevelt's decisive sweep of the state. Elmer A. Benson,
who had served as commissioner of banking in the Olson administration,
won the governorship; Ernest Lundeen triumphed over Theodore Christianson in the race for the Senate; five Farmer-Labor congressmen were
elected; and a liberal coalition was able to organize the state House of
Representatives.[36]

Two years later this triumph was abruptly reversed, and the Farmer-Labor
party suffered a catastrophic defeat from which it never recovered. After
winning a narrow victory over Hjalmar Petersen in the 1938 primary —
a bitter contest that shattered what remained of party unity — Benson lost
the final election to Harold Stassen, the thirty-one-year-old Republican
contender, by a margin exceeding 290,000 votes. The GOP also succeeded
in retiring four of the five Farmer-Labor congressmen, and conservatives
won decisive control of the state legislature. The Farmer-Labor era had
come to an end.[37]

Accepted interpretations of Farmer-Labor history may well have
exaggerated Governor Benson's personal responsibility for the disaster. The
marked difference between Olson and Benson is aptly expressed in an
often-repeated tale, possibly apocryphal but nevertheless illuminating. It
tells of a businessman discussing militant Farmer-Labor rhetoric shortly
after the 1936 election. He complained that "Floyd Olson used to say
these things; but this son of a bitch [Benson] believes them."[38] Olson's
flexible leadership might have reduced the dimensions of the defeat suffered
in 1938, but whether it could have surmounted the critical problems facing
the Farmer-Labor movement seems doubtful.

There was by then a widespread impression among Minnesota voters
that a corrupt political machine had achieved domination of the Farmer-Labor

movement either for the sake of patronage or for advancement of radical goals. Allied to this was a suspicion that the Farmer-Labor party was moving dangerously to the left — a serious handicap in a year of conservative reaction such as 1938. Both problems were to some extent legacies from the preceding administration. Olson had failed to resolve an ongoing conflict between a faction that wanted an appointment policy based on merit and the so-called "spoilsmen" who insisted that state jobs be allocated to deserving Farmer-Laborites. The movement's radical image, already reactivated by the 1934 platform, was further exaggerated by a nationwide Communist effort to infiltrate organizations like the Farmer-Labor party. This was launched in 1935 as part of Moscow's "popular front" strategy and had achieved high visibility by 1938. It not only intensified the image problem but further disrupted the already fragmented Farmer-Labor coalition.[39]

Other and less obvious factors reinforced the adverse tide. Since World War I party spokesmen had capitalized on resentments provoked by the loyalty crusade and pointed up the staunchly neutralist stand of the movement, but by 1938 such appeals had lost much of their force. Not only had memories of 1918 dimmed considerably, but a number of radical Farmer-Laborites, moved by intense hostility to German Nazism and Italian Fascism and a deep sympathy for the Loyalist cause in the Spanish civil war, were beginning to re-examine their neutralist premises. In comparison to other issues, the impact of foreign policy may have been minor, but it is interesting to note that from 1936 to 1938, Farmer-Labor fortunes declined more precipitously in German-American areas than in the state at large.[40]

The emergence of Harold Stassen placed a final seal of doom on the Farmer-Labor cause. Even a reactionary Republican might have won the governorship in 1938, but Stassen could not be so classified. As chairman of the Minnesota Young Republicans he had helped revitalize that organization as a force working for liberalization of the GOP. He won the gubernatorial nomination in a primary battle that placed him in opposition to the party's established leaders, who at the outset refused to take his candidacy seriously. According to Naftalin, the youthful Republican contender "appropriated the symbols of the Farmer-Labor movement . . . promised assurance of the rights of organized labor and programs of assistance to the farmers . . . [and] pledged active state government intervention in many areas of social welfare." This approach to public policy helped Stassen win the election and set the tone of his administration and those of his immediate successors, Thye and Youngdahl. It also contributed to the maintenance of Republican supremacy in Minnesota state government until 1954.[41]

The history of the state's politics between the two world wars suggests that the old progressive ethos retained a tenacious hold on the Minnesota mind. During those years political success for both Republican and Farmer-Labor parties depended largely on the ability of their leaders to establish a credible association with the traditions inherited from the progressive era. Whenever the GOP drifted perceptibly toward Old Guard conservatism, Republican election prospects dimmed. Similarly, the Farmer-Labor party courted disaster when it permitted the movement's radical tendencies to become overly conspicuous. Whatever may have been true elsewhere, in Minnesota the progressive impulse was weakened only temporarily during the period of conservative reaction following the first war.

There were, however, two significant breaks in continuity between the earlier years and the postwar era. The later period exhibited a stronger tendency toward polarization of opinion than its predecessor. Although the excesses of 1918 and 1920 were never surpassed, Republican and Farmer-Labor exchanges during the campaigns of 1924, 1934, and 1938 went beyond exaggerated rhetoric to implications that a cosmic struggle between good and evil was being waged in the political arena. Fortunately, the World War II period did not witness a repetition of 1917–18. However, the break between President Harry S Truman and Henry A. Wallace on the issue of American policy toward the Soviet Union, which culminated in Wallace's bid for the presidency on a third-party ticket in 1948, had disruptive repercussions within the recently formed Minnesota Democratic-Farmer-Labor party. The struggle between Wallace supporters led by Elmer Benson and an anti-Communist faction organized by Hubert H. Humphrey ended in victory for the latter and a virtual elimination of the Benson people from participation in the DFL.[42]

The second break in continuity was a sharpening of the role of partisanship in Minnesota politics. On the organizational level, Nonpartisan League efforts to capture the GOP encouraged Republican leaders to run a tighter ship. Managers of the Farmer-Labor movement also assigned high priority to organization; insofar as its purpose was to establish and maintain party discipline, the Minnesota Farmer-Labor Association resembled a conventional political machine. On the voter level, too, party affiliation apparently assumed more importance than it had enjoyed during the progressive era, although many citizens continued to proclaim their independence of party ties. The rise of the Farmer-Labor movement aroused strong emotion, a circumstance tending to reinforce loyalties on both sides.

Assertions that the Farmer-Labor party "disintegrated" following Benson's defeat in 1938 tend to obscure the fact that a solid core of third-party enthusiasts, accounting for more than one-third of the total electorate, voted the Farmer-Labor gubernatorial ticket in 1940 and again in 1942.[43] To the satisfaction of the politicians who negotiated the Democratic-Farmer-Labor merger of 1944, the bulk of these voters along with a considerably smaller bloc of Democratic loyalists transferred their allegiance to the new DFL party. Success at the polls did not follow immediately, although Roosevelt carried the state in 1944. Within ten years after the merger, however, Minnesota politics operated under a flourishing two-party system for the first time in the state's history. This development was attributable partly to the effective leadership of such DFL luminaries as Humphrey, Orville L. Freeman, and Eugene J. McCarthy, and partly to equalization of DFL and GOP competitive advantage following Youngdahl's resignation of the governorship in 1951 to accept a federal judgeship. A quantitative political study made by John H. Fenton found by 1960 an "overwhelming majority of the [Minnesota] voters associating themselves rather definitely with one of the two parties."[44]

Although the reactivation of partisanship in Minnesota mocked a few prophets of the first progressive generation, it did not signify either enthronement of machine politics or a drift toward blind party loyalty. The open primary — a sacrosanct institution in Minnesota — together with comprehensive statutory regulation of party activity could be circumvented and perverted, but they discouraged the crasser forms of political manipulation. So did the stringent civil service law enacted during Stassen's administration. The character of the state's electorate offered an even more substantial guarantee. Fenton's investigation revealed that, relatively speaking, Minnesota's voting public was keenly aware of social and political problems, committed to citizen participation in public affairs, and "better attuned to the performance of its candidates than [the electorate] in most states." These traits, according to Fenton, encouraged both the DFL and Republican parties to pursue an "issue-oriented" (as distinguished from a job-oriented) course.[45]

The profile emerging from Fenton's study points up the enduring impact of progressivism on the political culture of Minnesota. Whether the progressive movement itself was a resounding success is another question. Certainly it changed the course of American public policy to a significant extent. On the federal level it broadened governmental authority and responsibility in such areas as trust regulation, transportation, conservation, agriculture, public health, and education. National progressivism also helped sponsor four amendments to the United States Constitution — the income tax, direct election of United States senators, prohibition, and woman suffrage — which bear a relationship to the progressive era similar to that of the thirteenth, fourteenth, and fifteenth amendments to the reconstruction period. It is worth noting parenthetically that Congressman Andrew Volstead's authorship of the law implementing the eighteenth amendment established a putative link between Minnesota and prohibition that created an exaggerated impression of the state's commitment to the dry cause.

A second era of reform under the New Deal modified some of progressivism's approaches, abandoned at least one (prohibition), expanded others, and instituted a number of new programs, particularly in labor relations and social welfare. Although the two movements were sufficiently distinct to sustain a spirited argument on the question of whether the discontinuities separating them were more impressive than the continuities linking them, both operated on the premise that enlightened governmental intervention could correct the deficiencies inherent in modern capitalism, thereby obviating the need for a revolutionary change in the existing socio-economic system.

Action on the state level during the progressive era paralleled that taken by the federal government. The program adopted in Minnesota, if less well known than its Wisconsin counterpart, was fairly typical. Among other things, it theoretically democratized and purified the political process by instituting the direct primary and a strict code regulating campaign practices; liberated the legislature from onerous restrictions on the power to tax; subjected corporate enterprise to heavier taxation; extended state regulation of transportation, communication, banking, insurance, and public utilities; created a workmen's compensation system; tightened the legal protection afforded women and children; anticipated prohibition by adopting county option; broadened the scope of state services in such areas as highways, education, and agriculture; and worked for increased efficiency and professionalism in public administration. A number of cherished progressive goals, notably the grant to municipalities of full authority to regulate their public utilities, and the initiative, referendum, and recall, were never realized in Minnesota. Others, including occupation and royalty levies on iron ore and a state income tax, were achieved in the years immediately following the progressive period.

Minnesota progressivism also served as an educator — a role that may have been more important than the specific public policies which it launched. Its rhetoric reinforced a deep midwestern distrust of eastern seaboard capitalism (but not capitalism *per se*) and heightened sensitivity to the real and imagined evils of machine politics. Since neither Wall Street nor the country's political leadership were beyond reproach, these attitudes were not wholly

irrational. Unfortunately, however, the progressive mind occasionally responded to complex situations simplistically, attributing society's problems
to some monstrous conspiratorial force associated either with the "money
power" or the demons of the far left, Socialism and Communism. More
positively, progressivism also encouraged acceptance of such values and
beliefs as the compatability of liberty and equality, the capacity of a democratic society to order its own affairs, the moral obligation of citizens
to participate in government, and confidence in the basic rationality of
humanity at large.

Until the late 1960s most Americans possessing a sense of history tended
to assume that some variation of the reform tradition created by progressivism
and the New Deal could successfully meet the problems of modern industrial
society. In 1971 this optimistic confidence had been severely shaken. By
then virtually every claim made on behalf of the two movements appeared
vulnerable to challenge.

A case in point was the cause of women's rights. Fifty years after passage
of the nineteenth amendment, no one could seriously contend that the expectations generated by it had been realized. In Minnesota hopes had soared
immediately after suffrage was achieved. In 1922 Anna Dickey Olesen
became the Democratic candidate for United States senator, and though
outrun by Kellogg and Shipstead, she waged a highly professional campaign
that polled a vote far exceeding the rest of the Democratic ticket. In the
same year four women won election to the Minnesota House of Representatives. One of these, Myrtle A. Cain of Minneapolis, was a crusading
reformer who coupled advocacy of labor legislation with an effort "to
abrogate all the remaining common law disabilities of women . . . [and]
to restore to socalled illegitimate children these inherent rights now
denied them." On the grounds of opposition to "all special favors to any
class or sex," she voted against a bill requiring the governor to appoint
a woman to the Industrial Commission.[46]

These women failed to establish a trend in the state. Only a handful
ever followed Cain to the legislature; their voices were muted, and by
1971 their number had dwindled to one. The only woman elected to national
office was Coya Knutson, who represented the ninth district in congress
for two terms (1955–59). The Minnesota League of Women Voters wielded
considerable influence on policy making, and a few women achieved prominence in the affairs of both the DFL and Republican parties, but the

highest elective offices remained a male monopoly in Minnesota as elsewhere.

Other disappointing realities overshadowed the complaints of women's rights advocates. Most fundamental, perhaps, was the awesome concentration of wealth and power among a few corporations. Seventy years after the progressives declared war on monopoly, and despite the winning of many battles, the centralization of economic control in American life exceeded the worst fears of the early trust busters. The regulatory bodies created to protect the public interest were revealed in many cases to have yielded to this concentration of pressure and to have become in fact arms of the very industries they were intended to police. Critics claimed to find a consistent pattern of collusion between government officials and business leaders. Moreover, disclosure that scores of the most affluent Americans paid no income tax belied claims that implementation of the sixteenth amendment had redistributed the tax burden on the basis of ability to pay.

The fears of agrarian progressives seemed realized in the diminishing number of family farms and the steady migration of unemployed agricultural workers to the nation's overcrowded urban areas. Associated with this was the breakdown in existing welfare programs — most of which had originated under the New Deal but were clearly anticipated by the social justice forces of the progressive movement. Not only did these programs fail to meet the material needs of the poor, but the very professionalization of social work so earnestly sought by the generation of Jane Addams seemed to have produced a paternalistic bureaucracy which all too often resisted change and opposed attempts by the poor to assume control of their own lives. Meanwhile, spokesmen for minority groups stridently rejected the entire American reform tradition, charging that its so-called humanitarianism concealed a design to rob nonwhite groups of their racial and cultural identity.

The plight of American cities further undermined faith in the nation's reform tradition. Notwithstanding the innovations in municipal government promoted by the progressives and the urban planning and redevelopment programs pioneered by the New Deal, deterioration within the larger metropolitan centers had reached a point where some observers questioned whether the American city was not beyond redemption. Ironically, it was possible to argue that some cities still operating under classical machine control (Chicago being a prime example) were relatively more manageable than those whose political culture had been influenced by urban progressivism.

Temperance forces had retired in defeat after the failure of nationwide prohibition, and middle-class morality now faced a further challenge in the widespread proliferation of drug use. Once again American society invoked the progressive tradition by making personal abstinence a legal issue and, as before, its effectiveness appeared doubtful.

The euphoria of old conservationists who believed that Theodore Roosevelt and Gifford Pinchot had erected permanent safeguards against despoliation of the environment was mocked by a pollution crisis that threatened the very existence of industrial society. Critics pointed out with irony that the Tennessee Valley Authority, showpiece of the New Deal, had in fact encouraged destructive strip mining of the Kentucky hills in order to produce cheap power for the South's new industries.[47]

The trauma of American foreign policy also was shaking confidence in the country's reform tradition. "Defense of the Free World," the rationale justifying American global involvement in the years following World War II, was a logical extension of the Wilsonian crusade to "make the world safe for democracy" and Franklin Roosevelt's proclaimed determination to nourish the Four Freedoms "everywhere in the world." Although progressives of the old La Follette persuasion had vehemently rejected this definition of the American mission, most liberals came to accept it as a projection of progressivism to the rest of the world. By 1971, however, disenchantment with American globalism was rapidly accelerating. Either the pursuit of an objective like self-determination throughout the world was hopelessly utopian (a classical conservative premise which surprisingly few American conservatives argued) or progressive idealism had been distorted and rationalized to serve other ends. In any case American foreign policy was undergoing a painful reappraisal.

Inevitably, historians also re-examined accepted interpretations of the progressive era, analyzed its darker side, and produced less flattering and possibly more accurate portraits of it. They also revealed the extent to which its assumptions still permeated the thought and attitudes of concerned Americans. One question of supreme importance remained for the future to answer: was the reform tradition pioneered by progressivism and brought to fuller development in the New Deal era applicable to the crises of the 1970s? Or did American society have to find new and more radical responses to the revolutionary challenges of the late twentieth century?

Reference Notes

Chapter 1—THE RISE AND DECLINE OF AMERICAN PROGRESSIVISM—pages 1–8

[1] The literature on progressivism is voluminous and the range of interpretation broad. Two works in the New American Nation Series that span the period are George E. Mowry, *The Era of Theodore Roosevelt and the Birth of Modern America* (New York, 1958) and Arthur S. Link, *Woodrow Wilson and the Progressive Era, 1910–1917* (New York, 1954). Other works dealing interpretatively with progressivism include Richard Hofstadter, *The Age of Reform: From Bryan to F. D. R.* (New York, 1965); Robert H. Wiebe, *The Search for Order, 1877–1920* (New York, 1967); Gabriel Kolko, *The Triumph of Conservatism: A Reinterpretation of American History, 1900–1916* (Glencoe, Ill., 1963). All of these volumes carry extensive bibliographies or bibliographic essays.

[2] See Charles Forcey, *The Crossroads of Liberalism: Croly, Weyl, Lippmann, and the Progressive Era, 1900–1925*, xiii–xxix (New York, 1961), and Daniel Levine, *Varieties of Reform Thought* (Madison, Wis., 1964).

[3] Mowry, *The Era of Theodore Roosevelt*, 96. See also Robert H. Wiebe, *Businessmen and Reform: A Study of the Progressive Movement* (Cambridge, 1962).

[4] J. Joseph Huthmacher, "Urban Liberalism and the Age of Reform," in *Mississippi Valley Historical Review*, 49:231–241 (September, 1962). See also Huthmacher, *Senator Robert F. Wagner and the Rise of Urban Liberalism* (New York, 1968).

[5] For an interesting analysis of Jane Addams as a type, see Christopher Lasch, *The New Radicalism in America*, 3–37 (New York, 1967). See also p. 166 for a quotation revealing the attitude of many settlement workers toward the foreign born.

[6] George E. Mowry, *The California Progressives*, 92–94 (Chicago, 1963); Joseph G. Rayback, *A History of American Labor*, 213–226 (New York, 1966).

[7] Rayford W. Logan, *The Betrayal of the Negro, from Rutherford B. Hayes to Woodrow Wilson*, 341–392 (New York, 1965); David Noble, *The Progressive Mind*, 81–116 (Chicago, 1970); Gilbert Osofsky, "Progressivism and the Negro, New York, 1900–1915," in *American Quarterly*, 16:153–168 (Summer, 1964).

[8] William L. O'Neill, *Everyone Was Brave, the Rise and Fall of Feminism in America*, 49–77 (Chicago, 1969).

[9] Many regional and state histories of progressivism have been published. In addition to Mowry's work on California, cited above, the better known include: Richard Abrams, *Conservatism in a Progressive Age: Massachusetts Politics, 1900–1912* (Cambridge, 1964); Robert S. Maxwell, *La Follette and the Rise of the Progressives in Wisconsin* (Madison, 1956); Ransom E. Noble, *New Jersey Progressivism before Wilson* (Princeton, 1946); Russel B. Nye, *Midwestern Progressive Politics: A Historical Study of Its Origins and Development 1870–1950* (East Lansing, Mich., 1951); Hoyt L. Warner, *Progressivism in Ohio, 1897–1917* (Columbus, 1964).

[10] Link, *Wilson and the Progressive Era*, 79, 223–251.

[11] Forcey, *Crossroads of Liberalism*, 221–263; Lasch, *New Radicalism*, 181–193.

[12] For example, in condemning William Jennings Bryan for his neutralism in 1915, Walter Hines Page, U.S. ambassador to Great Britain, wrote: "Bryan . . . worked against national financial credit. Now he works against national honor. He has organized ignorance into treason." Quoted in Arthur S. Link, *Wilson: The Struggle for Neutrality, 1914–1915*, 427 (Princeton, 1960).

[13] Henry G. Teigan to Mrs. August Baumgartner, July 3, 1917, National Nonpartisan League Papers, in the Minnesota Historical Society.

[14] For a persuasive analysis of the impact of World War I on progressivism, see Forcey, *Crossroads of Liberalism*, 263–286. See also Lasch, *New Radicalism*, 193–250.

[15] On the postwar reaction, see Robert K. Murray, *Red Scare: A Study of National Hysteria 1919–1920* (Minneapolis, 1955).

[16] Stanley A. Cobden, *A. Mitchell Palmer: Politician* (New York, 1963); Robert L. Friedheim, *The Seattle General Strike*, especially 20–22 (Seattle, 1964).

[17] David A. Shannon, *Between the Wars: America, 1919–1941*, 3–33 (Boston, 1965).

[18] For a study of the relationship between progressivism and the New Deal, see Otis L. Graham, *An Encore for Reform: The Old Progressives and the New Deal* (New York, 1967).

Chapter 2 — THE RISE OF THE PROGRESSIVE MOVEMENT IN MINNESOTA — 1899-1909 — pages 9–21

[1] Theodore C. Blegen and Philip D. Jordan, *With Various Voices: Recordings of North Star Life*, 345 (St. Paul, 1949).

[2] John Lind, *Biennial Message to the Legislature* (St. Paul, 1899).

[3] Solon J. Buck, *The Granger Movement* (Cambridge, 1913); Martin Ridge, *Ignatius Donnelly: The Portrait of a Politician*, 149–164 (Chicago, 1962). For Kelley's early life see Rhoda R. Gilman and Patricia Smith, "Oliver Hudson Kelley: Minnesota Pioneer, 1849–1868," in *Minnesota History*, 40:330–338 (Fall, 1967).

[4] On the Farmers Alliance see Donald F. Warner, "Prelude to Populism," in *Minnesota History*, 32:129–146.

[5] *St. Paul Daily Pioneer Press*, September 2, 1886.

[6] The literature of Populism, like that of progressivism, is voluminous. The pioneer work is John D. Hicks, *The Populist Revolt: A History of the Farmers' Alliance and the People's Party* (Minneapolis, 1931). It remains indispensable. Later works include several chapters in Hofstadter, *Age of Reform;* Norman Pollack, *The Populist Response to Industrial America* (Cambridge, 1962); Walter T. K. Nugent, *The Tolerant Populists: Kansas Populism and Nativism* (Chicago, 1963); Robert F. Durden, *The Climax of Populism: The Election of 1896* (Lexington, Ky., 1965).

[7] On Bryan and the presidential election of 1896 see Durden, *Climax of Populism;* Stanley Jones, *The Presidential Election of 1896* (Madison, Wis., 1964); Paul W. Glad, *McKinley, Bryan and the People* (New York, 1964) and *The Trumpet Soundeth: William Jennings Bryan and His Democracy, 1896–1912* (Lincoln, Neb., 1960); Baolo E. Coletta, *William Jennings Bryan. I: Political Evangelist, 1860–1908* (Lincoln, Neb., 1964).

[8] *Minnesota Legislative Manual*, 1897, p. 416.

[9] A comprehensive history of Minnesota Populism remains to be published. The story can be reconstructed in part by consulting Hicks, *Populist Revolt*, and Ridge, *Ignatius Donnelly*. See also Carl H. Chrislock, "The Politics of Protest in Minnesota, 1890 to 1901: From Populism to Progressivism," Ph.D. dissertation, University of Minnesota, 1955.

[10] On Lind's career, see George M. Stephenson, *John Lind of Minnesota* (Minneapolis, 1935).

[11] William W. Folwell, *A History of Minnesota*, 3:242 (St. Paul, 1969).

¹² Folwell, *Minnesota*, 3:489–499; Stephenson, *John Lind*, 97–101; Harlan P. Hall, *Observations, Being More or Less a History of Political Contests in Minnesota from 1849 to 1904*, 242–245 (St. Paul, 1904).

¹³ *Legislative Manual*, 1897, p. 486; Stephenson, *John Lind*, 105–129.

¹⁴ Stephenson, *John Lind*, 140–158.

¹⁵ Quoted in Stephenson, *John Lind*, 145. Lind's acceptance speech was carried in full by the *Penny Press* (Minneapolis), October 11, 1898.

¹⁶ *Legislative Manual*, 1899, p. 500.

¹⁷ *Minneapolis Journal*, April 11, 18, 1899.

¹⁸ Stephenson, *John Lind*, 150, 178.

¹⁹ In the campaign of 1900 Lind continued his attack on "imperialism." See Stephenson, *John Lind*, 180.

²⁰ *Legislative Manual*, 1901, p. 532. For Van Sant's career, see James H. Baker, *Lives of the Governors of Minnesota*, 399–402 (*Minnesota Historical Collections*, 1908); Folwell, *Minnesota*, 3:256; Charles B. Cheney, *The Story of Minnesota Politics*, 7–10 (Minneapolis, 1947).

²¹ For a graphic account of the Northern Securities case, see Walter Lord, *The Good Years: From 1900 to the First World War*, 62–75 (Bantam edition, New York, 1960). A more scholarly treatment is B. H. Meyer, "A History of the Northern Securities Case," in University of Wisconsin, *Bulletins—Economics and Political Science Series*, 1:215–350 (Madison, 1904–06).

²² *St. Paul Pioneer Press*, January 11, 1902, p. 6; *Rock County Herald* (Luverne), November 29, 1902, p. 4. See also *Minneapolis Tribune*, January 2, 30, 1902; *Minneapolis Journal*, January 20, 1902; *St. Paul Dispatch*, January 22, 1902.

²³ Baker, *Lives of the Governors*, 410–413; Folwell, *Minnesota*, 3:260.

²⁴ *Legislative Manual*, 1903, p. 513.

²⁵ Folwell, *Minnesota*, 3:256–263. On the battle to raise the gross earnings tax, see Cheney, *Minnesota Politics*, 14.

²⁶ Folwell, *Minnesota*, 3:274.

²⁷ For a full account of the campaign of 1904, see Winifred G. Helmes, *John A. Johnson: The People's Governor*, 115–166 (Minneapolis, 1949).

²⁸ See Folwell, *Minnesota*, 3:286–292; Helmes, *John A. Johnson*, 174–183, 209–213, 288–295.

²⁹ His biographer comments: "Probably one of the main reasons for Johnson's success and power was that he was attuned to the popular mind. He seemed to know instinctively what the majority of the people favored, demanded, or opposed." Helmes, *John A. Johnson*, 246.

³⁰ Helmes, *John A. Johnson*, 208; James Manahan, *Trials of a Lawyer*, 50–68 (Minneapolis, 1933).

³¹ Helmes, *John A. Johnson*, 226–264; Manahan, *Trials of a Lawyer*, 95–97; Frank A. Day and Theodore M. Knappen, *Life of John Albert Johnson*, 189–198 (Chicago, 1910).

³² For the full text of the tonnage tax veto see Day and Knappen, *John Albert Johnson*, 382–388.

³³ Helmes, *John A. Johnson*, 292–294.

³⁴ George H. Mayer, *The Political Career of Floyd B. Olson*, 301 (Minneapolis, 1951).

Chapter 3 — THE DYNAMICS OF MINNESOTA
PROGRESSIVE POLITICS — pages 22–36

¹ For a discussion of Johnson's position on railroad legislation *vis à vis* that of his 1906 Republican opponent, Albert L. Cole, see *Minneapolis Journal*, October 2, 1906. On the 1908 campaign, see Helmes, *John A. Johnson*, 266–284.

[2] Brief profiles of Jacobson, a colorful personality, are carried in Cheney, *Minnesota Politics,* 30; Helmes, *John A. Johnson,* 268–270; O. N. Nelson, ed., *History of the Scandinavians and Successful Scandinavians in the United States,* 2:415 (Minneapolis, 1901).

[3] The thesis that progressivism was to a considerable extent generated by the "status" fears of influential middle-class groups is developed at length in Hofstadter, *Age of Reform,* 131–173, and Mowry, *The California Progressives,* 86–104.

[4] *Northfield News,* April 19, 1890, p. 2.

[5] *President's Address to the Minnesota Municipal and Commercial League, 1904,* 10, 12 (n.p., n.d.). Copy in the Leonard A. Rosing Papers, in the Minnesota Historical Society. Rosing was Van Sant's Democratic opponent in the gubernatorial contest of 1902.

[6] United States, *Statutes at Large,* 13:108. In 1908 approximately forty urban centers were designated as reserve cities. Minnesota had two, Minneapolis and St. Paul. However, there was "not a reserve city from Minneapolis to Spokane, Washington, and none between there and the Pacific Ocean." E. W. Davies to Knute Nelson, January 18, 1908, Nelson Papers, in the Minnesota Historical Society.

[7] The findings of the celebrated Pujo committee, created by the U.S. House of Representatives in 1912 to probe the "Money Trust," supported this line of reasoning. See Paul A. Samuelson and Herman F. Krooss, *Documentary History of Banking and Currency in the United States,* 3:2186 (New York, 1969).

[8] Davies to Nelson, January 27, 1908, Nelson Papers.

[9] *Congressional Record,* 60 Congress, 1 session, 2525.

[10] See comments in the *Northwestern Agriculturist* (Minneapolis), September 26, 1908, p. 8.

[11] *Commercial West* (Minneapolis), January 12, 1907, p. 8.

[12] *Minneapolis Journal,* January 25, 1895; Cheney, *Minnesota Politics,* 17. The best account of the Ames scandals is Lincoln Steffens, "The Shame of Minneapolis." This piece, first published by *McClure's Magazine* in 1903, constitutes a chapter in Steffens' *Shame of the Cities* (New York, 1904).

[13] *Minneapolis Journal,* September 11, 1906, p. 1.

[14] For the Voters' League address issued in 1908, see *Minneapolis Journal,* September. 24, 1908.

[15] For representative comments on the tariff issue in business-oriented periodicals, see *Minneapolis Tribune,* September 19, 1909; *Commercial West,* October 21, 1905, p. 9; December 9, 1905, p. 9; January 2, 1909, p. 7; February 27, 1909, p. 8; May 15, 1909, p. 8.

[16] *Commercial West,* November 23, 1901, p. 5. For further discussion of the reciprocity issue, see below, p. 43–45.

[17] George E. Budd to Knute Nelson, June 4, 1902, Nelson Papers.

[18] For a comprehensive treatment of the Payne-Aldrich battle, see Claude G. Bowers, *Beveridge and the Progressive Era,* 331–383 (New York, 1932).

[19] *Congressional Record,* 61 Congress, 1 session, 4755; *Commercial West,* January 8, 1910, p. 8; March 26, 1910, p. 8; September 10, 1910, p. 8; January 14, 1911, p. 8; March 11, 1911, p. 8.

[20] *Commercial West,* September 29, 1905, p. 59. See also issue of October 28, p. 15 and *Northwestern Miller,* 52:989 (November 13, 1901).

[21] For an analysis of agricultural discontent in the first decade of the twentieth century, see Theodore Saloutos and John D. Hicks, *Agricultural Discontent in the Middle West, 1900–1939,* 3–86 (Madison, Wis., 1951).

[22] Since the Citizens' Alliance shrouded its operations from public view, dependable information concerning its functioning is difficult to procure. There is a collection of its papers owned by the Minnesota Historical Society. These are helpful in revealing the motivations directing the organization, but less so in laying bare the details of its operations. For an exposé of its first year, written from labor's point of view, see *Union* (Minneapolis), July 24, 29, 1904; February 17, 1905.

[23] Neil Betten, "Strike on the Mesabi — 1907," in *Minnesota History,* 40:340–347 (Fall, 1967); Hyman Berman, "Education for Work and Labor Solidarity: The Immigrant Miners and Radicalism on the Mesabi Range," 38–46, unpublished manuscript, copy in the Minnesota Historical Society.

[24] *Union,* June 16, 1905; *Minnesota Union Advocate* (St. Paul), June 15, 1906; Helmes, *John A. Johnson,* 199.

[25] Helmes, *John A. Johnson,* 224; Betten, in *Minnesota History,* 40:346; Charles B. Cheney, "A Labor Crisis and a Governor," in *Outlook,* 89:24–30 (May 2, 1908).

[26] Helmes, *John A. Johnson,* 222.

[27] The *Minnesota Union Advocate* was highly critical of Johnson's strike policy, maintaining that his intervention was both ineffective and tardy. See issues of September 6, 20, 27; October 4; November 1; December 20, 1907.

[28] Lynn Haines, *The Minnesota Legislature of 1909,* 105 (Minneapolis, 1909).

[29] Minnesota, *Laws,* 1915, p. 24–34.

[30] *Union,* May 4, 18, 1906; *Minnesota Union Advocate,* May 29, 1908; October 7, 1910.

[31] Minnesota Census, 1905, p. 196–198.

[32] The election returns for 1888, for example, demonstrate a high degree of straight party voting. See *Legislative Manual,* 1889, p. 399. On ethnic voting patterns in Minneapolis and St. Paul before 1890, see Michael Barone, "The Social Basis of Urban Politics: Minneapolis and St. Paul, 1890–1905," 2, unpublished manuscript in the Minnesota Historical Society.

[33] See J. F. Rosenwald to Knute Nelson, October 28, 1912, Nelson Papers. On Swedish-American loyalty to the Republican party, see Stephenson, *John Lind,* 118.

[34] See Barone, "Social Basis of Urban Politics," 9, 21.

[35] Barone, "Social Basis of Urban Politics," 12. In 1906, for example, the nine counties comprising the third congressional district (principally the Minnesota Valley), which never had elected a Democratic congressman, chose twelve Democratic and eleven Republican state legislators.

[36] Haines, *The Minnesota Legislature of 1911,* 99–120 (Minneapolis, 1912). While Haines does not make this point explicitly, he does characterize the records of legislators from Brown, Carver, Le Sueur, Stearns, and Scott counties as reactionary. Here and in later works on the U.S. congress he employed the La Follette technique of compiling and classifying roll call votes.

[37] As early as 1892 Knute Nelson felt heavy Scandinavian pressure to join the dry cause. See L. G. Almen to Nelson, July 17, 25, 1892, Nelson Papers. See also translation of an editorial published originally in *Skandinaven* (Chicago), quoted in *Minneapolis Journal,* June 25, 1892.

[38] Samuel N. Nichols to Nelson, March 6, 1899, Nelson Papers.

[39] Quoted in Day and Knappen, *John Albert Johnson,* 285.

Chapter 4 — THE PROGRESSIVE TIDE RISES, 1909–1912 —
pages 37–46

[1] The *Minnesota Legislative Manual* for 1945 includes a brief obituary sketch of Eberhart written by Henry N. Benson. Since the governor and lieutenant governor were not on the same ticket in Minnesota, the election of men belonging to different parties was not unusual.

[2] Haines, *Legislature of 1909,* 22.

[3] Cheney, *Minnesota Politics,* 43; Stephenson, *John Lind,* 205.

[4] Cheney, *Minnesota Politics,* 43. Haines charged that Smith's influence over Eberhart was such that Smith in fact had exercised the lieutenant governor's prerogatives. *Legislature of 1909,* 22.

[5] Cheney, *Minnesota Politics,* 43; Haines, *Legislature of 1909,* 12. See also *Minneapolis Journal,* July 7, 1910.

[6] Haines, *Legislature of 1911*, 8.

[7] Haines, *Legislature of 1911*, 6. For Smith's own interpretation of his career, see *The Philosophy of a Politician: An Epistolary Biography of Edward E. Smith, Edited by His Son, Rollin L. Smith* (Minneapolis, 1932).

[8] Stephenson, *John Lind*, 199.

[9] Stephenson, *John Lind*, 202–204. Gray was a journalist by profession. His son of the same name gained prominence as a Minnesota writer and historian.

[10] *Legislative Manual*, 1911, 476– 479, 482, 536; Cheney, *Minnesota Politics*, 37; *Minnesota Union Advocate*, September 30, November 11, 1910.

[11] Haines, *Legislature of 1911*, 8; *Minneapolis Journal*, April 19, 1911.

[12] George E. Mowry, *Theodore Roosevelt and the Progressive Movement*, 73–80 (Madison, Wis., 1946). The Twin Cities newspapers of late August and early September, 1910, gave complete coverage to the Conservation Congress.

[13] *St. Paul Pioneer Press*, September 7, p. 3; September 8, p. 10, 1910.

[14] For an able study of the first district contest, see Roger E. Wyman, "Insurgency in Minnesota: The Defeat of James A. Tawney in 1910," in *Minnesota History*, 40:317–329 (Fall, 1967). A sympathetic sketch of Tawney's career is George Authier, "From the Forge to Congress," in *Minneapolis Tribune*, September 12, 1910.

[15] *St. Paul Dispatch*, September 18, 1909, p. 6. The *Evening Tribune* (Albert Lea), September 18, 1909, carried the full text of Taft's address; for reactions of Congressmen Charles A. Lindbergh and Charles R. Davis, see *Minneapolis Tribune*, September 21, 1909. See also editorial in the same paper, September 24, 1909.

[16] *St. Paul Pioneer Press*, September 6, 1910; *Minneapolis Journal*, September 6, 1910, p. 9 (quotation).

[17] *Minneapolis Tribune*, September 7, 8, 1910; *St. Paul Pioneer Press*, September 7, 1910; *Legislative Manual*, 1911, p. 484; Wyman, in *Minnesota History*, 40:325.

[18] Perhaps the most crucial test of a Republican congressman's insurgency came in March, 1910, with the House vote on a resolution introduced by George W. Norris of Nebraska stripping Speaker Cannon of most of his power. It was passed by a coalition of Democrats and dissident Republicans. Five of Minnesota's eight GOP congressmen — Lindbergh, Miller, Halvor Steenerson, Charles R. Davis, and Andrew J. Volstead — together with Hammond, the delegation's lone Democrat, voted aye. Nye of Minneapolis, Frederick Stevens of St. Paul, and Tawney voted nay. Nye was placed on the defensive by this vote and won renomination in 1910 by a narrow margin. In 1912 he declined to run for re-election, ostensibly because he felt out of harmony with the Republican party. *Congressional Record*, 61 Congress, 2 session, 3435; Nye to Knute Nelson, August 6, 1910, Nelson Papers; *Minneapolis Journal*, September 8, 11, 1910; *St. Paul Daily News*, August 19, 1912.

[19] See *Minneapolis Journal*, on the Buckman-Lindbergh contest, September 9, 11, 19, 20, 26, 1906; on McCleary and Hammond, September 26, October 1, 1906; and on Bede and Miller, September 8, 11, 1908; L. M. Willcutts to Nelson, September 25, 1908, Nelson Papers.

[20] For an account of the reciprocity fight, see Mowry, *Theodore Roosevelt and the Progressive Movement*, 157–167. Senator Nelson confidentially informed a trusted supporter that he was working with protectionist "standpatters" in an effort to prevent reciprocity from coming to a vote. Nelson to Ole O. Canestorp (copy), March 9, 1911, Nelson Papers.

[21] With the exceptions of the *St. Paul Daily News* and the *Minneapolis Daily News*, the Twin Cities daily papers supported reciprocity. For a comment concerning the effect on Taft's renomination, see *Commercial West*, June 29, 1912, p. 8.

[22] J. H. Nordby to Nelson, September 13, 1912. See also Paul V. Collins to Nelson, February 1, 1911, both in Nelson Papers.

[23] Leaders of the movement included Collins, editor of the *Northwestern Agriculturist*, Henry Feig, Ole O. Canestorp, and R. W. Wilkinson. See Collins to Nelson, May 1, June 15, 1911, Nelson Papers; *Northwestern Agriculturist*, February 11, p. 16; May 20, p. 1; May 27, p. 10, all 1911; January 13, p. 12; June 8, p. 19, both 1912.

[24] *Commercial West*, May 29, 1909, p. 8.
[25] *Commercial West*, May 15, 1909, p. 7.

Chapter 5—THE CAMPAIGN OF 1912—pages 47–58

[1] For La Follette's own account, see his *Autobiography*, 204–226 (Reprint edition, Madison, Wis., 1960). See also Mowry, *Theodore Roosevelt and the Progressive Movement*, 157–82.

[2] Mowry, *Theodore Roosevelt and the Progressive Movement*, 183–283; La Follette, *Autobiography*, 227–321. For a lively and readable account of the Bull Moose movement by a participant, see William Allen White's *Autobiography*, 427– 496 (New York, 1946).

[3] Cheney, *Minnesota Politics*, 32.

[4] *Minneapolis Journal*, May 11, 13, 14, 15, July 6, 15, 22, 1912; *Northwestern Agriculturist*, September 21, 1912, p. 1.

[5] *Minneapolis Journal*, May 15, 16, 1912; *Northwestern Agriculturist*, May 25, 1912, p. 8. In his *Journal* column of May 15 Cheney attributed Roosevelt's victory to the strategy of aligning his cause with the anti-Eberhart movement.

[6] Cheney, *Minnesota Politics*, 43; *Minneapolis Journal*, May 17, June 4, 1912. The latter issue contains Eberhart's message to the special session.

[7] *Minneapolis Journal*, June 18, 1912, p. 16. See also issues of June 11, 12 for coverage of the politics of the special session.

[8] Minnesota, *Laws*, Special Session, 1912, p. 4–22.

[9] *Legislative Manual*, 1913, p. 348–351; *Northwestern Agriculturist*, October 12, 1912, p. 5; *Minneapolis Journal*, September 26, 27, 28, 1912.

[10] Cheney, in *Minneapolis Journal*, June 23, 24, 1912.

[11] *Minneapolis Journal*, July 3, 1912; *St. Paul Daily News*, July 3, 1912. By September 11 eight of the eleven presidential electors selected by the state GOP convention had resigned and two more had announced an intention to do so. The one remaining elector was for Taft. The Republican state central committee appointed replacements. *Minneapolis Journal*, September 11, 1912.

[12] Cheney, in *Minneapolis Journal*, July 18, 1912; *Northwestern Agriculturist*, July 20, 1912, p. 2.

[13] See *Northwestern Agriculturist*, July 27, 1912, p. 9, for text of official call.

[14] *Northwestern Agriculturist*, August 10, 1912, p. 4.

[15] *Minneapolis Journal*, September 3, 4, 1912; *Northwestern Agriculturist*, September 14, 1912, p. 3.

[16] *Minneapolis Journal*, September 21, 1912; *Northwestern Agriculturist*, September 28, 1912, p. 17.

[17] For examples of Collins' campaign rhetoric, see *Northwestern Agriculturist*, October 5, 12, 1912, both p. 1.

[18] *Legislative Manual*, 1913, p. 512; 1915, p. 544.

[19] *Minneapolis Journal*, September 11, 1912. Burnquist ran ahead of Eberhart by about 18,000 votes and polled a plurality of approximately 60,000 over his Democratic opponent.

[20] Usher L. Burdick, *The Life of George Sperry Loftus: Militant Farm Leader of the Northwest*, 35, 49–56 (Baltimore, 1940); Manahan, *Trials of a Lawyer*, 48.

[21] Manahan, *Trials of a Lawyer*, 183; *Northwestern Agriculturist*, September 28, 1912, p. 17; *Minneapolis Journal*, September 21, 1912.

[22] Quoted in Manahan, *Trials of a Lawyer*, 192.

[23] *Dawson Sentinel*, November 1, 1912; Millard L. Gieske, "The Politics of Knute Nelson, 1912–1920," 51–112, Ph.D. thesis, University of Minnesota, 1965, copy in the Minnesota Historical Society.

[24] A Nelson campaign circular dated October 15, 1912, stated: "While I have . . . been a member of the Republican party, I have never been a blind follower of the party. . . . As examples of this, I refer you to my vote against the Payne-Aldrich tariff bill, and against the so-called Canadian Reciprocity scheme, and several instances of less note could be cited." While the senator's stand on these two regional issues drew insurgent support, his part in the Ballinger investigation repelled some progressives. In writing to Nelson, the editor of the *Minneapolis Journal* observed, "The Ballinger matter hurt you in the state." Letter from Herschel V. Jones, July 31, 1912, both in Nelson Papers.

[25] *Legislative Manual*, 1913, p. 342. For Bull Moose support, see Andrew A. D. Rahn to Nelson, August 22, 1912; I. A. Caswell to, August 27, 1912; W. W. Heffelfinger to, September 10, 1912; Walter H. Newton to, September 10, 1912; P. V. Collins to, September 19, 1912. For Peterson's campaign, see Henry Rines to L. M. Willcutts, August 27, 1912 (copy); Edward Rustad to Nelson, August 28, 1912; Julius E. Haycraft to, August 26, 1912, all in Nelson Papers. Haycraft reported that there was "some opposition due principally to the so called Ballinger episode," but that "Mr. Peterson is unsatisfactory to such opposition."

[26] William T. Coe to George L. Treat, October 22, 1912 (copy), Nelson Papers.

[27] *Legislative Manual*, 1913, p. 502.

[28] See, for example, *Minneapolis Journal*, September 5, 1912.

[29] *Northwestern Agriculturist*, November 25, 1911, p. 1–13; March 9, 1912, p. 11; September 14, 1912, p. 4.

[30] Arthur S. Link, *Wilson: The Road to the White House*, 506 (Princeton, N. J., 1947).

[31] See, for example, *Minneapolis Journal*, July 22, 1912; *La Follette's Weekly Magazine*, July 27, 1912, p. 1. On October 12, 1912, p. 6, this magazine carried an article by Louis D. Brandeis excoriating the Roosevelt trust program. Brandeis was known as a Wilson spokesman.

[32] Frank M. Eddy to Nelson, August 30, October 8, 1912; Henry W. Elliott to, October 20, 1912, Nelson Papers. For Democratic politics, see Cheney, in the *Minneapolis Journal*, May 2, 14, 27, 28, 30, June 3, 4, 6, 7, 26, July 24, 1912; *St. Paul Daily News*, September 7, 1912.

[33] *Minneapolis Journal*, July 13, 1912; L. M. Willcutts to Nelson, October 1, 1912, Nelson Papers.

[34] *Legislative Manual*, 1913, p. 500; 1909, p. 537. In 1908 Debs polled 14,524 votes.

[35] Stephenson, *John Lind*, 206.

[36] *Legislative Manual*, 1913, p. 500.

[37] The 1912 vote for state officers by counties is given in the *Legislative Manual*, 1913, p. 504–507.

[38] For Ringdal's platform, see *St. Paul Daily News*, August 14, 1912. During the primary campaign, one of Nelson's friends noted a link between Ringdal and Nelson's opponent, Peterson. See L. M. Willcutts to Nelson, September 3, 1912, Nelson Papers.

[39] A. C. Hatch to Nelson, October 5, 1912; Nelson to Simon Michelet, October 12, 1912, Nelson Papers.

[40] Haines, *Minnesota Legislature of 1911*, 100. For the text of the Prohibitionist platform, see *Park Region Echo* (Alexandria), July 18, 1912.

[41] For a biographical sketch of Løbeck, see Nelson, ed., *History of the Scandinavians*, 1:435.

[42] *Legislative Manual*, 1913, p. 368, 406, 476, 512, 514.

[43] See Nelson to Jacob A. O. Preus, November 9, 1912, Preus Papers, in the Minnesota Historical Society.

[44] A Lincoln County Republican circular, dated November 1, 1912, and filed among Nelson's papers, virtually ignored the national ticket. It asserted that space limitations did "not permit of a lengthy elucidation" of this aspect of the campaign. According to Cheney, the Roosevelt bolt was not a complete embarrassment to Republican office seekers. Taft, he thought, was so unpopular that few candidates for state office wanted to support him,

and to back Wilson amounted to an outright bolt. Roosevelt, a lifelong Republican, offered safe middle ground. See Cheney, in *Minneapolis Journal*, July 10, 1912.

[45] Mowry, *Theodore Roosevelt and the Progressive Movement*, 282.

Chapter 6—PROGRESSIVISM TRIUMPHANT—pages 59–65

[1] *Commercial West*, November 9, 1912, p. 7.

[2] *Legislative Manual*, 1913, p. 146.

[3] Cheney, *Minnesota Politics*, 42. For his summary of the 1913 legislature, see *Minneapolis Journal*, April 24, 1913.

[4] Minnesota Rate Cases, 230 *United States Supreme Court Reports* 352 (1913); Minnesota, *Laws*, 1913, p. 77–81, 789–793.

[5] The discussion here and in the following paragraphs is based largely on Charles R. Adrian, "The Origins of Minnesota's Nonpartisan Legislature," in *Minnesota History*, 33:155–164 (Winter, 1952).

[6] See G. Theodore Mitau, *Politics in Minnesota*, 57–79 (Minneapolis, 1960). This chapter is entitled "A Nonpartisan Partisan Legislature."

[7] *Minneapolis Journal*, February 2, 1914; *Minneota Mascot*, February 6, 1914.

[8] *Minneota Mascot*, February 13, 1914, p. 4.

[9] *Minneapolis Journal*, March 19, 1914; *Minneota Mascot*, March 27, 1914.

[10] Sageng was under pressure from Democratic as well as Bull Moose and Republican progressives to run for governor. See Frank A. Day to Sageng, [early 1914]; Hugh Halbert to, March 6, 13, 1914; Hans P. Bjorge to, March 14, 1914, all in Ole O. Sageng Papers, in the Minnesota Historical Society.

[11] *Minneapolis Tribune*, April 15, 1914; *Legislative Manual*, 1915, p. 536.

[12] *Minneota Mascot*, April 24, 1914; May 8, 1914, p. 1 (quotation).

[13] Stephenson, *John Lind*, 199–203; *Minneota Mascot*, January 30, 1914.

[14] *Minneapolis Journal*, March 31, 1914; *Minneota Mascot*, April 10, 1914.

[15] *Legislative Manual*, 1915, p. 193.

[16] *Minneota Mascot*, June 19, 1914, p. 4; *Legislative Manual*, 1915, p. 184.

Chapter 7—MINNESOTA'S INITIAL RESPONSE TO WORLD WAR I—pages 66–76

[1] Arthur S. Link, *Wilson the Diplomatist: A Look at His Major Foreign Policies*, 5 (Baltimore, 1957). Walter Lippmann, too, later confessed that he "came out of college thinking . . . that war was . . . not something serious minded progressive democrats paid any attention to." Quoted in Forcey, *The Crossroads of Liberalism*, 223.

[2] Lord, *The Good Years*, ix.

[3] Professor Link comments: "To say that the outbreak of war in Europe in 1914 came as a shock to the American people would be an understatement of heroic proportions." *Woodrow Wilson and the Progressive Movement*, 145.

[4] *Minneota Mascot*, August 14, 1914, p. 4.

[5] Link notes the difficulty of formulating accurate generalizations explaining American reaction to the war. See *The Struggle for Neutrality*, 7.

[6] Mowry, *Theodore Roosevelt and the Progressive Movement*, 310.

[7] *Red Wing Daily Republican*, August 5, 1914, p. 2; *St. Paul Pioneer Press*, August 3, 1914, p. 4.

[8] *Blue Earth County Enterprise* (Mapleton), August 7, 1914, p. 4.

[9] *Minneapolis Tribune*, August 20, 1914, p. 6.

[10] See, for example, *Minneapolis Journal*, August 4, 1914.

[11] *Brown County Journal* (New Ulm), August 8, 1914, p. 4; *Minneota Mascot*, August 14, 1914, p. 1.

[12] Translation in *Brown County Journal*, September 12, 1914, p. 4.

[13] *Park Region Echo*, September 17, 1914; *Brown County Journal*, November 28, 1914, p. 1 (quotation).

[14] *Brown County Journal*, September 19, p. 1 (quotation), 26, 1914.

[15] The Nelson Papers, particularly under the dates November 11, 12, 13, 1914, contain a number of letters from Scandinavian-Americans, some in identical language, protesting the effect of the British blockade on Scandinavia.

[16] For a detailed analysis of this financial crisis, see Link, *The Struggle for Neutrality*, 77–104.

[17] Quoted in *Red Wing Weekly Republican*, August 5, 1914, p. 7.

[18] *Minneapolis Journal*, August 3, 1914, p. 9; *Blue Earth County Enterprise*, August 7, 1914, p. 4.

[19] For relations with Britain, see Link, *The Struggle for Neutrality*, 105–136.

[20] Link, *The Struggle for Neutrality*, 161–167.

[21] Quoted in *Minneota Mascot*, September 4, 1914, p. 4.

[22] Ray Allen Billington, "The Origins of Middle Western Isolationism," in *Political Science Quarterly*, 60:44–64 (March, 1945); Hofstadter, *The Age of Reform*, 90–91; Ignatius Donnelly, *The Golden Bottle*, 308 (Reprint edition, New York and London, 1968).

[23] Stephenson, *John Lind*, 145.

[24] *Commercial West*, September 26, 1914, p. 10.

Chapter 8 — PROGRESSIVISM CRESTS — pages 77–88

[1] *New Ulm Review*, September 23, 1914, p. 4; *Sherburne County Star-News* (Elk River), October 8, 1914, p. 4. Both papers were quoted in the *Minneapolis Journal*, October 10, 1914.

[2] *Legislative Manual*, 1913, p. 506; 1915, p. 536.

[3] See statement of George B. Safford, superintendent of the Anti-Saloon League, in *Minneota Mascot*, September 25, 1914.

[4] The speech is reported in the *Minneapolis Journal*, September 15, 1914, p. 4. All quotations are from this source.

[5] His speech is reported in the *Minneapolis Journal*, September 29, 1914, p. 8. The quotation is from this source.

[6] *Legislative Manual*, 1915, p. 534–537.

[7] For coverage of the campaign, see Cheney, in *Minneapolis Journal*, September 24, 30, October 2, 3, 5, 19, 1914. For the position of the Democratic drys, see *Journal*, September 24, October 19, 1914. Sageng, campaigning for Lee, asserted that "The election of Mr. Hammond would be . . . a victory for whisky." (*Journal*, October 20, 1914, p. 1.) Hans P. Bjorge, a prominent northwestern Minnesota progressive, disagreed with this statement. See Bjorge to Sageng, November 5, 1914, Sageng Papers.

[8] For the Democratic platform, see *St. Paul Pioneer Press*, April 1, 1914.

[9] *Pioneer Press*, October 2, 1914, p. 7; *Legislative Manual*, 1913, p. 504–507; 1915, p. 534–537. Compare especially Ramsey, Hennepin, Dakota, Rice, Washington, Carver, Sibley, and Blue Earth counties.

[10] *Minneapolis Journal*, October 8, 11, 1914.

[11] See biographical sketch in *Legislative Manual*, 1893, p. 593.

[12] A biographical sketch of Hammond is at the front of the 1917 *Legislative Manual*.

[13] *Minneapolis Journal*, September 26, October 1, 10, 20, 1906.

[14] Cheney, *Minnesota Politics*, 38.

¹⁵ Cheney, *Minnesota Politics*, 37; *Pioneer Press*, September 29, 1914, p. 4.
¹⁶ Cheney, in *Minneapolis Journal*, September 24, 1914, p. 12; *Minneota Mascot*, November 13, 1914.
¹⁷ *Legislative Manual*, 1915, p. 542–544.
¹⁸ *Minneapolis Journal*, November 5, 1915, p. 6.
¹⁹ *Minneota Mascot*, November 13, 1914, p. 4.
²⁰ John H. Fenton, *Midwest Politics*, 75–116 (New York, 1966).
²¹ *Inaugural Message of Governor Winfield S. Hammond* (n.p., 1915). Quotations here and in the following paragraphs are from this source. A copy is in the library of the Minnesota Historical Society.
²² Sam Y. Gordon to Sageng, December 3, 1914, Sageng Papers. For Cheney's summary of the 1915 legislature, see *Minneapolis Journal*. April 22, 1915.
²³ A. L. Hanson to Sageng, November 10, 1914, Sageng Papers; Minnesota, *Senate Journal*, 1915, p. 212.
²⁴ Cheney, *Minnesota Politics*, 36; Minnesota, *House Journal*, 1915, p. 479; Minnesota, *Laws*, 1915, p. 24 –34.
²⁵ *Senate Journal*, 1915, p. 783; *House Journal*, 1915, p. 1382–1388; *Laws*, 1915, p. 205.
²⁶ *Senate Journal*, 1915, p. 479; *Park Region Echo*, June 10, 1915; Cheney, in *Minneapolis Journal*, April 22, 1915.
²⁷ *Laws*, 1915, p. 166–170, 208–215.
²⁸ *Laws*, 1915, p. 133–136, 268–275, 285–300.
²⁹ *Journal*, April 22, 1915, p. 14; *Pioneer Press*, April 23, 1915.
³⁰ *Blue Earth County Enterprise*, June 18, July 16, 1915; Cheney, *Minnesota Politics*, 36.
³¹ Cheney, *Minnesota Politics*, 38.

Chapter 9 — FOREIGN POLICY BECOMES AN ISSUE: A STRAIN ON PROGRESSIVE SOLIDARITY — pages 89–105

¹ The account here and in the following paragraphs is in the main based on Link, *Woodrow Wilson and the Progressive Era; Wilson: The Struggle for Neutrality*; and *Wilson the Diplomatist*. Other works dealing with the period include Ernest R. May, *The World War and American Isolation, 1914 –1917* (Cambridge, Mass., 1950); and Charles C. Tansill, *America Goes to War* (Boston, 1938). The latter is critical of Wilson.
² For the text of Wilson's February 10, 1915, note, see Albert Fried, ed., *A Day of Dedication: The Essential Writings and Speeches of Woodrow Wilson*, 215–217 (New York, 1965).
³ Fried, ed., *Writings and Speeches of Woodrow Wilson*, 225.
⁴ For an abbreviated interpretation of the complex relationship between Wilson's efforts to negotiate the *modus vivendi* and to open the way for American mediation of the war, see Link, *Wilson the Diplomatist*, 57–59.
⁵ Wilson summed up the content of this note in an address to congress on April 19, 1916. For this address, see Fried, ed., *Writings and Speeches of Woodrow Wilson*, 247–252. For the text of the note, see Robert Lansing to James W. Gerard, April 18, 1916, in United States Department of State, *Papers Relating to the Foreign Relations of the United States*, 1916 Supplement, 232–234 (Washington, 1929).
⁶ For Wilson's position on the Gore-McLemore resolutions, see Wilson to Senator William Stone, February 24, 1916, in Fried, ed., *Writings and Speeches of Woodrow Wilson*, 245–247.
⁷ Link, *Woodrow Wilson and the Progressive Era*, 183.

[8] For an account of the presidential campaign of 1916, see Link, *Woodrow Wilson and the Progressive Era*, 223–251.

[9] See, for example, Irving J. Lowell to Nelson, January 21, 1916; W. L. Harney to, January 25, 1916; Frank Hense to, January 12, 1916, Nelson Papers. The latter was "sure that every four out of five Minnesotans" favored an arms embargo.

[10] In June, 1915, Nelson gave a speech in southwestern Minnesota at which it was hoped and expected that he would discuss U.S. relations with Germany, but the audience was "doomed to disappointment." At the Mille Lacs County fair in September he spoke of the willingness of the foreign-born to rally on behalf of the United States, citing the German-American record in the Civil War, but still maintained a noncommittal stance on the issues then in the forefront of controversy. See *Rock County Herald*, July 2, 1915, p. 8; *Princeton Union*, September 23, 1915.

[11] See, for example, *Minneapolis Journal*, April 27, 30, 1915.

[12] Franklin F. Holbrook and Livia Appel, *Minnesota in the War with Germany*, 1:27 (St. Paul, 1928).

[13] *Park Region Echo*, July 29, 1915, p. 5; *Blue Earth County Enterprise*, October 13, 1916, p. 4.

[14] Harold U. Faulkner, *American Economic History*, 581 (New York, 1960); Mayer, *Floyd B. Olson*, 20. For further analysis of the northwestern Minnesota farm situation, see Robert H. Bahmer, "The Economic and Political Background of the Nonpartisan League," Ph.D. thesis, University of Minnesota, 1941 (photocopy in the Minnesota Historical Society); E. C. Johnson and W. L. Calbert, *Adjusting Farm Debts* (University of Minnesota, *Special Bulletins*, No. 157 — December, 1932).

[15] Stimson was quoted in the *Labor World* (Duluth), February 5, 1916. See also the issues of June 26 (quotation, p. 4), July 24, 31, October 16, 1915; August 5, 1916; *Minnesota Union Advocate*, January 7, April 28, June 23, 30, July 28, September 1, 1916; *New Times* (Minneapolis), July 23, 1915; L. Stinton, recording secretary of Minneapolis Trades and Labor Assembly, to Nelson, August 26, 1915, Nelson Papers.

[16] Holbrook and Appel, *Minnesota in the War with Germany*, 1:27.

[17] *Labor World*, October 23, 1915, p. 4.

[18] Edward H. Hewitt to Nelson, February 25, 1916; H. H. Blades to, February 28, 1916, Nelson Papers; *Commercial West*, September 18, 1915, p. 8; July 1, 1916, p. 7.

[19] Carl Resek, ed., *War and the Intellectuals: Essays by Randolph S. Bourne, 1915–1919*, 5 (New York, 1964).

[20] J. H. Beek, secretary, St. Paul Association of Commerce, to Nelson, February 28, March 16, 1916, Nelson Papers; *Commercial West*, November 28, 1914, p. 30; January 2, 1915, p. 11; May 22, 1915, p. 17. An exception among conservatives was ex-Congressman James A. Tawney, who was a strong neutralist and vigorous opponent of preparedness. See *Minneapolis Tribune*, May 10, 1915; *Blue Earth County Enterprise*, May 14, 1915.

[21] Carl F. Wittke, *German-Americans and the World War*, 62–67 (Columbus, Ohio, 1936).

[22] Holbrook and Appel, *Minnesota in the War with Germany*, 1:7; *St. Paul Volkszeitung*, February 12, 13, May 8, May 10 (quotation) 1915. See also *Der Wanderer* (St. Paul), January 20, February 24, March 2, 9, 1916. For all translations from German-language publications the author is indebted to Miss Hermina Poatgieter of the Minnesota Historical Society staff.

[23] *New Ulm Review*, June 30, 1915, p. 1 (quotations); *Brown County Journal*, July 3, 1915.

[24] Wittke, *German-Americans and the World War*, 25.

[25] *Brown County Journal*, July 3, 1915, p. 4 (quotation); October 16, 30, 1915; *New Ulm Review*, December 6, 1916; *Commercial West*, October 2, 1915, p. 7.

[26] Nelson to C. J. Swanson, February 29, 1916 (copy), Nelson Papers.

[27] William Huper to Nelson, February 21, 1916, Nelson Papers.

[28] Ex-Congressman Frederick C. Stevens reported that he and Nelson had sought to persuade the Minnesota congressional delegation to oppose the Gore-McLemore resolutions, "But

could not get one. They stick close to the German vote." Stevens to Frank B. Kellogg, March 9, 1916, Kellogg Papers, in the Minnesota Historical Society.

[29] Theodore Roosevelt, *Fear God and Take Your Own Part*, 138–164 (New York, 1916); Ray Stannard Baker and William E. Dodd, eds., *The Public Papers of Woodrow Wilson: The New Democracy*, 1:390 (New York, 1926); *Minneota Mascot*, February 4, 1916, p. 4.

[30] *New Times*, July 3, 1915; *Minneapolis Tribune*, July 5, 1915; *St. Paul Pioneer Press*, September 10, 1915; *Princeton Union*, September 23, 1915; W. F. Decker to Nelson, July 8, 1915, Nelson Papers.

[31] *New Ulm Review*, November 1, 1916, p. 4; Wittke, *German-Americans and the World War*, 3. The *Minneapolis Journal* commented editorially: "A people speaking one language are a unity; speaking two languages, they are a division. Americans in their optimism have felt they could ignore what no other nation can afford to ignore." June 8, 1916, p. 14.

[32] *Minneapolis Tidende*, January 23, March 1, 1916.

[33] An article by Edward Goldbeck, printed in the *Minneapolis Journal*, argued that German-Americans would abandon the hyphen when Anglo-Americans did so. Meanwhile, Goldbeck added, "Let the exodus of the Anglo-Americans start at once! Let all those people go who think that America is a new England." July 16, 1916, editorial section, p. 2.

[34] George M. Stephenson, "The Attitude of Swedish Americans toward the World War," in Mississippi Valley Historical Association, *Proceedings*, 1918–1919, vol. 10, part 1, p. 79–94; F. A. Scherf to Nelson, February 1, 1916, Nelson Papers; *Bemidji Herald*, January 27, March 16, May 25, 1916.

[35] *Minneapolis Tribune*, February 14, 1916; *St. Paul Daily News*, July 26, 1916.

[36] McGee to Nelson, March 7, 11, 29, 1916; McGee to George R. Smith, March 1, 1916 (copy); Nelson to McGee, February 4, 1916; to Peter Shippman, March 10, 1916; Z. L. Begin to Nelson, December 17, 1916; draft of a letter evidently prepared in response to neutralist missives from constituents, January 11, 1916, all in Nelson Papers. See also McGee to Senator Moses Clapp. February 14, 1916 (copy), in Jacob A. O. Preus Papers, in the Minnesota Historical Society.

[37] Jacob A. O. Preus to S. S. Scott, February 16, 1916, Preus Papers.

[38] *St. Paul Volkszeitung*, June 11, 1915; *Fairmont Daily Sentinel*, June 28, 1915, p. 2. See also the issue of July 6, 1915.

[39] *Minneota Mascot*, May 14, June 25, 1915; March 10, December 15, 1916. Other examples are: the *Fairmont Sentinel*, which was neutralist on nearly every issue but occasionally quoted antihyphenist expressions with approval (see issue of July 13, 1915); the *Blue Earth County Enterprise*, which also followed a neutralist line but disagreed with the Gore-McLemore resolutions (see issue of April 7, 1916); and the *Labor World*, which defended the peace movement and attacked ultrapreparedness but consistently supported Wilson and strongly opposed the Gore-McLemore proposition (see issues of August 21, October 15, 1915; March 11, 1916).

[40] *St. Paul Pioneer Press*, January 13, 1915, p. 1 (quotation); *Minneapolis Journal*, January 13, 1915.

[41] *Fairmont Daily Sentinel*, March 19, 1915; *Red Wing Weekly Republican*, April 21, 1915; *New Ulm Review*, March 3, 1915; *Minneapolis Journal*, January 13, 1915.

[42] The *Fairmont Daily Sentinel* remarked: "The Germans are today hopelessly estranged from the democratic party. If you doubt it ask the first one you meet." (April 2, 1915, p. 2.) The *Daily Journal-Press* (St. Cloud) asserted that "President Wilson would lose Stearns county, if the election were held today." (April 27, 1915, p. 4.)

[43] *St. Paul Volkszeitung*, May 8, 1915.

[44] *Minneapolis Journal*, May 8, 1915, p. 4. Northrop was quoted in the *Fairmont Daily Sentinel*, May 10, 1915, p. 2. For other editorial comment, see *St. Paul Pioneer Press*, May 8, 1915; *Commercial West*, May 15, 1915, p. 7; *New Times*, May 15, 1915; *New Ulm Review*, May 12, 1915.

[45] *Fairmont Daily Sentinel*, May 17, 1915, p. 2; August 2, 1915, p. 2. A Mankato attorney, writing to Nelson in May, commented that German population in his locality was large, "and they all have imbibed the spirit of the Kaiser." Ivan Bowen to Nelson, May 12, 1915, Nelson Papers.
[46] *Union Labor Bulletin* (Minneapolis), July, 1915, p. 1.
[47] For the House vote, see *Congressional Record*, 64 Congress, 2 session, 3720.
[48] *New York Times*, March 22, 1916, p. 12.
[49] *Duluth Herald*, March 8, 1916, p. 2; *Le Sueur News*, March 9, 1916, p. 2; *Princeton Union*, March 23, 1916, p. 6; *Minneapolis Journal*, March 13, 1916, p. 10.

Chapter 10 — DOMESTIC DISCORD — pages 106–118

[1] Edward C. Blackorby, *Prairie Rebel: The Public Life of William Lemke*, 26 (Lincoln, Neb., 1963).
[2] James A. Everitt, *The Third Power: Farmers to the Front*, 69 (Indianapolis, 1905); Saloutos and Hicks, *Agricultural Discontent*, 113–116, 121.
[3] Theodore Saloutos, "Farmer Movements since 1902," 35–66, Ph.D. thesis, University of Wisconsin, 1940, copy in the Minnesota Historical Society.
[4] Saloutos and Hicks, *Agricultural Discontent*, 135.
[5] Saloutos and Hicks, *Agricultural Discontent*, 137; Manahan, *Trials of a Lawyer*, 207; *Commercial West*, March 22, 1913, p. 7 (quotation); August 24, 1914, p. 72–74.
[7] Manahan, *Trials of a Lawyer*, 207–210.
[8] *House Journal*, 1913, p. 1749; *Senate Journal*, 1913, p. 1768. Manahan served as counsel for the Minnesota House committee before taking his seat in Congress.
[9] Robert L. Morlan, *Political Prairie Fire: The Nonpartisan League, 1915–1922*, 19 (Minneapolis, 1955); Blackorby, *Prairie Rebel*, 30.
[10] Morlan, *Political Prairie Fire*, 20.
[11] Morlan, *Political Prairie Fire*, 21 (quotations); Herbert E. Gaston, *The Nonpartisan League*, 42–44 (New York, 1920).
[12] Morlan, *Political Prairie Fire*, 23.
[13] Morlan, *Political Prairie Fire*, 23; Gaston, *Nonpartisan League*, 45–51; interview with Arthur C. Townley by Lucile M. Kane and Russell W. Fridley, St. Paul, Minn., December 11, 1956 (typewritten transcript), in the Minnesota Historical Society. Quotation, p. 2.
[14] Townley interview, p. 3.
[15] Morlan, *Political Prairie Fire*, 23; Elwyn B. Robinson, *History of North Dakota*, 329 (Lincoln, Neb., 1966). Henry G. Teigan, a prominent leader first in the North Dakota Socialist party and later in the league, declared: "it was due to the work of Socialists, very largely, that the League did develop so rapidly." Teigan to J. C. Hogan, January 30, 1917, Nonpartisan League Papers.
[16] Morlan, *Political Prairie Fire*, 24; Gaston, *Nonpartisan League*, 51–54.
[17] Morlan, *Political Prairie Fire*, 25 (quotations); Gaston, *Nonpartisan League*, 55–57.
[18] Morlan, *Political Prairie Fire*, 26.
[19] Ray McKaig, "The Nonpartisan Champion," in *Public*, 22:518 (May 17, 1919) (quotation); Townley interview, 9; Gaston, *Nonpartisan League*, 57–80; Morlan, *Political Prairie Fire*, 36–38; Manahan, *Trials of a Lawyer*, 229.
[20] Morlan, *Political Prairie Fire*, 51–75; Blackorby, *Prairie Rebel*, 35–55.
[21] Walter E. Quigley, "Out where the West Begins," 25, manuscript in the collection of the Minnesota Historical Society; *Minneapolis Journal*, July 5, 1916; *Northfield News*, September 1, 1916. Two days before the North Dakota primary, in which league candidates captured Republican nominations throughout the state, Cheney remarked in his *Journal* column:

"It is predicted that the [Nonpartisan League] movement will spread by another year to Minnesota and South Dakota." June 26, 1916, p. 6.

[22] Saloutos and Hicks, *Agricultural Discontent*, 169.

[23] Minnesota Federation of Labor, *Proceedings*, 1908, p. 14; 1911, p. 48; 1912, p. 17; 1913, p. 26; 1914, p. 17; 1915, p. 22; 1916, p. 14.

[24] Minnesota Federation of Labor, *Proceedings*, 1915, p. 21; *Union Labor Bulletin*, August, 1915, p. 18.

[25] See Joseph G. Rayback, *A History of American Labor*, 250–260 (New York, 1959).

[26] Harlow H. Chamberlain (president, Boyd Transfer & Storage Co.) to Knute Nelson, July 3, 1918, Nelson Papers.

[27] See *The Citizens Alliance of Minneapolis* (n.p., 1927), a pamphlet in the Citizens Alliance of Minneapolis Papers, in the Minnesota Historical Society. The society also has an incomplete file of the organization's monthly *Bulletin*, running from August, 1917, to May, 1932.

[28] While the alliance was being organized, a few Minneapolis businessmen complained of receiving unsolicited memberships and assessments. William F. Brooks to George K. Belden, July 29, 1903; J. B. Bushnell to O. P. Briggs, August 26, 1903, Citizens Alliance Papers.

[29] *Minnesota Union Advocate*, January 20, 1911; *New Times*, July 29, 1911; July 23, 1915; *Labor World*, August 5, 1916; *Union Labor Bulletin*, August, 1915, p. 24; July, 1917, p. 8; Minnesota Federation of Labor, *Proceedings*, 1915, p. 84. In reporting a Socialist rally the *Union Labor Bulletin* added this comment: "There is little doubt but that meetings of this kind do much good in a general way. It [*sic*] gives the worker an opportunity to hear much that is good for him and some things that are not good for him. . . . Most any kind of agitation is good for the public, because — it agitates. Water bounding over a rock-strewn bed is much more wholesome than that drawn from a stagnant pool." April, 1916, p. 6.

[30] For a full discussion of the streetcar strike of 1917–18, see below, chapter 12. On 1916 strikes, see *New Times*, April 1, 8, June 10, 17, July 18, 1916; *Minneapolis Journal*, July 1, 2, 1916; *Union Labor Bulletin*, February, p. 6; June, p. 8; July, p. 7, 1916.

[31] Two weekly newspapers gave full coverage to Socialist activity in Minneapolis: the *New Times*, and *Gaa Paa* [Forward], a Norwegian-language organ.

[32] *Minneapolis Journal*, October 25, 1916, p. 6.

[33] *New Times*, October 9, 1915; *Minneapolis Journal*, November 8, 1916; *Legislative Manual*, 1915, p. 543.

[34] "Twin Cities," in *Fortune*, April, 1936, p. 118, 193.

[35] *New Times*, July 15, 1916; Minnesota Federation of Labor, *Proceedings*, 1914, p. 51; 1915, p. 91; 1916, p. 17, 40; Henry G. Teigan to James A. Peterson, October 16, 1919, National Nonpartisan League Papers.

[36] Berman, "Education for Work and Labor Solidarity," 47.

[37] Berman, "Education for Work and Labor Solidarity," 43.

[38] On the tax controversy, particularly as it affected Hibbing, see *New Times*, September 18, 1915; *Commercial West*, September 18, 1915, p. 8; December 4, 1915, p. 7; *Labor World*, August 7, October 2, 1915, September 16, 1916. On labor policies of mining companies, see *Labor World*, January 22, 1916.

[39] Berman, "Education for Work and Labor Solidarity," 51–55. For a detailed account of the 1916 strike, see Neil Betten, "Riot, Revolution, Repression in the Iron Range Strike of 1916," in *Minnesota History*, 41:82–94 (Summer, 1968).

[40] A report on the strike written by George P. West of the United States Industrial Relations Commission was highly critical of the mining companies, as was one prepared by Lenora Austin Hamlin of the Women's Welfare League. For these and other statements on the strike, see *St. Paul Daily News*, August 1, 1916; *Labor World*, July 22, August 19, September 23, 1916; *Union Labor Bulletin*, September, 1916, p. 9.

[41] Berman, "Education for Work and Labor Solidarity," 53. The state investigators, like

others who reported on the strike, were sympathetic to the miners, although they did find IWW instigation to be a factor. Their report was printed in full in the *Duluth News Tribune*, August 17, 1916.

[42] *Daily News*, July 27, 1916, p. 6; *Journal*, July 5, 1916, p. 10; *Northfield News*, August 4, 1916, p. 1; *Enterprise*, July 14, August 4, 1916.

[43] Blackorby, *Prairie Rebel*, 57.

Chapter 11 — THE CAMPAIGN OF 1916 — pages 119–129

[1] *Legislative Manual*, 1917, p. 509, 512, 518–520.

[2] Lindbergh had formally announced his candidacy. See *Brown County Journal*, October 9, 1915.

[3] *Legislative Manual*, 1917, p. 568.

[4] Haines, *The Minnesota Legislature of 1911*, 42–47, 103; *Minneapolis Journal*, January 12, 1915; A. L. Hanson to Sageng, November 10, 1914, Sageng Papers.

[5] *Echo*, January 13, 1916, p. 1; *Mascot*, January 7, 1916, p. 4; *Brown County Journal*, March 4, 1916, p. 2.

[6] *Legislative Manual*, 1917, p. 190.

[7] *St. Paul Daily News*, July 31, August 1, 1916; *Mesaba Ore* (Hibbing), July 22, 29, 1916; *Labor World*, July 15, 1916.

[8] A substitute motion requesting Burnquist to "send a representative from the Labor department to investigate the strike" prevailed. Burnquist acceded to this request (see above, p. 118). Minnesota Federation of Labor, *Proceedings*, 1916, p. 76 (quotation); *Labor World*, August 19, 1916.

[9] Such a statement is not easily susceptible to either proof or disproof. In any case, many of Burnquist's contemporaries underwent a similar evolution. Alleged threats to assassinate the governor and dynamite the State Capitol also may have had an impact on his response. On rumors of violence, see *Princeton Union*, July 13, 1916.

[10] Frank M. Eddy to Nelson, September 26, 1916 (quotation), Nelson Papers; W. E. McKenzie to Frank B. Kellogg, August 12, 1916; E. A. Bancroft to, August 21, 1916; Frank M. Eddy to, August 22, 24, 1916, Kellogg Papers.

[11] *Minneapolis Journal*, January 22, May 25, 31, June 13, 1916.

[12] *Northfield News*, June 30, 1916, p. 8 (quotation); Cheney, in *Minneapolis Journal*, June 30, July 6, 1916.

[13] *Northfield News*, August 18, 1916, p. 4 (quotation); October 27, 1916; Cheney, in *Minneapolis Journal*, June 22, 1916, p. 10.

[14] *Northfield News*, July 28, 1916, p. 2 (quotation), August 25, September 15, 1916; Eddy to Nelson, September 26, 1916, Nelson Papers; *Legislative Manual*, 1917, p. 512.

[15] Cheney predicted a Hughes victory by a margin of 75,000 votes. *Minneapolis Journal*, June 30, 1916.

[16] E. V. Moore to Nelson, October 18, 1916. As early as August 23, 1916, John E. Diamond informed the senator: "I fear Pres. Wilson is stronger than our fellow Republicans think he is." Both letters in Nelson Papers.

[17] Day to Ole O. Sageng, October 23, 1916, Sageng Papers. Commenting on Sageng's support of Hughes, Day remarked: "I'm awfully sorry you have lined up with the Special Interests Crowd. . . . Men of your stamp every where are with Wilson." For the other quotations, see Fremont S. Brown to Frank B. Kellogg, October 19, 1916, Kellogg Papers; B. H. Bowler to Sageng, October 12, 1916, Sageng Papers.

[18] *Union Labor Bulletin*, September, 1916, p. 8; Philip S. Converse to Nelson, October 9, 1916; L. M. Willcutts to, October 14, 1916, Nelson Papers.

[19] Magnus Martinson to Nelson, October 16, 1916 (quotation); I. A. Caswell to, October 17, 1916; H. C. Jackson to, October 20, 1916, Nelson Papers.

[20] Moos to Eric L. Thornton, October 19, 1916 (copy), in Kellogg Papers.

[21] *Minneapolis Journal*, October 11, November 8, 15, 1916; *Northfield News*, November 24, 1916; *Union Labor Bulletin*, October, 1916, p. 8. The latter commented: "If the laboring men . . . are as solidly united on the Wilson policies as the labor press there can be no doubt of the outcome in the coming election."

[22] *Legislative Manual*, 1917, p. 508.

[23] For examples of Republican campaign polemics, see *Duluth News Tribune*, October 22, 1916; *Northfield News*, September 8, 22, November 3, 1916.

[24] Link, *Woodrow Wilson and the Progressive Movement*, 250.

[25] *Legislative Manual*, 1917, p. 198, 518; *Minneapolis Journal*, June 20, 21, 1916. Lundeen's margin over Smith was paper-thin — less than 500 votes.

[26] *Journal*, June 20, 1916, p. 12.

[27] Kellogg to Charles Evans Hughes, June 30, 1916 (copy); Theodore Roosevelt to Kellogg, June 21, 1916, Kellogg Papers.

[28] *Legislative Manual*, 1917, p. 190, 510–513; Calderwood to Sageng, September 11, 1916, Sageng Papers; *Ugeblad* (Fergus Falls), September 27, 1916.

[29] Raynal C. Bolling to Kellogg, March 8, 1916. On Manahan's role, see Kellogg to C. J. Moos, March 11, 1916 (copy); Fletcher Maddox to Kellogg, September 11, 1916; Frank M. Eddy to, October 9, 1916, Kellogg Papers; *Princeton Union*, October 5, 1916. On Power's role, see *Minneapolis Journal*, July 6, 1918. For others, see John E. Casey to Kellogg, March 6, 1916; A. C. Weiss to, November 7, 1916; Tom Davis to, August 1, 1916, Kellogg Papers; William E. Lee to Sageng, June 23, 1916; C. J. Moos to, June 24, 1916, Sageng Papers.

[30] *Brown County Journal*, October 7, 1916, p. 4; Moos to Kellogg [undated, 1916] in which Moos discloses that he had secured the agreement of Emil Leicht, publisher of a number of German-language newspapers, to run articles favorable to Kellogg. According to Moos, the Leicht arrangement assured Kellogg "the support of every german paper in the state." Kellogg Papers.

[31] *Commercial West*, September 9, 1916, p. 7; George M. Gillette to Nelson, September 7, 1916; John Washburn to, September 1, 1916; W. H. Williams to, September 1, 1916; McGee to, September 11, November 15 (quotation), 1916, Nelson Papers.

[32] *New Times*, March 18, November 11, p. 1 (quotation), 1916; *Minneapolis Journal*, October 16, 20, 22, 25, 26, 27, 1916. Frederick H. Whitin, an antivice crusader from New York, was quoted as saying that he "hadn't been in Minneapolis 10 minutes before I was invited to go to a disorderly house. . . . The disorderly houses here are about as open as Minnesota lakes." *Journal*, May 25, 1916, p. 15.

[33] Morlan, *Political Prairie Fire*, 92–108. Since the North Dakota Senate was not controlled by the league, it was able to block full enactment of Townley's program. This, however, appeared to be only a temporary frustration.

[34] *Commercial West*, February 3, 1917, p. 7, 8.

[35] Link, *Woodrow Wilson and the Progressive Movement*, 261.

[36] Gordon A. Craig, *The Politics of the Prussian Army, 1640–1945*, 320–322 (New York, 1964).

[37] Fried, ed., *Writings and Speeches of Woodrow Wilson*, 281–287.

Chapter 12 — STORM AND STRESS — pages 130–144

[1] *New Times*, February 10, 1917, p. 1, 2.

[2] *Minneapolis Tribune*, February 6, 1917; *New Times*, February 17, 1917, p. 1; *Union Labor Bulletin*, February, 1917, p. 4; John S. McLain to Knute Nelson, February 16, 1917, Nelson Papers.

[3] Nelson to Woodrow Wilson, February 21, 1917 (copy), Nelson Papers; *Union Labor Bulletin*, February, 1917, p. 4 (quotation).

[4] Minnesota, *Laws*, 1917, p. 872; Edward MacGaffey, "A Pattern for Progress: The Minnesota Children's Code," in *Minnesota History*, 41: 229–236 (Spring, 1969).

[5] Minnesota, *Laws*, 1917, p. 374.

[6] *House Journal*, 1917, p. 1615, 1712; *Senate Journal*, 1917, p. 1036, 1196, 1428. On the history of the Safety Commission, see Folwell, *Minnesota*, 3:556–575; O. A. Hilton, *The Minnesota Commission of Public Safety in World War I* (Stillwater, Okla., 1951).

[7] The *New Times*, April 14, 1917, p. 1, predicted the commission would "Prussianize Minnesota and establish here that military autocracy against which we are supposed to be fighting in our war with Germany."

[8] McGee to Nelson, April 11, 1917, Nelson Papers.

[9] The *Union Labor Bulletin*, a voice of conservative unionism, complained that "Labor was . . . entirely ignored in the makeup of the commission, so labor will get its orders without consultation from a commission that, with a possible exception, represents organized capital from start to finish." June, 1917, p. 4.

[10] *St. Paul Daily News*, April 5, 1917, p. 1, 5 (quotations); *Labor World*, March 2, 1918; Minnesota Commission of Public Safety, *Report*, 22 [St. Paul, 1919].

[11] *Commercial West*, February 17, 1917, p. 7; *Martin County Sentinel*, March 2, 1917, p. 4. (The *Fairmont Daily Sentinel* appeared in a semiweekly edition as the *Martin County Sentinel*.) In the *Minneota Mascot* Bjornson said: "When it comes to murdering people in order that a few of the human hogs, that call themselves American, may have more millions to spend upon lust and lap-dogs, then let us pray that we may have the moral courage to say, as once did President Wilson, that we are 'too proud to fight.' " (February 16, 1917, p. 4.) The *Park Region Echo* of March 27 published George Washington's 1793 proclamation of neutrality, and Moen, who was a member of the state legislature, asserted in *Ugeblad*: "These are great times for the militarists." March 28, 1917, p. 3. (Translations from this and other Norwegian-language sources are by the author.) See also the *New Ulm Review*, February 14, 21, March 21, 1917.

[12] The Macalester College incident is described in Holbrook and Appel, *Minnesota in the War with Germany*, 1:44–47. All quotations in this and the next paragraph are from this source. The Knute Nelson Papers for February, 1917, contain many petitions protesting the drift toward war, a preponderance of them from labor groups, German-American societies, and small-town leaders. Countering these efforts, patriotic societies based in the Twin Cities and mainly led by businessmen with the backing of the Twin Cities daily papers carried on a campaign to "stand by the president." Charles W. Farnham, president of the Patriotic League of St. Paul, asserted that the purpose of his organization was to "offset the activities of various unpatriotic propagandists" in the cities. *St. Paul Pioneer Press*, April 4, 1917, p. 14. On the national peace movement at this time see Link, *Woodrow Wilson and the Progressive Movement*, 275.

[13] *New Ulm Review*, April 4, 11, 1917; *Pioneer Press*, April 1, 4, 1917; *Martin County Sentinel*, April 6, 1917, p. 4.

[14] *Congressional Record*, 65 Congress, 1 session, 413; *Legislative Manual*, 1919, p. 254; Cheney, *Minnesota Politics*, 69. For Republican reaction to Lundeen's stand, see Hovey C. Clarke to Lundeen, April 6, 1917 (copy); McGee to Nelson, April 5, 1917, Nelson Papers. Also in the Nelson Papers, filed under date of November 7, 1917, are copies of an interesting exchange between Lundeen and Theodore Roosevelt in which the former sought

to justify his course by citing a mail poll of fifth congressional district residents that registered an overwhelming majority against the decision for war. Lundeen achieved political reincarnation in the 1930s, when he was elected to congress and later to the U.S. Senate on the Farmer-Labor party ticket. See Cheney, *Minnesota Politics*, 69.

[15] *Minneota Mascot*, March 16, p. 4, August 10, p. 4, 1917.

[16] *Minneota Mascot*, August 24, 1917, p. 4; February 1, 1918, p. 4.

[17] Both quotations are from Charles Hirschfeld, "Nationalist Progressivism and World War I," in *Mid-America*, 45:146 (July, 1963). The *Martin County Sentinel* remarked: "Sure as there is a God in Israel (,) out of the cruel war will come two incomparable blessings — prohibition and woman suffrage, twin messengers of christianity and civilization." (May 22, 1917, p. 4.)

[18] *Gaa Paa*, September 22, 1917.

[19] *Gaa Paa*, July 14, 1917; *New Times*, October 20, November 3, 1917. Those convicted included Jacob O. Bentall, Socialist candidate for governor in 1916, and Abraham L. Sugarman, secretary of the Minnesota Socialist party. See also H. C. Peterson and Gilbert C. Fite, *Opponents of War 1917–1918*, 37, 184 (Madison, Wis., 1957).

[20] Hugh E. Leach to Nelson, March 18, 1918, Nelson Papers; *New Ulm Review*, May 30, 1917. Peterson was convicted in Federal District Court, but in 1920 the United States Supreme Court set the conviction aside on grounds of procedural irregularities. See *Folkets Røst* (Minneapolis), October 23, 1920; Peterson and Fite, *Opponents of War*, 184.

[21] Van Lear defined these concerns in an address to the 1917 convention of the National Editorial Association. See *New Times*, July 14, 1917.

[22] *Commercial West*, August 18, 1917, p. 8. On various peace proposals, see Link, *Wilson the Diplomatist*, 99–102.

[23] *New Times*, June 30, 1917, p. 1; *New Ulm Review*, July 4, 1917, p. 8.

[24] *New Times*, July 28, August 4, 11, 1917.

[25] *New Times*, August 25, 1917; *Minneapolis Journal*, August 14, 17, 20, 1917; Commission of Public Safety, *Report*, 33; Carl L. Wallace to Nelson, August 28, 1917, Nelson Papers.

[26] *Labor World*, September 8, 1917, p. 1.

[27] See P.G.G. Lorenz to Nelson, June 21, 1917, Nelson Papers. This letter from a German-American Lutheran clergyman strikingly reflects the trauma of many German-Americans.

[28] *Martin County Sentinel*, February 20, 1917; Holbrook and Appel, *Minnesota in the War with Germany*, 1:50 (quotation).

[29] Commission of Public Safety, *Report*, 32.

[30] Stevens to Nelson, April 18, 1917; Lynch to, April 13, 1917; McGee to C. B. Miller, May 22, 1917 (copy). See also McGee to Nelson, May 31, 1917, all in Nelson Papers. McGee's anxiety was not shared by Lind, his colleague on the Safety Commission. In a letter printed in the *New Ulm Review* the former governor wrote that he was "not . . . much worried that our German friends would shoot up their neighbors or destroy their own property." In an obvious reference to McGee, he remarked that all commissions inevitably had some "bell-ringers" within their ranks. (June 6, 1917, p. 4.)

[31] *Brown County Journal*, June 9, 1917, p. 1; *New Ulm Review*, April 25, May 2, June 27 (quotation, p. 4), July 11, 1917.

[32] *New Ulm Review*, July 25, 1917; *Brown County Journal*, July 28, 1917, p. 1. For the attitude of the *Brown County Journal*, whose editor, Philip Leisch, was a fervent Republican, see the issue of April 14, 1917, which carried a strong prowar editorial.

[33] *New Ulm Review*, August 29, 1917; Haines, *Minnesota Legislature of 1911*, 101, 113. The generalization about Pfaender is true to a less striking degree in Lundeen's case. Before the war Lundeen was known as a progressive, but he enjoyed little favor with Minneapolis Socialists. His vote against the war and subsequent opposition to conscription heightened his reputation within Socialist circles. See *New Times*, April 28, 1917; *Gaa Paa*, July 21, September 18, 1917.

[34] *Brown County Journal*, July 28, 1917, p. 1. The account here and in the next two paragraphs is based primarily on the *Journal*, which gave the event full and apparently objective

coverage. See also the *New Ulm Review*, August 1, 1917, which reported on similar meetings in other southwest Minnesota towns, and the *Minneapolis Journal*, July 26, 27, 1917.

[35] Lawler was quoted in *Labor World*, August 25, 1917, p. 3; *Princeton Union*, August 9, p. 4; 16, p. 4, 1917; *Ugeblad*, August 29, 1917; *Gaa Paa*, August 25, 1917; *New Times*, August 4, 1917. Dunn's reference to the Sioux recalled the noted siege of New Ulm by the Indians in 1862.

[36] Commission of Public Safety, *Report*, p. 49; *Brown County Journal*, August 25, 1917, p. 3 (quotations), September 29, October 6, 1917.

[37] *New Ulm Review*, August 22, October 3, December 5, 1917; *Brown County Journal*, September 15, 22, 1917; Commission of Public Safety, *Report*, 48–51.

[38] *New Ulm Review*, September 5, 1917; *Brown County Journal*, September 8, 1917, p. 4 (quotation).

[39] *New Ulm Review*, March 13, 20, 27, April 3, 1918; *Brown County Journal*, March 23, 30, April 6, 1918.

[40] *Minnesota in the War*, May 4, 1918, p. 1 (quotation); Holbrook and Appel, *Minnesota in the War with Germany*, 2:84.

[41] Holbrook and Appel, *Minnesota in the War with Germany*, 2:52–55, 76; *Commercial West*, September 15, p. 7. Another editorial in the same issue (p. 8) hailed the recently created American Alliance for Labor and Democracy: "With Samuel Gompers . . . heading this alliance, and endorsed by such prominent socialists as John Spargo . . . this Minneapolis convention of labor men should go a long way towards preventing any further disloyal propaganda."

Chapter 13 — THE RISE OF THE LOYALTY ISSUE — pages 145–163

[1] *Martin County Sentinel*, February 2, p. 4; 16, p. 4, 1917.

[2] Morlan, *Political Prairie Fire*, 127; Blackorby, *Prairie Rebel*, 65.

[3] *Princeton Union*, September 20, 1917; *Park Region Echo*, September 4, 11,1917.

[4] Morlan, *Political Prairie Fire*, 127; *Princeton Union*, April 5, 1917; *Labor World*, April 28, 1917.

[5] John R. Serrin, president of the Glenwood Commercial Club, told Senator Nelson that members of that organization were studying the Equity Association and the Nonpartisan League before taking a position on their activities. (Serrin to Nelson, January 31, 1917, Nelson Papers.) At first small-town papers were similarly ambivalent. Generally speaking, sympathetic interest in the Nonpartisan League waned and hostility increased as the months of 1917 passed. See, for example, *Princeton Union*, February 17, 1916; January 11, 25, February 8, May 27, June 28, July 19, 1917. The *Northfield News* showed a similar evolution. On March 31, 1917 (p. 4), the *Blue Earth County Enterprise* advised lawmakers to take action on rising railroad rates "or others will be chosen. . . . Even the coming of the non-partisan league will be welcomed." The *Enterprise* was to become later a harsh critic of the league.

[6] *Minneota Mascot*, October 19, 1917, p. 1. Earlier the *Mascot* had reported sympathetically on the progress of the league, and later it noted that N. S. Randall, a prominent league lecturer, was less inclined "to array class against class" than Townley. December 8, 1916; January 25, 1918, p. 1. For IWW rumors, see Ole O. Sageng to Nelson, December 20, 1917, Nelson Papers.

[7] On early league business enterprises, see Morlan, *Political Prairie Fire*, 115–120. For a striking reflection of small-town social and economic "status fears" see editorial from an unidentified North Dakota newspaper quoted in Saloutos and Hicks, *Agricultural Discontent*, 159.

[8] W. E. Verity to Kellogg, November 11, 1916, Kellogg Papers; Snyder to Nelson, August 18, 1917, Nelson Papers.

[9] Teigan to Mrs. August Baumgarten, March 6, June 16, July 3 (quotation), 1917; Mrs.

Baumgarten to Teigan, June 7, 9, 1917, National Nonpartisan League Papers, in the Minnesota Historical Society.

[10] For quotations from Townley's speeches, see Gaston, *Nonpartisan League*, 181–185.

[11] Teigan to Charles Ludwig, July 26, 1917 (quotation); to E. W. James, July 25, 1917, League Papers. For an account of Baer's campaign, see Blackorby, *Prairie Rebel*, 68–74.

[12] Blackorby, *Prairie Rebel*, 74; *Commercial West*, June 16, 1917, p. 8; Teigan to S. A. Harris, June 11, 1917, League Papers. The failure of North Dakota to meet its first liberty loan quota — a performance redeemed in subsequent drives — was attributed by some to the Nonpartisan League. *Princeton Union*, July 5, 1917.

[13] Quigley, "Out where the West Begins," 34; Teigan to Oscar Anderson, March 13, 1919, League Papers.

[14] *Minneapolis Journal*, August 24, 1917; *Princeton Union*, August 30, 1917; *Minneota Mascot*, October 19, 1917; *New Ulm Review*, February 27, 1918; Teigan to Elizabeth Freeman, July 3, 1917; to Daniel O'Connell, August 9, 1917; to James Dolsen, September 27, 1917, League Papers.

[15] Gaston, *Nonpartisan League*, 197–207.

[16] Morlan, *Political Prairie Fire*, 142.

[17] Material and quotations here and in the following three paragraphs are from Belle Case La Follette and Fola La Follette, *Robert M. La Follette*, 2:762–768 (New York, 1953).

[18] La Follette and La Follette, *Robert M. La Follette*, 2:770. Eight months later the Associated Press retracted the original version of its dispatch. Morlan, *Political Prairie Fire*, 144.

[19] *Commercial West*, September 29, 1917, p. 7.

[20] Charles W. Ames to Nelson, September 28, 1917; Louis Keane to, February 19, 1918, Nelson Papers; *Fairmont Daily Sentinel*, October 20, 1917, p. 4. The *Minneota Mascot* (September 28, 1917, p. 4) commented: "There were, of course, many loyal sentiments expressed at the meeting, but these seem to be lost in the overwhelming seditiousness of the talk given by one United States Senator from Wisconsin, whom it is needless to name."

[21] *St. Paul Pioneer Press*, September 22, 1917; *New York Times*, September 26, 1917; La Follette and La Follette, *Robert M. La Follette*, 2:776, 911.

[22] *Duluth News Tribune*, September 26, 1917; Morlan, *Political Prairie Fire*, 145.

[23] *Park Region Echo*, October 2, 1917, p. 1. The *Courier-News* is quoted in the *Echo* for October 9, 1917, p. 1.

[24] Material and quotations in this and the following two paragraphs are from the *Duluth News Tribune*. October 8, 1917, p. 1, 12. George W. Lawson, secretary of the Minnesota Federation of Labor, was among the labor representatives.

[25] *Labor World*, November 24, 1917; *St. Paul Daily News*, November 8, 1917; *Park Region Echo*, November 27, 1917; Lynn Haines to Teigan, November 30, 1917, League Papers. Shortly before the La Follette address, Cheney suggested there might be a substitution of bipartisan "loyal" tickets for the customary Republican-Democratic contests in 1918. See *Princeton Union*, September 20, 1917.

[26] *Nonpartisan Leader*, April 1, 1918, p. 13 (quotation). The *Leader* was published in Fargo, N. D., until December 31, 1917, and thereafter in St. Paul. *Labor World*, February 23, 1918; *St. Paul Daily News*, November 16, 17, 18, 1917. Senator Nelson personally requested President Wilson to address the gathering. See telegram, Nelson to Wilson, October 20, 1917, Nelson Papers.

[27] *Park Region Echo*, December 4, 1917; *Labor World*, February 2, 1918; Charles E. Russell, *The Story of the Non-Partisan League*, 244 (New York, 1920).

[28] Nelson to Creel, April 8, 1918 (copy). The printed text of Creel's reply, from which the quotations in the following two paragraphs are taken, is filed with Nelson's letter in the Nelson Papers.

[29] *Union Labor Bulletin*, August, 1917, p. 22. See also *Labor World*, June 30, 1917.

[30] See resolution adopted April 15, 1917, by the executive council of the MFL. *Labor World*, April 21, 1917, p. 3. The Minneapolis Trades and Labor Assembly, which remained under radical control throughout the war, showed less enthusiasm than either the MFL or the AFL. In April, 1917, it endorsed Senator La Follette's opposition both to arming merchant ships and declaring war, and later it went on record in opposition to conscription. The radical *New Times* subsequently complained that the leaders of the Minneapolis body were persuaded by Samuel Gompers to soften their opposition to the war. *Union Labor Bulletin*, April, 1917, p. 22; January, 1918, p. 3; *New Times*, July 28, 1917; Leslie Stinton to Nelson, April 18, 1917, Nelson Papers.

[31] *Labor World*, July 21, 28, September 1, 15, 1917; *Union Labor Bulletin*, July, 1917, p. 4–6; August, 1917, p. 22; *New Times*, July 28, August 18, September 8, 1917; *Gaa Paa*, July 21, 1917; Robertson to Nelson, January 16, 1918, Nelson Papers.

[32] *Bulletin*, December, 1917, p. 16.

[33] *Mesaba Ore*, September 28, 1917, p. 1; *Union Labor Bulletin*, January, 1918, p. 4.

[34] *Union Labor Bulletin*, October, 1917, p. 4–6; *New Times*, September 29, October 13, 1917; *Gaa Paa*, September 15, 29, 1917.

[35] Commission of Public Safety, *Report*, 39, 146 (quotation); *Minnesota Union Advocate* (St. Paul), November 23, 30, 1917; *Gaa Paa*, December 1, 1917.

[36] The Safety Commission Order No. 30, issued on March 30, 1918, gave this policy firm legal status. Commission of Public Safety, *Report*, 108. See also *Labor World*, June 8, 1918, for an analysis of the clash between state and federal policies.

[37] *Union Labor Bulletin*, December, 1917, p. 17; Manahan, *Trials of a Lawyer*, 224–232; Frederick C. Stevens to Nelson, December 22, 1917 (quotation), Nelson Papers. Nelson had requested Stevens to provide him with a comprehensive report of the strike situation.

[38] *Minnesota Union Advocate*, December 7, 1917; Commission of Public Safety, *Report*, 41; *St. Paul Daily News*, December 5, 1917. A copy of Baker's telegram is in the Nelson Papers under date of December 4, 1917.

[39] Commission of Public Safety, *Report*, 40; *St. Paul Daily News*, December 13, p. 1 (quotation), 14, 1917. A copy of Burnquist's telegram is in the Nelson Papers under date of December 13, 1917.

[40] Reprinted copy of a letter from J. H. Walker to Joseph C. Colgan, March 13, 1918, enclosed with O. P. Briggs to Nelson, March 18, 1918, in Nelson Papers. See also *Minnesota Union Advocate*, March 15, 1918.

[41] *Park Region Echo*, February 19, 1918; Nelson to President Wilson, December 17, 1917 (quotation attached). Apparently both Nelson and Kellogg did what they could to discourage federal intervention. See Nelson and Kellogg to Burnquist (copy), December 7, 1917; Nelson to A. M. Robertson (copy), December 4, 1917, all in Nelson Papers.

[42] Briggs to Nelson, December 31, 1917; March 18, 1918, Nelson Papers.

[43] Briggs to Nelson, March 18, 1918; *Commercial West*, December 8, 1917, p. 8.

[44] *Labor World*, February 23, 1918, p. 2 (quotation); *Minnesota Leader* (St. Paul), April 27, 1918. On the significance of the streetcar strike in promoting farmer-labor co-operation, see also remarks of William Mahoney in James M. Youngdale, ed., *Third-Party Footprints: An Anthology from Writings and Speeches of Midwest Radicals*, 190 (Minneapolis, 1966).

[45] Morlan, *Political Prairie Fire*, 167–173; Folwell, *Minnesota*, 3:571–575. All but one of these prosecutions were on the state level. The single league worker tried in a federal court was speedily acquitted. Teigan to Upton Sinclair, August 10, 1920, League Papers. For a dramatic account of Gilbert's trial in Lakefield, see Manahan, *Trials of a Lawyer*, 232–238.

[46] *Blue Earth Post*, January 15, 1918, p. 5.

[47] R. C. Muir to A. E. Bowen, January 18, 1918, League Papers; *Freeborn County Standard* (Albert Lea), March 4, 1918.

[48] *Park Region Echo*, January 8, July 2, 16, November 6, 1918; Bob —— to Nelson, June 19, 1918. Earlier Nelson had conveyed to the postmaster general and had heartily endorsed

a recommendation by the Safety Commission that the *Echo* be deprived of its mailing privileges. Nelson to A. S. Burleson, August 11, 1917 (copy), Nelson Papers.

[49] National Nonpartisan League, *Memorial to the President of the United States Concerning Conditions in Minnesota, 1918*, 95, 96.

[50] *Minnesota in the War*, March 30, 1918, p. 2.

Chapter 14 — THE CAMPAIGN OF 1918 — pages 164–181

[1] See, for example, *Commercial West*, March 16, 1918, p. 7.

[2] *Minneapolis Tribune*, March 12, 1918, p. 1, 4.

[3] Morlan, *Political Prairie Fire*, 51–59, 189–192.

[4] *Nonpartisan Leader*, April 1, 1918; *Minneapolis Tribune*, March 17, 18, 19, 20, 1918.

[5] *Minneapolis Tribune*, March 20, 22, p. 4 (quotations), 1918.

[6] *Minnesota Leader*, April 6, 1918, p. 6.

[7] *St. Paul Daily News*, May 9, 1918, p. 4.

[8] Quigley, "Out where the West Begins," p. 4; *Gaa Paa*, March 23, 1918; *Daily News*, June 13, 1918, p. 1; *Mesaba Ore*, June 21, 1918, p. 1.

[9] Lindbergh, *Why your Country is at War*, 6, 117 (Washington, D. C., 1917).

[10] Lindbergh, *Why your Country is at War*, 7.

[11] *St. Paul Pioneer Press*, May 2, 1918.

[12] *Minneapolis Tribune*, March 20, 1918, p. 7 (quotation); *St. Paul Daily News*, May 1, 1918.

[13] *Commercial West*, December 8, 1917, p. 7. A *Nonpartisan Leader* editorial of February 11, 1918, affirmed that Bolshevik pressure had encouraged a clarification of Allied war aims and questioned the alleged pro-German orientation of the new regime. See also *Gaa Paa*, May 4, 1918.

[14] *Commercial West*, March 9, 1918, p. 7, 8.

[15] *Commercial West*, July 13, 1918, p. 7.

[16] Burnquist appointed his secretary, Gustaf Lindquist, as state chairman, a selection that failed to arouse the enthusiasm of many Republicans. As a member of the state central committee, Smith played an important but not overly conspicuous role as mediator among contending GOP factions. The Nelson Papers contain a mass of informative correspondence on the internal Republican situation. See especially Magnus Martinson to Frank B. Kellogg, October 4, 1917 (copy); also F. H. Carpenter to Nelson, February 19, June 21, 1918; E. E. Smith to, April 22, May 11, 23, June 6, 12, 27, July 18, 25, September 25, October 8, 1918; L. M. Willcutts to, May 4, June 15, 27, July 13, 19, 27, August 1, 23, September 25, 1918; Nelson to Smith, July 1, 12, 22, October 11, 1918; to Willcutts, June 26, 27, July 1, 11, August 5, 1918; to Gustaf Lindquist, July 23, 1918. For Nelson's comment on his own relationship to Burnquist, which was not particularly amicable, see Nelson to J. A. O. Preus, July 8, 1918.

[17] *St. Paul Daily News*, May 6, p. 2; June 16, p. 12, 1918. Some of the governor's editorial supporters stated his case in a higher key. The *Princeton Union*, for example, asserted editorially: "Every disloyalist and near traitor, every I.W.W. thug, every anarchist and malcontent, native and foreign born, in the state are arrayed against Governor Burnquist. Loyal Americans love him for the enemies he has made." (May 23, 1918, p. 4).

[18] Quoted in Lynn and Dora Haines, *The Lindberghs*, 281 (New York, 1931).

[19] *St. Paul Pioneer Press*, May 5, 1918, section 2, p. 4 (quotation); McGee to Nelson, April 25, 1918; A. C. Hatch to Nelson, April 22, 1918, Nelson Papers. Hatch, a Battle Lake hardware merchant who was active in the GOP campaign, reported that McGee was "doing more to promote the union of the farmer labor vote than a thousand Townleys could do." On May 10, 1918, the *Minneota Mascot* called for McGee's resignation.

[20] For comment on these indictments, see *Commercial West*, June 8, 1918, p. 7.

[21] L. M. Willcutts to Nelson, May 30, 1918, Nelson Papers; *Minneapolis Journal*, June 7, 1918.

[22] *St. Paul Daily News*, June 16, 1918, p. 4.

[23] *Legislative Manual*, 1919, p. 252; *Daily News*, June 18, 1918, p. 6. For the conservative reaction, see *Commercial West*, June 22, 1918, p. 7.

[24] *St. Paul Daily News*, May 12, 17, June 16, August 29, p. 3 (quotation), 1918.

[25] *Labor World*, July 20, August 31, 1918; *Minnesota Union Advocate*, July 26, August 30, 1918; *Gaa Paa*, August 31, 1918.

[26] *Minnesota Leader*, August 31, 1918.

[27] *Minnesota Union Advocate*, September 7, 1918.

[28] For text of Le Sueur's letter, see Asher Howard, ed., *The Leaders of the Nonpartisan League: Their Aims, Purposes and Records*, 65 (Minneapolis, 1920). For comment on release of the letters by the Safety Commission, see *St. Paul Daily News*, October 20, 1918; *Minnesota Leader*, September 21, 28, 1918.

[29] Dar. S. Hall to Nelson, October 19, 1918; Julius A. Schmahl to, October 16, 1918; L. M. Willcutts to, October 19, 1918, Nelson Papers.

[30] *St. Paul Daily News*, June 23, 1918; *Public*, 21:876–878 (July 13, 1918). As early as July 13 (p. 8), *Commercial West* questioned the wisdom — though not the morality — of banning league meetings. See also Henry G. Teigan to Leon Durocher, October 2, 1918; to Edward Teigan, October 18, 1918, League Papers.

[31] *Minnesota Leader*, September 28, 1918.

[32] *Minnesota Leader*, September 28, 1918.

[33] *Minneota Mascot*, October 11, 1918, p. 4.

[34] *Minneota Mascot*, October 11, 1918, p. 4.

[35] *Minneapolis Tribune*, March 29, 1918; Marcus Johnson to Nelson, December 12, 1917; B. F. Nelson to, January 11, 1918; L. M. Willcutts to, March 28, April 3, 24, 1918; E. E. Smith to, April 11, 1918; John Jenswold to, April 30, 1918; A. C. Weiss to, May 1, 1918; Daniel Lawler to, May 9, 1918; Simon Michelet to, October 18, 1918; Nelson to Michelet, July 27, 1918, Nelson Papers. The total Minnesota vote was Nelson, 229,923; Peterson, 89,464. In Douglas County it was Peterson, 1,956; Nelson, 1,520. *Legislative Manual*, 1919, p. 250, 252.

[36] According to Nelson's biographer, "it became known that President Wilson had written a letter to Minnesota Democrats, requesting that no candidate be placed . . . against him [*Nelson*]." Martin W. Odland, *The Life of Knute Nelson,* 259 (Minneapolis, 1926).

[37] A copy of the telegram is in the Nelson Papers under date of October 23, 1918.

[38] Nelson to T. Gulbrandsen, October 29, 1918 (quotation); to L. M. Willcutts, November 12, 1918; B. F. Nelson to Nelson, November 5, 1918, Nelson Papers.

[39] Nelson to L. M. Willcutts and to J. R. Morley, June 20, 1918 (copies); to E. E. Smith, July 1, 1918 (copy); to C. A. Thompson, July 30, 1918 (copy); Calderwood to Nelson (telegram), October 30, 1918, Nelson Papers.

[40] Simon Michelet to Nelson, October 24, 1918; E. E. Smith to, October 26, 1918, Nelson Papers; *Minnesota Leader*, October 26, 1918; *Minneapolis Tribune*, October 29, p. 6.

[41] *Legislative Manual*, 1919, p. 670 (insert); Anson Evans to W. D. Jamieson, November 2, 1918 (copy); Charles E. Johnson to Democratic voters of Minnesota, November 2, 1918 (copy); B. F. Nelson to Nelson, October 29, 1918; Kellogg to, November 1, 5, 1918; Fred Wheaton to, November 11, 1918, Nelson Papers.

[42] *Legislative Manual*, 1919, p. 210–217; *Labor World*, August 31, September 22, 1918; *Minneapolis Tribune*, March 20, 1918.

[43] *Labor World*, February 24, 1917; April 12, September 27, 1919.

[44] *Gaa Paa*, June 29, 1918; *Labor World*, March 23, 1918. According to Henry Teigan, the Bohemians "were extremely hostile" to the league in 1918 but considerably less so a year later. Teigan to Signe Lund, April 22, 1919, League Papers.

[45] *Legislative Manual*, 1919, p. 671; *Labor World*, August 3, 17, 24, 31, 1918.

[46] *Labor World*, October 26, 1918, p. 4. Miller's friends also believed that the national administration threw its influence back of Carss. See L. M. Willcutts to Nelson, November 9, 1918, Nelson Papers.

[47] *Minnesota Leader*, November 9, 1918; Commission of Public Safety, *Report*, 32 (quotation).

[48] *Legislative Manual*, 1919. For general election returns by county and precinct, see p. 514–669; for complete primary returns, p. 84–249.

[49] Nelson to Thomas W. Gregory, March 16, 1918, Nelson Papers; Quigley, "Out where the West Begins," 26. Teigan professed to believe that "The League's position on financing the war . . . is instrumental in bringing the cautious Germans into the organization." Teigan to Judson King, July 19, 1917, League Papers.

[50] See H. Locheed to Nelson, October 28, 1918, Nelson Papers.

Chapter 15 — THE AFTERMATH OF MINNESOTA PROGRESSIVISM — pages 182–203

[1] Arthur Naftalin, "A History of the Farmer-Labor Party of Minnesota," 58, Ph.D. thesis, University of Minnesota, 1948, copy in the Minnesota Historical Society.

[2] Naftalin, "The Farmer-Labor Party," 59–63. The primary vote was Preus, 133,832; Shipstead, 125,861. In the final election Preus polled 481,805 votes to Shipstead's 281,402. *Legislative Manual*, 1921, p. 100, 526. Two factors may have increased Preus's strength in the fall: voter resentment of Shipstead's second try and the drawing power of the Harding-Coolidge national ticket.

[3] Naftalin, "The Farmer-Labor Party," 84.

[4] Quoted in Stephenson, *John Lind of Minnesota*, 344.

[5] Samuel Lubell, *The Future of American Politics*, 142 (New York, 1951); Naftalin, "The Farmer-Labor Party," 73; Mayer, *Floyd B. Olson*, 13; John H. Fenton, *Midwest Politics*, 77 (New York, 1966).

[6] *Legislative Manual*, 1929, p. 84. The vote in 1926 was 38,008; in 1928, 213,734.

[7] *Minneota Mascot*, April 18, 1919, p. 4. See also issues of January 3, February 7. September 26, 1919. The *Minneapolis Journal* (September 20, 1919, p. 4) called Burnquist's action on the tonnage tax "a mistake in judgment," given the large majority mobilized for the measure in the House and the impossibility of acting on the veto.

[8] Minnesota, *Laws*, 1919, p. 43. The regular session also passed a stringent sedition law (p. 91).

[9] *Princeton Union*, May 13, 1920, p. 1; Naftalin, "The Farmer-Labor Party," 60. The convention is reported in *Minneapolis Journal*, May 8, 9, 1920, both p. 1. The iron ore tax plank, though carried overwhelmingly, was vigorously debated on the convention floor.

[10] *Minneota Mascot*, October 15, 1920, p. 4.

[11] *Minneapolis Tribune*, April 21, 1921, p. 1; Buell, *The Minnesota Legislature of 1921*, 7 (n. p., n. d.).

[12] Minnesota, *Laws*, 1921, p. 25–33, 150, 274 (quotation), 274–277, 524, 999, 1000–1002.

[13] Minnesota, *Laws*, 1921, p. 328–337, 401–406, 646; Buell, *Legislature of 1921*, 38–49.

[14] Naftalin, "The Farmer-Labor Party," 76–88; Buell, *The Minnesota Legislature of 1923*, 7 (n.p., n.d.); *Legislative Manual*, 1923, p. 452.

[15] *Inaugural Message of Governor J. A. O. Preus to the Legislature of Minnesota, Jan. 3, 1923*, 6–8, 24–28 (St. Paul, 1923); Minnesota, *Laws*, 1923, p. 124–126, 246–257, 258–260.

[16] Naftalin, "The Farmer-Labor Party," 90–92.

[17] *Dawson Sentinel*, July 26, August 23, 1912; Manahan, *Trials of a Lawyer*, 187–189; Mayer, *Floyd B. Olson*, 33. A factor in the steel company's uncertainty about Christianson was his opposition to highway construction on grounds of economy — a stand that did not encourage expansion of the market for steel.

[18] Theodore Christianson, *Minnesota, The Land of Sky-Tinted Waters*, 2:445 (Chicago and New York, 1935). The governor's description (2:451) of his recommendations to the 1925 legislature is also revealing. He recalled that he told the session "to hold appropriation totals below those of 1923; to establish no new state institutions, create no new state activities, authorize no new state obligations, and accept no new form of Federal aid conditioned on state expenditures; to refuse all requests for salary increases; to make no appropriations for new buildings not urgently needed; and to consider whether there were not some state activities that might better be discontinued." Although it is difficult to agree with the characterization of Burnquist which Christianson gives in this work, his description of Preus's response to the Nonpartisan League challenge shows real insight.

[19] In 1926 Christianson prevailed over Magnus Johnson by a plurality of nearly 130,000 votes. Two years later his plurality exceeded 300,000. *Legislative Manual*, 1927, p. 184; 1929, p. 194.

[20] Mayer, *Floyd B. Olson*, 50, 51; Naftalin, "The Farmer-Labor Party," 162, 178; Cheney, *Minnesota Politics*, 61, 71.

[21] Martin Ross, *Shipstead of Minnesota*, 21–24, 28, 31–35 (Chicago, 1940).

[22] Ross, *Shipstead of Minnesota*, 36–39. The *Glenwood Herald* did not report the incident described by Ross, but its files do disclose that the Pope County Safety Commission banned Nonpartisan League meetings within its jurisdiction during the late winter and spring of 1918. The ban was partially lifted following protests by a number of Glenwood citizens. See issues of February 7, May 16, 1918. The vote in the congressional primary was Volstead, 19,552; Shipstead, 16,775. *Legislative Manual*, 1919, p. 255.

[23] For samples of Shipstead's campaign oratory, see text of a speech at Glencoe, May 19, 1920, Shipstead Papers, in the Minnesota Historical Society; *Minneota Mascot*, September 24, 1920; *Park Region Echo*, March 10, 1920. Years later, Preus attributed Kellogg's defeat to the stand he had taken on the war. See interview with Lucile M. Kane and June D. Holmquist, 1960 (typewritten transcript), p. 47, in the Minnesota Historical Society.

[24] Jon M. Wefald, "Congressman Knud Wefald: A Minnesota Voice for Farm Parity," in *Minnesota History*, 38:177–185 (December, 1962); Saloutos and Hicks, *Agricultural Discontent*, 321–403. The identity between progressivism and the farm bloc should not be pushed too far. While one wing of the latter carried impeccable progressive credentials (Senators La Follette, Norris, Borah, and Burton K. Wheeler, for example) defense of the agricultural interest overshadowed ideological considerations. It is significant that the conservative Farm Bureau, an organization frequently under attack by La Follette progressives, strongly backed the McNary-Haugen bill. Moreover, support of the measure committed farm bloc members "to a policy of high and ruthless tariff protection" (Saloutos and Hicks, 374). This was a shift from the insurgent stance in 1909, when the Payne-Aldrich bill was up for consideration. On the other hand, farm bloc rhetoric was clearly in the progressive tradition, as was the demand that government intervene against the excesses of speculators, packers, and other putative exploiters of the farmer.

[25] Quoted in Naftalin, "The Farmer-Labor Party," 92.

[26] The episode discussed here and in the next three paragraphs is treated fully in Naftalin, "The Farmer-Labor Party," 94–121. See also Saloutos and Hicks, *Agricultural Discontent*, 355–360; Mayer, *Floyd B. Olson*, 31–33; and James M. Youngdale, " 'VOTE AS YOU WOULD STRIKE,' the Story of the Minnesota Working People's Non-Partisan Political League," 27–44, an unpublished manuscript made available through the kindness of Mr. Youngdale.

[27] Mayer, *Floyd B. Olson*, 33–36; *Legislative Manual*, 1925, p. 318.

[28] Naftalin, "The Farmer-Labor Party," 131–156, 147 (quotation).

[29] Mayer, *Floyd B. Olson*, 45 (quotation); Naftalin, "The Farmer-Labor Party," 169. For the full text of the platform, see *Farmer-Labor Leader*, April 15, 1930.

[30] *Legislative Manual*, 1931, p. 190. For the story of the campaign, see Mayer, *Floyd B. Olson*, 46–56.

[31] Mayer, *Floyd B. Olson*, 62. The full text of the message is in John S. McGrath and

James J. Delmont, *Floyd Bjørnsterne Olson, Minnesota's Greatest Liberal Governor*, 177–183 (St. Paul, 1937).

[32] Mayer, *Floyd B. Olson*, 139–142.

[33] Mayer, *Floyd B. Olson*, 222. For further coverage of the truck strike, see Thomas E. Blantz, "Father Haas and the Minneapolis Truckers' Strike of 1934," in *Minnesota History*, 42:5–15 (Spring, 1970).

[34] Naftalin, "The Farmer-Labor Party," 244–246.

[35] Mayer, *Floyd B. Olson*, 10 (quotation), 9–11, 175–177, 239, 295–298. For the text of Olson's keynote speech, see McGrath and Delmont, *Floyd Bjørnsterne Olson*, 249–254.

[36] *Legislative Manual*, 1933, p. 200; 1935, p. 204; 1937, p. 206, 382–384. Olson's plurality in 1932 was 188,357; in 1934, 72,453.

[37] *Legislative Manual*, 1939, p. 214, 390–392.

[38] Quoted in James M. Shields, *Mr. Progressive: a biography of Elmer Austin Benson*, 86 (Minneapolis, 1971).

[39] Shields, *Mr. Progressive*, 161; Naftalin, "The Farmer-Labor Party," 341–352.

[40] In Brown County, for example, Benson's share of the vote declined from 68 per cent in 1936 to 26 per cent in 1938. In the state as a whole, the decline was from 62 per cent to 34 per cent. *Legislative Manual*, 1937, p. 220; 1939, p. 228. For a discussion of the foreign-policy issue, see George W. Garlid, "The Antiwar Dilemma of the Farmer-Labor Party," in *Minnesota History*, 40:365–374 (Winter, 1967).

[41] Naftalin, "The Farmer-Labor Party," 364, 381 (quotation).

[42] G. Theodore Mitau, "The Democratic-Farmer-Labor Party Schism of 1948," in *Minnesota History*, 34:187–194 (Spring, 1955).

[43] Hjalmar Petersen was the nominee on both occasions. In 1940 the gubernatorial vote was Republican, 654,686; Farmer-Labor, 459,609; Democrat, 140,021. In 1942 Stassen polled 409,800 votes to Petersen's 299,917 and 75,151 for the Democratic candidate. *Legislative Manual*, 1941, p. 226; 1943, p. 272.

[44] Fenton, *Midwest Politics*, 95, 100 (quotation).

[45] Fenton, *Midwest Politics*, 107. One informed student of recent Minnesota political history feels that although Fenton's analysis is "essentially correct," it tends to overstate the author's case. See review by Millard L. Gieske in *Minnesota History*, 40:90 (Summer, 1966).

[46] Buell, *Legislature of 1923*, 8. Olesen's vote was 123,624 compared with 79,903 for the Democratic candidate for governor. *Legislative Manual*, 1923, p. 452.

[47] "Appalachian Inferno," in *Ramparts*, June, 1971, p. 10.

Index

THIS BOOK, *designed by Alan Ominsky, is photo-composed in Mergenthaler V.I.P. Times Roman and lithographed on Bergstrom Ibsen eggshell. The work was produced by the North Central Publishing Company, St. Paul, Minnesota.*